Christmas '92

To DONNA:

Light the candles, put on the [...]
Light the incense, read the book
Listen to the CD, think, Drink the wine
"& remember".

All my Love
Mike

FRAGILE EDGE

FRAGILE EDGE

Maria Coffey

Chatto & Windus
LONDON

Published in 1989 by
Chatto & Windus Ltd
30 Bedford Square
London WC1B 3SG

A CIP catalogue record of this book is available
from the British Library.

ISBN 0 7011 3407 0

Photoset by Rowland Photypesetting Ltd
Bury St Edmunds, Suffolk
Printed in Great Britain by
Mackays of Chatham plc, Chatham, Kent

For Joe, in memory

ACKNOWLEDGEMENTS

During the writing of this book I have received help in generous measure, and I am especially indebted to the following people:
Hilary Boardman, Dorothy Boardman, and Chris and Wendy Bonington, for the encouragement which spurred me on beyond a first draft.
George Greenfield, Vivienne Schuster of John Farquharson Ltd, and Rupert Lancaster of Chatto & Windus, for their support and good advice.
Alison Samuel, my editor, for her hard work and sensitivity.
My husband Dag, for understanding so much.

My grateful thanks for permission to reproduce material also go to:
Lorna Burgess, Carolyn Estcourt, Hilary Boardman and Daniel Bonington, for the extracts from their letters.
Charlie Clarke, for the extracts from *Everest: The Unclimbed Ridge*, Hodder & Stoughton Ltd, 1983.
Jane May Griffith, for the extract from *The Book of Love and Other Poems*.
Unwin Hyman Ltd, for the lines from *Chinese Poems*, translated by Arthur Waley.
Rex Collings, for the lines from Tony Harrison's translation of *The Oresteia*.
Hilary Boardman, Chris Bonington, Charlie Clarke, Sarah Richard, Marie-Noelle Kingsley and *Mountain Magazine* for their photographs.

PROLOGUE

Infertile brown hillocks rolled by, beyond them the purple hues of higher ground and glimpses of snow peaks. An infinity of sky and a sharp, brilliant light. Everest, its summit shrouded in cloud, came into sight at the crest of a pass. Dong leaned on the side of the truck and pointed.

> 'Chomolungma, that's its Tibetan name.'
> His words were whipped around by the wind.
> 'What does it mean?' I shouted.
> The reply sent a shiver through me.
> 'Goddess Mother of the World.'

PART ONE

. . . I suppose he was my destiny
a brilliant sparkle of stars
a few brief years long in memory
so soon gone . . .

Jane May Griffith

ONE

That February night in 1982 is still clear in my memory. Joe sitting on the living-room floor of his Derbyshire house, surrounded by photographic equipment and engrossed in the workings of a newly-acquired movie camera. He was shortly to leave on a mountaineering expedition to the Tibetan side of Everest and, in his usual way of biting off huge chunks of life at a time, had taken on the role of cameraman as well as climber. Film footage was to be sent back from the mountain for national news programmes, and Joe was worried about the responsibility and the demands of this double challenge.

Curled up comfortably on a goatskin rug in front of the log fire, I watched his lean, wiry frame bent in concentration. His hair was thinning, I could see his scalp through the reddish-blonde wispy curls. Years of high-altitude climbing had helped that along and had brought premature lines to the fine skin on his forehead and around his eyes. He looked up and those blue eyes met mine. Usually they were bright, twinkling, full of mischief, but on that evening they revealed tiredness and worry. It was six months since his return from his last climbing trip to Mount Kongur in China and since then he had written a book, done a lecture tour, sorted out business commitments and begun renovations to his house. And continued a relationship with me. Behind all of it had been the constant and building pressure of this latest expedition. 'The big one,' he called it. A small team, led by Chris Bonington, was to attempt the unclimbed East-North-East Ridge of Mount Everest, without oxygen.

Joe was driven by ambition, by the constant need to meet bigger and more taxing challenges. I had never met such a determined and disciplined man. One of a world class of mountaineers, his years of hard work and adventure were blossoming into book publications, lecture tours, film work and television appearances. Yet he could not sit back and rest on these achievements.

'I'm only as good as my next climb,' he would say. 'It's all so insecure.'

We had eaten dinner earlier that night in the big, comfortable kitchen, where Joe rarely ventured past the table towards the stove. He hated cooking.

'You're so much *better* at it than me,' was his frequent plea, and he smirked with satisfaction when my friends expressed amazement at the previously hidden domesticity that was emerging in me.

After the meal and the wine I relaxed by the fire while he returned to work. He lived under the constant pressure of his numerous commitments. 'There is never enough time' – he said it so often, it was his motto, really. And he was away a lot: three expeditions already in the course of our two-year relationship. Pakistan, Nepal, China – big mountains and dangerous climbs.

The first had been the worst: K2 had almost claimed his life. The day he returned I met him in the flat he lived in at the time. He was sitting on the floor, talking on the telephone, when I walked in and I had a few moments to gaze at him before we moved shyly towards each other. The man I watched was almost a stranger. There seemed to be barely any flesh left on his body and the long, unruly hair and beard accentuated a haunted, hollowed face. It was two weeks before he began to relax and to lose the residue of horror, the waking nightmare of the avalanche that had engulfed him, and his struggle for survival in its aftermath. Hitherto unsuspected nurturing instincts arose in me then. I wanted to care for him, feed him and restore his strength. A calmness settled over me, a totally new feeling of contentment. The roller-coaster I had been on for years slowed down and I sighed with relief, not having realized how ready I was for it to stop.

'Good thing I came along,' Joe used to tease, 'otherwise who knows *what* would have become of you!'

But he had appeared on cue, because amidst all the wild times, the people and the travelling, I had grown lonely. With him had come a sense of belonging; it was as if I had suddenly and unexpectedly arrived at a familiar place where I felt at ease, and I no longer needed to rush around in pursuit of happiness.

I put another log on the fire.

'Wish I had time to do a proper film-making course before we leave,' muttered Joe.

6

I reached over for the book he had brought home the previous day, Bonavia's *Tibet*, and laid it on the Indian silk carpet that covered most of the floor. Joe loved comfort and, in contrast to the deprivation to which he subjected himself in the mountains, he was surrounded in his house by things that provided luxury and ease – the heating turned up high, a log fire and an unending supply of hot water – as if he were trying to soak up the warmth and comfort, to store it for the harsh months ahead.

Within days we were to leave his warm house and drive to Heathrow Airport. I would say goodbye again and watch him disappear through the doorway to passport control, away into a part of his life, a large part, to which I was only tenuously connected by his letters. When he left on expeditions he tried to turn his emotions off. He told me that he could not perform efficiently in the mountains if his head and his heart were engaged elsewhere. And so the letters I received, long after they had been written, were usually rather detached and factual, not full of the love and longing that I felt. Knowing how much he looked forward to my replies, I sent him news and gossip and tried to connect him to my daily life. But I held back from really exposing my feelings, confused as usual about how openly I should express my love for him.

Joe was central to my life, but his primary commitment was to mountaineering. He was honest with me in this respect, he made no promises and did not lead me to expect more than he was prepared to give. He reassured me that he wanted me in his life but he made his major decisions, including those concerning the expeditions, without consulting me.

'If I really considered your feelings,' he had said a few nights before, 'or what would happen to you if I had an accident on the mountain, I probably wouldn't go.'

Being his girlfriend was a difficult agenda to meet: give time and space for his work, go easy on the emotional demands. I tried, I tried too hard, but the tough, self-contained image that I projected to him and to the world was a veneer barely covering my longing for him to need me as much as I needed him.

On that Sunday evening, though, there were no conflicts or uncertainties. Warm and relaxed, I was happy to soak in the contentment, to watch him absorbed in his work, to imprint the memory for recall in the weeks ahead.

'Joe, these photographs are amazing.'

He left his camera and flopped down on the rug next to me. His beard grazed my cheek as we looked at the pictures of mountains, high plains, monasteries and people, images that were filled with clear, brilliant light, iridescent colours and mystery. He put an arm around my shoulders and his hand hung limply, its long fingers loose and at rest. The completeness with which he could unwind and let go of tension matched his ability for intense, concentrated work. A colourfully-dressed Tibetan girl smiled broadly from the page, her hair braided and ribboned against her scalp.

'You should do yours like that,' said Joe, pushing back a strand of hair that had fallen across my face. In contrast to the driven determination of his professional life he was physically a very tender man, often touching me, a hand resting briefly on my shoulder as we passed in the house, stroking my hair while we watched television or putting an arm around my waist when he was deep in conversation with a friend in the pub. It was a touch that said what he could not find words for, and it brought me back to equilibrium time and time again.

I was envious of his trip to Tibet. 'I wish I could go there too,' I grumbled.

'But why?' he said. 'It's just like anywhere else. I'd just as soon stay here. I'm going there to do a job, you know.'

Tibet – it was a place out of my reach, distant and, to me, mysterious. I had no inkling that before the end of the year I would be travelling through that high, mystical land, seeing images remembered from the book of photographs, following in Joe's footsteps to Everest, Chomolungma, 'Goddess Mother of the World'.

TWO

It was by chance that I met Joe Tasker in 1979, but the circumstances leading up to our meeting had been developing for a number of years.

My eldest brother, Mick, had been rock-climbing and mountaineering since the 1960s. He knew Joe long before I did. After university, while I was living in Peru, I received a letter from an undergraduate friend who had moved to North Wales.

'Come and see me when you get back,' he wrote. 'It's a wild scene here and there are lots of people who know your brother.'

Soon after returning to England I went up to Llanberis and met Mick's friends, all of them directly or peripherally involved in the world of climbing.

It was an attractive world in those easy days of the mid-seventies. The danger of the sport seemed to draw certain characters whose spirits were capable of freeing themselves from convention. Daytime activity on the rock was mirrored by night-time abandon when the adrenalin of the sport would spill over into the pubs and parties, with feelings of risk and daredevilry spinning through the air. It was fun to be there; I would return from frequent weekends in Wales to my house and teaching job in Manchester, thoroughly exhausted.

In 1978 I received a call from Tim, who ran a climbing magazine in Sheffield. I had met him both in Wales and in London at my brother's place. He told me that the British Mountaineering Council, based in Manchester, had just employed a new National Officer because Pete Boardman was resigning to take up the directorship of a climbing school in Switzerland.

'You have lodgers in your place, don't you? Got any space for another one? The new bloke's moving over from Leeds and he doesn't know many people in Manchester.'

I volunteered that I would have a spare room in a month's time, which Tim took as agreement.

'What's he like?' I asked.

'Well.' Tim gave one of his hoarse laughs. 'We call him "Dirty Alex", actually.'

I began to protest.

'No, honestly, Coffey, I can vouch for him. He's a great bloke.'

Alex McIntyre arrived. Beneath an unruly mop of black, ringleted hair were dark eyes and a wicked grin. His small, lean frame exuded fitness and energy and was clad in an assortment of mismatched and unkempt clothing. He was extremely untidy, hence the nickname, but this seemed to be part of his general disregard for convention and authority. Alex had trained for a career in law but was wholeheartedly embracing a lifestyle which allowed him to mountaineer. He was as tenacious and daring in his climbing as he was in his social and professional worlds. Clever and quick-witted, he would jump into an argument, firmly take a side and hang onto his point of view to the bitter end, like a terrier. His stubbornness and supreme self-confidence infuriated me and we fought a lot, but we respected and liked each other and became good friends. Within the month he was a lodger in the house, although his work and the expeditions meant he was away as often as he was there.

My home was frequently a weekend base camp for Alex's rock–climbing mates. They would roll in on a Friday night when the pub closed, crawl into sleeping-bags on the living-room floor and remain comatose for eight hours before cooking huge, greasy breakfasts and driving off to the Derbyshire crags. They and Alex advised me on my tilting romances, teased and flirted with me and took me out for cheering-up sessions when my spirits were down.

Towards the end of 1979, on a grey Saturday afternoon, I sat morosely in the house mulling over my ill-starred love life. For months I had juggled with three unsatisfactory relationships; everyone thought it a hilarious situation, but I was miserable. The night before I had had a final argument with one of the men. Another, a long-standing boyfriend, had just telephoned from Llanberis, suggesting we meet there to sort things out.

'There's no point in just sitting here and festering,' said Alex. 'It's time you got rid of the lot and started again. I'm off to North Wales anyway. Jump in the car, you can do another hatchet job tonight.'

Shouting at each other over the car stereo, we drove to Al Harris's cottage near Llanberis, the hub of the climbing-party scene. I had become close to Julie, Al's girlfriend. She survived four years in his house, where the ear-shattering stereo, strobe lighting and sparse furnishings were always ready for another onslaught. There was no party in full swing the night Alex and I arrived, though. Julie and Al were sitting in their kitchen with a smiling, bearded man.

'Come and listen to this story Joe's telling,' Al greeted us.

So that was how we met. He was recounting an epic descent from Mount Dunagiri, in the Himalayas, with Dick Renshawe. It had been a desperate and, I later learned, near-fatal situation, but he told the story with humour, to amuse his audience. His name was familiar to me.

'Don't you know Joe Tasker?' Julie had asked some weeks before, when she was visiting me in Manchester. 'He only lives about twenty miles away from you; he's got that climbing equipment shop in Hope. He's lovely,' she had added, 'you'd like him.'

She and Alex had set off from my house the next night for a party Joe was giving in the flat above his shop. There had been a sharp frost and I opted for the warmth of the local pub instead of Alex's heaterless car. They joined me there for last orders; black ice had made the steep hill before Joe's village impassable.

'I don't think he's got a girlfriend at the moment,' Julie had said, smiling mischievously over her glass. 'He visits us a lot in Wales. You should get a lift up with him some time.'

'Matchmaker!' I had retorted. 'I've got enough on my plate right now, thanks!'

I telephoned him once, though, late on a Friday afternoon when my car had broken down and I was trying to get to Llanberis for a party. He was a voice on the end of the line, with no plans to go to Wales that weekend but obviously intrigued by the call from a strange female.

'You don't know me,' I'd said by way of introduction, 'but we have a lot of friends in common.'

Now the five of us were close together in the small, low-ceilinged kitchen. Al handed me a mug of tea; I warmed my hands on it and sipped, studying Joe over the rim and through the steam, aware of an instant attraction.

'So Dick was huddled on this ledge with frost-bitten fingers, we'd run out of food and had no fuel to make drinks. I asked him how he was feeling. He just said, "Could be worse."'

His eyes widened and he laughed with remembered astonishment.

'"*Could be worse!*" Can you imagine the restraint? Years in a Jesuit seminary didn't give me that much control. The man's remarkable.'

He turned to me.

'Are you Mick Coffey's sister?'

'Er, yes.' Suddenly tongue-tied.

'I've known Mick for years. When I'm in London I sometimes stay at his place.'

At that moment, my boyfriend arrived and we all drifted into the living room and sat around the fireplace. It was built of slate and had stone seats at either side of the chimney. Joe crouched on the hearth and the flames showed through his sparse curls, catching the red tints. He was pouring hot water into a funny wooden pot with a straw coming through its lid.

'Nepalese tea,' he said. 'We pass it round.'

'Are you sure it's tea?' inquired Al.

'Yes, sorry to disappoint you.'

I stretched on the couch, watching Joe shyly. The attraction was not physical, not at first. It was something else, a vitality and vivacity that shone from his eyes and through his smile as he talked, and that kept his face alight while the rest of his body was relaxed and at ease. My distraction made my boyfriend more attentive than usual.

'I got the wrong impression,' Joe told me later. 'I thought you two were really close. But I still wanted to hold you, all that evening. Was that awful?'

Alex decided to stay on in Wales for a few days and Joe drove me to Manchester the following night, through a heavy storm. Cocooned in his car, with loud music swirling about us and the darkness of the Welsh backroads speeding by, we talked non-stop for the two-hour drive. Memories returned, pieces of a jigsaw clicked into place.

'You were at a party at Pete Boardman's house in Derbyshire,' he said. 'I was in the kitchen getting a drink, and you came in through the back door with some people and went straight over to the food table. I watched you bending over, picking things off plates; your hair looked nice.' The compliment was simple, direct and open, typical of Joe. I dipped my head, embarrassed.

'I wasn't invited,' I admitted. 'Some friends took me along.'

Pete was only a name to me then, as part of the British team that climbed Everest in 1975 and as Alex's predecessor at the British Mountaineering Council. I had not even spoken to him on that occasion. Not that it mattered, one didn't bother much with invites in those days, a few people could be asked to a party and the speedy communication network of the climbing world ensured that a crowd would turn up. I had become an acolyte, part of the social satellite orbiting around the sport. I thought back to the party, the kitchen, I scanned the room in my memory but could not locate Joe.

'I bet you don't remember me at the Estcourts' do either,' he teased.

Nick Estcourt was another mountaineer; he and his wife Carolyn had invited me to a party to celebrate the opening of their shop near Manchester. It was early autumn, two years before, and a van full of the Welsh crew had turned up with a supply of freshly picked magic mushrooms.

'You walked past me and looked in my direction a couple of times,' said Joe, 'but I suppose you thought I was a lizard or something.'

The headlights picked out individual raindrops. Windscreen wipers swept across my vision in a steady, rhythmic beat. Suddenly it was there, clear and distinct, my first awareness of Joe. Arriving at my parents' place once for Sunday dinner, going up to the bathroom and leafing through a Sunday supplement magazine that was lying on the floor. Across the centre pages, Joe Tasker and Pete Boardman atop a Himalayan mountain. I read the article with interest because of my brother's climbing, and admired the photographs. Now, in the car, I remembered Joe's iced-up beard, and how the rest of his face had been hidden by a hood and sunglasses.

He stopped off at my house for tea and toast.

'I've been here before,' he remarked.

I was surprised.

'I called in to see Alex one weekend – you were away somewhere. I like this place. Where are the wallhangings from?'

It was late, and he left quickly, away to his home twenty-five miles away in the Derbyshire hills, leaving me to wonder about him.

On the last day of that year there was a heavy snowfall. The hills surrounding my friends' Derbyshire farmhouse were blanketed and softly white in the wintery sunshine. People arrived throughout the day, leaving cars at the bottom of the hill and trekking up the fields carrying bottles and sleeping-bags. Tim was there, the climbing magazine friend who had introduced me to Alex.

'Clint and Annie's stereo isn't loud enough,' he said. 'I'll phone Tasker and ask him to bring his over.'

The half-mile track up to the farmhouse was steep and rutted. It wound through sharp curves and squeezed between stone walls before dropping precipitously down a steeply-banked drive to the yard. My Beetle could make it – in good conditions. We heard the revving of an engine and seconds later the kitchen door swung open to reveal a red-cheeked Joe. Tim stared at him.

'You *drove* up?'

'Yes, I saw your car at the bottom. That made me go for it. Come and help carry the stereo in.'

Joe was more of an observer than a participant at the party: he seemed preoccupied and tired. I hardly spoke to him, and gave him a chaste kiss on the cheek at midnight. He took photographs and joined in with some of the climbing banter.

'If you, Boardman and Renshawe get chopped on K2,' shouted someone, 'I'll move three rungs up the mountaineering ladder!'

Sick, I thought, but Joe just laughed.

The car had to be dug and pushed out of a snowdrift the next day.

'Call in for a brew!' We just caught the words as the big brown Granada Estate skidded off along the track. The remains of the party tramped down the hill and drove over in convoy for a lunchtime session at The Moon, a climbers' drinking hole on the way to Sheffield. At three o'clock we were turfed out and the group split. Two carloads set off back to Manchester.

'Let's drop in on Joe,' suggested Julie. 'It's on the way.'

The village of Hope was once all winding streets and old stone houses, clustered around an ancient church and graveyard; in more recent years one side has been stretched like chewing gum into a new road and modern houses have sprouted up on either side of it. 'Magic Mountain' stood back from this road, almost at the boundary of the village. We parked the cars right in front of the shop window.

'Thomas Mann,' I said.

'Who? What?'

'He wrote *The Magic Mountain.*'

'Oh, yes, Joe's the intellectual type all right.'

Above the shop, along a corridor littered with climbing boots, ropes and boxes of freeze-dried food, was a comfortable flat. A log fire blazed, wicker furniture was softened with Eastern-looking cushions, there was a comfortable sofa, and Indian rugs lay over the carpet. Two silk-screen prints of couples in extremely unlikely sexual positions hung on one wall.

A woman was with Joe; she made us tea and then sat against his knee on the floor, smiling. I wondered why she had not been at the party but did not ask. Joe rested a hand on her shoulder; they seemed content and comfortable together. It was a feeling I barely remembered. The man with me leaned over to run a finger across my eyebrow, seeming to sense my envy.

A few weeks later, early in February, I visited the same friends in their farmhouse and we went along to a climbing club disco at the local pub. Squeezing through the press of people on the way to the bar I caught sight of Joe. He waved and mouthed 'Hello' to me across the noisy babble of voices. The pub was packed, but when I returned with the drinks Annie had found us a wall to lean against. I could see his head and torso through the crowd. Arms across his chest, a pint of beer in one hand, leaning back slightly and laughing a lot. The sleeves of his sweater were pushed up and his forearms looked taut and strong. Our eyes kept meeting: he was watching me too. Suddenly he was at my side.

'I've got some good photos of you from the New Year's party,' he said. 'Come to the "do" at The Moon tomorrow night and I'll show you them.'

I opened my mouth to reply but he carried on.

'I talked to your brother on the phone today. I'm giving a lecture in London next Saturday and staying at his place. I told him I'd met you. Why don't you come along and visit him? It's good to have company in the car.'

My face flushed.

'Annie, this is Joe. Joe Tasker.' A weak attempt to cover my confusion with an introduction.

'Maria, we've already met. At the farm on New Year's Eve. He brought the stereo. Remember?' She shook her head, bemused.

Well done Maria, I thought, watching his retreating back as he went off to get drinks, you really impressed him there.

'He seems like a nice man,' said Annie.

I agreed, and quickly changed the subject.

On the following evening Annie suggested that we go to The Moon, but I demurred, fearful of how strongly I felt drawn to Joe. Going to London and back in his company seemed less threatening; I phoned and arranged it.

Once again we sat together in a car and talked for hours, stealing glances at each other's profiles. He told me about his Himalayan expeditions, five over the past four years. And how his training for the priesthood in a Jesuit seminary helped him to cope with the deprivation he faced in the mountains.

'How long were you there?'

'Seven years. Almost.'

'*Seven years?*'

'How long were you at convent school, then?'

'I started there when I was eleven . . . uumm . . . seven years. But that's different. I went home every night. How old were you when you got out?'

'Sounds like prison. Twenty.'

'Hhmmm.'

'I know what you're thinking.'

'Do you?'

'I had most success with girls when I was training as a priest. I'd go home in the holidays and they'd be after me.'

'Why?'

'Thanks! Well, for the same reason you went "Hhmm." They were fascinated because I was unattainable, and because they presumed I was a virgin.'

'Were you? Until your twenties?'

'I'm not saying. I've still got a lot of catching up to do, though.'

It was hard to pin him down and get to his real feelings.

'Why did you leave?'

'I decided that I didn't want to be a priest. I'd known for a while, but it was a terribly hard decision.'

'Do you regret it? Locked away for all those teenage years?'

'In some ways. But not really. It happened, it's part of who I am now. And I got an excellent classical education. With my background I simply wouldn't have had the chance otherwise.'

Our upbringings were similar – Catholic families, far from well off but secure and supportive.

'Tell me about when you lived in Peru.'

I described Arequipa, where I had worked, and the beautiful

volcano Misti that towers above the town. I told him about my trips through the Andes, across Bolivia and down to Patagonia. We were intrigued by each other.

While Joe lectured at the Alpine Club my brother introduced me to his latest haunt, a bar where the waiters slid around on roller skates and served deadly cocktails.

. 'So, what are the sleeping arrangements tonight?' he asked.

'I'll have the spare room to myself,' I replied. 'We're just friends.' By the time Joe returned to Mick's flat I was in bed and asleep; I was not sure why, but I did not want to see him when I was drunk and less in control of my feelings.

He brought me tea in the morning and said quizzically, 'I thought you were the original owl. What happened to you last night?'

We left after a late breakfast and called into a trade show in a London suburb, where a company selling paper shredders was using one of Joe's photographs on their stand. He was friendly and businesslike with the representative and I watched him, admiring his ease and self-confidence. As we wandered around the other stands together I had an urge, which I quickly repressed, to reach out and hold his hand.

Later, at a motorway service station, he loped back to the car after paying for petrol, his stride easy and relaxed and his arms cradling bottled drinks and bags of sweets and crisps.

'How's the hangover? Fancy coming along to the lecture this evening?' A scout group on the outskirts of Manchester had asked him to show some slides and present an award. 'They wanted Pete Boardman, I'm second best really.'

A wooden hut, foldaway chairs, anxious and overawed scouts; the occasion held no financial reward or kudos for Joe yet he performed as well as I saw him perform on future occasions, in major London halls or on television, and he made each of the boys feel important. I was impressed and hardly noticed the slides and his account of climbing Kangchenjunga. We said goodbye in the car park, and kissed briefly.

'Give me a ring,' he said. 'Let's go and watch a film together.'

While I drove home through neon-lit streets my mind swung through its own curves; an involvement with Joe seemed to be inevitably approaching, I sensed it was within my reach, and yet I had misgivings. He had told me about the woman I had seen at his flat. Force of circumstance had driven them apart: she was married and, although she and Joe wanted to be together, she had recently made the difficult decision to stay with her husband and keep their family intact. It was obvious that, despite the impossibility of the situation, she was still firmly in Joe's heart.

'The best relationship I've ever had . . . am still having,' he said. And within two months he would be leaving for Pakistan to climb K2. This was to be his second attempt on it.

The first had been the expedition in which Nick Estcourt lost his life. I remembered the sunny afternoon in Manchester eighteen months before, loud pop music coming from the radio in my brother John's kitchen. At half past the hour there had been a news broadcast and Nick's death in an avalanche on K2 was announced. John came into the room.

'Estcourt? Isn't he your mate from Altrincham – the one with the shop?'

A mate; only an acquaintance really and yet the feeling was strong, that stunned realization that someone is gone, suddenly consigned to the past and to memory. It was the first time anyone I knew had died in the mountains. I thought about his wife and children, how it must be for them. I tried to put a letter together to send my condolences, but could not find the words. From then on I would sympathize with the women involved with mountaineers, imagining the worry and strain they dealt with while the men were away following their dreams. I had marvelled at how calmly Alex's girlfriend bade him farewell as he left my house for one of his frequent expeditions.

'I was holding on,' she told me later. 'You should have seen me when he'd gone and I was driving away down the motorway.'

And my mind spun back to Mick, my brother Mick falling into a crevasse during an expedition in the early 1970s. That was a close one, I thought, as I waited at the traffic lights. I was nearly home. I remembered reading the headline: 'Climber Rescued from Tomb of Ice', in a newspaper I had bought in Liverpool, at Lime Street Station. It had taken me a few seconds to realize the familiarity of the names and photographs in the article. I had rushed to phone my parents. Someone in the press had had the forethought to contact them just before the papers came out, to make sure they knew, but my mother had not been able to reach me in time.

I was strongly drawn to Joe, yet I knew enough about the world of mountaineering to realize that loving him would bring separation and stress along with happiness. I was wary of a relationship complicated by other emotional ties. And he was soon to be going away on an expedition . . .

By the time I drew up outside my front door the decision was made: we would be friends, and nothing more.

The doorbell rang one evening, some days later, and Joe was on the step, wrapped in his sheepskin coat and leaning against the wall. He was on his way to give a lecture in Manchester, he explained, and one of his car headlights had failed. He was anxious about being stopped by the police. Could he borrow my car to drive into the city centre, and perhaps stay over that night so that he could return to Derbyshire in daylight the following morning? I agreed and in minutes he was gone, leaving me dazed. My friend Catriona, a lodger in the house since Alex had moved out, laughed heartily.

'Well, it's obvious, Maria,' she said. 'He *likes* you!'

Having decided against the telephone call and the film, I had expected to see him, if at all, only at one of the several parties that were always thrown prior to an expedition. This sudden reappearance stirred up a whole host of mixed feelings. A new relationship appealed, the wildness of the social scene I moved in was beginning to pall and a need for some peace and quiet was creeping up on me. Joe liked to have a good time but he had a seriousness and a sense of responsibility about him also. And I enjoyed being with him, he was amusing and kind and intelligent and . . . and he was a mountaineer who went away for months at a time on dangerous climbs. Catriona chewed over these thoughts with me.

'Well, I think he's a cracker,' she teased. 'If you don't want him I'll have him.'

When he returned at eleven I was ready for bed.

'You can sleep down here,' I told him, throwing a sleeping-bag onto the sofa and ignoring the slight surprise that registered in his eyes. I quickly gave him tea and bade him goodnight.

Catriona ran downstairs during the early hours to get a glass of water. She was stark naked.

'I put the light on and went into the kitchen,' she recounted. 'On the way back through the living room I heard this rustle – there was Joe, propped up on one elbow like a big grinning caterpillar, enjoying the view. He's a cheeky man! And anyway, how was I to know you were making him sleep down there!'

Breakfast was rushed; Joe had to get back to open up his climbing equipment shop and I was late for work.

'I'll let myself out,' he said, getting up from the table. 'I have a meeting in Manchester this afternoon. How about dinner and a film later on?'

I decided to cook a meal and, needing moral support, I asked Catriona and her boyfriend to join us.

'What's *wrong* with you?' she teased. 'You said he's just a friend and now you're acting like a teenager on a first date!'

How could I explain myself – something important in my life seemed to be irresistibly underway despite my misgivings, but it was intangible, nothing had yet happened that I could point to. She was right: I had not felt so nervous about going out with a man in years.

Joe phoned early in the evening. His meeting was still on: he would be an hour late. Catriona's boyfriend found the situation, and my nervousness, hilarious.

'This is turning into a real courtship,' he said. 'Here, smoke some of this, it will calm you down.'

Joe arrived to find me in a near-catatonic state, a result of the drug and my general anxiety. Bottles of wine were drunk, another joint was passed around after dinner and we left for the local cinema on foot, neither of us capable of driving by then.

The film was *Manhattan*. I had seen it before but now I could not follow the plot at all. He'll think I'm a total idiot, I said to myself. Joe leaned over.

'What on earth is going on?' he whispered.

'No idea,' I admitted.

'I thought you said you'd seen this before.'

'I have!'

His arm came round my shoulders and he hugged me.

'I'd better keep you off the grass next time we watch a film.'

I leaned against him, breathed out and began to relax.

THREE

It wasn't always easy, right from the start. I stood on the sidelines, gazing in at the world of top mountaineers where egos were large and personalities well defined.

'Do *you* climb?' was a frequent question and I would resent the assumption behind it; but deep down I wished the answer was yes, because of that fullness of experience, that edging closer to life's boundaries which shone through the eyes of those people and for which I envied them. The climbing community drew me in: I was no longer just a girl who turned up at parties but now an integral and accepted member and, like any good family, it offered security, squabbling and fun. It was there for me to turn to when I was alone, which was often.

Six weeks we had, Joe and I, after becoming lovers and before he left for K2, but it was not a time of leisurely learning about each other; our romance was squeezed in amongst all his pressing commitments. His shop was to be in the hands of a manager for the months he would be away so there was much for him to finalize and arrange. And there was a last-minute panic about finances. The expedition was short of the money it needed by thousands of pounds and it fell to Joe to sort this out. While he fielded telephone calls and rushed around by car for meetings or for television and radio appearances to publicize the expedition, I would be in the background, cooking for him and waiting for when he would finally stop, usually around ten at night, and relax. It was a change in my lifestyle, to say the least, but it passed almost unnoticed at first because few people realized that Joe and I were together. We were both moving out of other relationships and decided to keep quiet about our blossoming one for the time being.

For me it was a relief to be finally still, to be centred on one person and not part of a social whirligig. Falling in love occurred quickly, despite my caution. Joe was perplexed.

'I didn't mean this to happen,' he mumbled helplessly into my neck, when we woke in the dark at the same moment and reached for each other. Here was a sudden sense of his life swerving out of control: it was something he had not accounted for in his plans. That night, in my bed, I could almost visualize the way he applied the brakes on his feelings.

'I can't commit myself,' he said. 'You have to realize and accept that or we can't continue.'

'So what do you want?' I asked. 'We're obviously not just friends.'

I felt him shake his head.

'I don't know what to say. It's partly that I still have strong feelings for someone else. Is it possible to love more than one person? But it's also the climbing. I'm going away soon. I just don't know how I'll feel once I'm out there. This must all sound awful. Does it?'

It was confusing. Strength and independence were qualities Joe had perceived in me and been attracted to: they complemented his desire for freedom and latitude within a relationship. The second time I had cooked a meal for him he arrived two hours late. I had heard a radio report about the motorway jam and presumed that was the reason for his tardiness.

'Aren't you cross?' he asked as he walked in.

'No,' I replied truthfully, 'but I got hungry so I went ahead and ate. I've kept yours warm and I haven't started on the wine yet.'

His mouth hung open. He was flabbergasted.

'You mean . . . you've already had dinner . . . you didn't sit here and fume?'

'Don't be silly,' I laughed, amazed at his admiration and flattered that he should find my behaviour unusual.

'You give the impression of being unattainable,' he had said at the beginning, and I realized how much my initial holding back had made him eager to win me over. He always liked to work for his rewards. But he hadn't bargained for the unpredictable nature of human emotions. He hadn't realized that my self-possession was not the whole story, or that the strength and the independence covered insecurities and a deep-seated loneliness. When my defences were down, when I made it clear that I needed him, he backed away, alarmed by the vulnerability that love drew out in me. I was faced with a choice – to accept this man and the uncompromising and uncertain future he offered me, or to leave before our love affair became more involved. I found that I could not and did not want to turn away.

The seriousness of the climb he was preparing for dawned on me gradually. K2 is the second highest mountain in the world, only a few hundred feet lower than Everest. Its reputation as being difficult to scale, with an attendant list of accidents and deaths, was something I gleaned from conversation and from dipping into the literature around Joe's flat; I could not bring myself to make direct enquiries. He spoke little of his previous climb there, in 1978, but we came close to a row once when he told me of how hard it had been to decide to abandon that expedition after Nick Estcourt's death in an avalanche.

'Wasn't it the only thing to do, Joe? I mean, why did you need to discuss it? How could you have carried on after that?'

I recalled listening to the news broadcast, to the announcement that they were on their way home, a sign, it seemed to me at the time, of respect for Nick and his family. Joe responded crossly, on the defensive.

'Maybe Nick would have wished us to continue. Have you thought of that?'

'Does it matter what he would have wished? Surely your priority should have been the feelings of Carolyn and his kids? How would they have felt if you had carried on?'

'Don't push me into this role of unfeeling male, Maria. It wasn't as easy for me, or for any of the others, as you obviously think it was.'

The argument was short–lived: it was a subject uncomfortably close to the heart, to our own reality.

The six weeks before the expedition began were intense. We discovered each other fast and our times together were compressed like small but bulging packages. If I could not see Joe for a day or two, he would telephone and we would chat and gossip. Within the harsh boundaries that he set on the relationship there was a tenderness and caring, a special quality that made me aware that this was no fleeting love affair – the feeling would last, whatever was to happen between us. He came to stay at my house whenever he could, finding a respite there from his hectic schedule.

'It's marvellous to know that when the phone rings it's not for me.'

Shortly before he left we went to see *Apocalypse Now*. Visually, musically, and through its message, the film stunned Joe. I bought him the two books on which the screen play was based, *Heart of Darkness* and *Dispatches*, and he was already a devotee of the music of Jim Morrison and The Doors. A common theme ran through them all – the fine line between order and chaos, and the unknown territory that one faces if the line is crossed. This seemed to tap into Joe's deepest feelings about his climbing, and we talked about it a lot during his last days in England.

'Do you know what it's like, to be so close to the edge, to almost let go of control?' he asked, as much of himself as of me.

I told him of how I had once nearly drowned and of my awareness, in the minutes before losing consciousness, that I was actually holding onto life, that I could easily give up the fight and let myself slip away. And we had both experimented with LSD during student days. For me it was only twice but on both occasions my senses seemed to open up and become powerfully attuned to everything around. Joe's experiences had been more extreme.

'I saw things that just weren't there.'

'Were you afraid?'

'No, it was weirdly fascinating. A part of my mind knew what was going on and just let it happen; it was like watching a film of myself having the hallucinations. I never completely let go of control. It was the same coming down off Dunagiri – I saw people who weren't there. But somehow I made it down and so did Dick.'

They had spent four nights and five days descending from that mountain, without food or water.

'If you'd let go of control then, if you'd let yourself go into those hallucinations, you wouldn't have survived,' I said. 'It's the same with the drugs – allow yourself totally into the experience and you risk madness.'

Joe was looking at me thoughtfully.

'For an old hippy you're quite wise,' he said, his face breaking into a grin.

Our first parting was a bewildered one. I left him outside his shop, early on a May morning. He was to drive to London that afternoon and fly to Pakistan the following day. It would be three months at least before we would see each other again, and somewhere deep inside I acknowledged the possibility of his not returning. During the final days he had withdrawn from me emotionally and, with

24

no understanding back then of how he prepared himself for an expedition, I took his detachment personally. He had been covering his feelings well, but I realized that he still cared for the woman who had left him four months before. I knew that they still wrote to each other and it was a situation which made me insecure. I clung to him outside his shop, and my defences fell away.

'What will happen when you get back? Will we be together?'

He paused before answering and chewed his lip.

'Let's see what happens,' he replied.

I cried all the way back to Manchester. Al Harris was in town, and that night he and Catriona's boyfriend took me to a punk concert. The anarchy of the music matched my inner turmoil and I let myself be pushed around by the excited crowd. Joe rang from the airport, early the next morning. There was so much to say to him, words formulated the previous day, but all I did was weep down the telephone.

Then came the first of the long and uncertain periods that I was to become more used to, when I was one of the women I used to pity: a climber's girlfriend, left at home, watching for mail.

'It's like wartime,' said my friend Viola, who came to live with me while Joe was away and who was openly puzzled at the turn my life had taken. It took weeks for his first letter to arrive.

'Emotionally I am in a bit of a limbo,' he wrote. 'I know it must be awful for you and I can see that my whole behaviour must seem weird. On a trip like this, when all outside stimulus is removed, I find I am very detached. If I do think about what I am doing I am puzzled and bewildered, but thinking about things which are so far away in space and time can become a torture, so I just drift.'

He wrote regularly then, sounding off his frustrations over the progress of the expedition and saying little in the way of romance, but at least reassuring me that he hoped I would be there when he returned.

The previous Christmas I had begun a new job, teaching English to Vietnamese refugees in a Manchester reception centre. Whole family groups arrived from Hong Kong and stayed at the centre until houses were found for them. To cope with the constant turnover of students, English lessons were to be held year round and we teachers had the luxurious perk of being able to organize our thirteen weeks of annual holidays in rotation with each other. I decided that travelling while Joe was away would help me to cope with the separation. I flew to the States, met up with four friends, and drove cross-country with them in an old limousine. A few days after my return a letter arrived from Joe which wiped away the post-vacation euphoria. It had been written from the K2 Base Camp, and dated 17-8-80; in his confusion he had been a month ahead of himself.

'I don't quite know how to start this letter,' he wrote. 'It's not any romantic, emotional reason, it's just that I feel plain and simply wiped out. I couldn't have written yesterday and as it is I have to suppress a lot and not look at the events of the past few days directly in order to get by.

'Yesterday Pete, Dick and I arrived back here after what will probably, I hope, be one of the most profound experiences ever for us. It affects us all differently, but I know that I haven't come to terms with its implications and last night I went to sleep twitching at the slightest rustle of the tent, or rattle of a stone outside, imagining rocks plying away from ice, and slipping into dreams of hospital wards and personal Apocalypses.

'On the night of July 13th Pete, Dick and I were hit twice, at 26,500 ft, by avalanches. We were lucky to be alive, but I think it was the next three days struggling to survive that induced this state of shock. The weather, in spite of forecasts, was bad, and having decided to retreat, though only about six hours from the summit, we found our retreat barred by thigh-deep, avalanche-prone slopes. We hadn't the food or fuel to stay put so we had to try to get down. For three days, growing more and more exhausted, we struggled down in appalling weather – the mountain was totally in control.

'When we stumbled into Base Camp yesterday some American friends were there who had joined our Base Camp, and so was Georges Bettembourg from our Kanch expedition and I was glad, as we stumbled into this welcome committee (they had followed our painful progress by walkie-talkie without being able to help), of my reflective sunglasses, no one could see the tears of relief and gratitude in my eyes.'

The blue aerogramme was lying on my hallway carpet when I came home from work. I ripped it open on the way through to the living room. Standing stock still by the table, I rested a steadying hand on the brown chenille cloth, trembling as I read. Only recently, lying in American sunshine, I had tried to visualize Joe in freezing temperatures and howling winds. Now there was no effort, the image of tons of snow and ice engulfing him wiped away the reality of the sticky summer day in the city. His letter was like a telegram account of his experience, and it filled my mind with pictures. 'Avalanche'. The word brought a chill of horror, the deep-seated fear of nature taking hold, taking control, as Joe had said. As a child I had imagined an avalanche to be a rush of soft hissing snow that swept its captive along and over some unseen edge. Now I knew a little more: I knew that the snow was more often like wet concrete and held huge blocks of ice, that death was usually by suffocation, and that it was a terror for those who gambled in the mountains. Nick Estcourt had pitted himself against K2 just as Joe was doing now, and had lost. An avalanche took him away, over that edge, as he carried supplies up to where Joe and Pete were camped. He crossed a slope at the wrong time; he decided to take the lead only minutes before; it could so easily have been someone else or no one at all. The stakes were high: Alex had once quoted a fatality rate to me of one in ten among high-altitude mountaineers. And those at home, all the families and the lovers, they had their futures hanging in the balance too. Ah, but Joe had not been claimed this time — he was alive.

There was nothing, no previous experience or foreknowledge, to prepare me for his closing paragraph.

'We decided on the way down not to discuss going back up until we reached Base Camp. Really we should all be back for one reason or another and our visas run out on July 31st, but we were so close we will probably have one more go. We will be all right this time. Tara for now. Love Joe.'

Again and again I read the words. '. . . we will probably have one more go. We will be all right this time . . .' It was the beginning of August. They had planned to be back by now; Dick's baby was almost due to be born; how could they even consider going back up the mountain after escaping death so narrowly? The fact that he had written from Base Camp and that, before the closing sentence, I presumed he was out of danger, had allowed me in those minutes to open up to the reality of the danger he faced, moment to moment, while climbing K2. This letter was two and a half weeks old; he could already be making another summit attempt. It was too late to close down my channels of imagination: all the possibilities generated by the slip of paper in my hand took hold. There was no way of knowing if Joe, or any of the others, were dead or alive.

Desperation and anger hit me in turn. I paced through the house clutching the letter, rereading it until I almost knew it by heart, asking myself why, why would they go back up the mountain and

27

risk so much, why did they climb at all, why had my life led me to this moment of rising, anchorless panic? It was hard to know what to do, whom to turn to. The need to talk and to share the worry grew strong, but my neighbour registered incomprehension at what I told her. Alex was away on an expedition, so I phoned a couple of other climbers.

'Nothing to be done, love,' said the one I reached, 'but no news is good news.'

For nine days I hung onto that well-used cliché, until Joe rang me from Islamabad.

'We didn't make it on the second try but we're all fine. I'll be home on the twelfth.'

Once again I was wordless at the end of the telephone, this time aware of nothing except overwhelming relief.

When Joe returned from the later expeditions there would be a resurgence of feeling between us, an excitement as fresh and keen as when we were first together. But after K2 he had psychological wounds that were deep and still open. Holding him in bed on the first night, I felt bones where the fleshy part of his buttocks should have been, and a picture formed in my mind of his body running out of resources during his ordeal and beginning to consume itself. Throughout that night he shuddered and groaned, and sometimes clutched me to him fiercely, a source of comfort and security amid whatever darkness possessed him as he slept. Physical love was impossible.

'The avalanche . . . and coming down off the mountain . . . it was really awful.' He searched for words to explain. 'We only just survived; I feel as if I've looked into an abyss . . . and whenever I begin to let go of control, when I'm drifting into sleep or we begin to make love, it looms up before me again. I'm sorry, there's nothing I can do, it's going to take time.'

My present for him from America was a pair of rainbow-coloured braces, intended only as an item of fashion. Joe had lost so much weight that he really needed them to hold up his trousers.

'Don't be surprised,' I warned Viola, who had never met him, as we waited for Joe's arrival at my house one evening. 'He looks funny at the moment.'

In he came, a pinched, sunken face framed by newly-trimmed beard and hair, and jeans that were suspended around his waist by the new braces. But he was on the mend by then, a twinkle had returned to his eyes and Viola was charmed.

As Joe began to recover, physically and mentally, so our relationship took on as much normality as was possible in the circumstances. In just over three months he would be leaving again for another expedition; he had a shop to run, articles to write and lectures and interviews to give, before even beginning to think about preparing for the next trip. Our time together was frustratingly limited. He did not ask me to do it, but I began to bend my life around his so as to be with him whenever possible, capitalizing on the flexibility of my job and making him a priority in the planning of my days. For Joe there was little compromise: he had a busy schedule and I squeezed in where I could. There was no question of his changing any of his plans because of a relationship; from the beginning I had realized that it was a 'take it or leave it' situation.

'You were attracted to me because of my energy and my drive,' he said, when we discussed this on more than one occasion, 'and if I changed I wouldn't be the same person and you might not like me any more.'

As an argument it was hard to fault. His past love affairs had usually foundered on the rocks of this single-mindedness, and I had gone in with open eyes and no illusions; all my forethought, and the fact that he was careful not to make demands upon me, made it hard for me to complain too loudly.

'At least you've finally stopped rushing around the country,' commented a friend. And it was true, I was more at peace than ever before. Joe's shop and flat were in a valley, surrounded by rolling hills of heather and sheep and stone walls. On Saturday mornings, while he opened up 'Magic Mountain', I would lie in bed, listening to the muffled tones of his voice below and the ping of the shop bell. And then I would hike or drive over to visit my friends in their farmhouse, until he was free. The scarcity of our time together lent it a quality I had never known. Just being by the fire, eating, laughing, drinking, watching a late-night film were the best moments, the ones most treasured in memory.

Domesticity continued to creep up on me. I would catch myself happily pottering around his flat or my house and wonder at the transformation. In some ways it was what I had wanted, to be more settled, but there was also an element of seeking to adapt to the role into which I had been cast. Joe was the adventurer, the risk-taker, and his life was compartmentalized into 'expedition' and 'at home'. I could not share in his climbing; those experiences were his alone. He was critical of mountaineers who took wives or girlfriends along to Base Camp on trips, seeing it as a dilution of their energy and commitment. Becoming the nurturer, keeping a place warm and dry and comfortable for him to return to, this went against the grain of all that I had claimed to believe in, against years of active feminism and freewheeling independence, and yet it was what happened. If we were to be together, if our lives were to intermingle and each give extra meaning to the other, then my part in the relationship had to be the more passive, for if I were as busy and committed as he, we would simply never see each other. Joe was incensed when I voiced this, and he claimed that I was overreacting.

'I'm not looking for a housekeeper, for Christ's sake.'

He had no expectations of me, domestically – he was capable and willing to look after himself – yet he was always glad nonetheless to come home, after an expedition or simply a day at work, to meals, a comfortable environment, and a person to whom he could relate and talk through his problems and successes.

'This is marvellous,' he would say. 'I'm really grateful, but don't feel you have to do it.'

And I would reflect that perhaps it would be easier if he did expect more of me, because this 'honest' stance of no true commitment and no real demands was frustrating and somehow unreal: it was an avoidance of compromise and sharing, the basic fabric of relationships. I enjoyed caring for him and did not feel trapped by it or resentful in any way, but I was moulding myself around his preoccupations without complementary movement on his part, and it put us off balance. Attempts to discuss this usually led to heated feelings. Joe reacted with anger at any show of what he mockingly referred to as 'femininism', the extra syllable a sign of his disparagement. And I would become infuriated by his refusal even to consider what seemed to me the very simple and easily analysed pattern that was emerging between us. But I was afraid of fighting; it seemed a waste within our limited timescale and too often I bottled up feelings, unaware of how quickly they seeped through some chink in my reserve.

'I'm not a mind-reader,' Joe would say, trying to pry out of me whatever was closing up my face and heart to him. There was no easy answer. We had to work things out as we went along, amid the busy times and the separations.

When he was at home he wanted to miss nothing: the parties were fun, there was camaraderie in the pubs and we were well matched for the social life we led. We both had a gregarious side to our natures and his love of controversy suited my often outlandish dress sense, which he encouraged. He returned once from a trade show bearing a large plastic bag.

'Have a look in there.'

Inside was a garish suit jacket with pictures of Marlboro cigarette packets printed all over it.

'Ugh, it's *awful*, Joe!'

'What do you mean? Don't you like it? It took me ages to persuade the girl on the stand to let me have one. I thought it was your sort of thing – I got it for you.'

It fitted him anyway so we reversed roles and he wore the jacket to the pub. The amused comments it provoked seemed to spur him on. Instead of the occasional cigarette he would usually accept from a friend, that night he bought a packet of his own and chain-smoked until closing time.

Perhaps because they had a keen awareness of their own mortality, the mountaineers often gave the impression of taking nothing and nobody seriously, especially themselves. We all laughed a lot, and the hilarity and teasing would reach a pitch just before and after expeditions when tension, and then relief, would rise to the surface and bubble over.

Three weeks after Joe returned from K2 there was a party at his flat for a group of visiting Japanese climbers. Alex arranged for funds from the British Mountaineering Council and invited lots of people, and, with Viola, I prepared a lavish buffet and bar. It was a Saturday afternoon, and guests would begin to arrive around six, when the day's rock-climbing was over. Joe popped up from the shop to see how we were getting on.

'Oooo, Fifi!' He had discovered Viola's nickname and would call her nothing else. 'What are you planning to do to these poor Japanese boys? They don't drink alcohol, you know.'

'Don't they? Hmmmm. Can you think of something they might prefer? What do Japanese boys like?'

'That depends, Fifi. What are you good at?'

31

'Hmmmmm! Well, I'm fairly capable all round, actually.'

Bliss for Joe, a girl who would thrust and parry to his teasing. It was a while before I could get any sensible conversation out of them again, but he eventually produced the cases of non-alcoholic beer given to him by the company that had sponsored the K2 trip. There was no room for them in the fridge so they were left where he put them, on the living-room floor.

The first guests arrived, hungry and thirsty after climbing on nearby crags, and the flat began to fill with the noise of quickly inebriated people. By the time Alex ushered in twelve shy young Japanese men the party was in full swing. I went in search of the non—alcoholic beer and found an empty case at the feet of two guffawing friends, both renowned for their drinking prowess.

'Er, would you two like some real beer?' I suppressed a grin. 'There's lots in the kitchen.'

'Real beer? What's this then?' said one, squinting at the label. 'Bloody hell!' he exploded, 'I've had six of these and I feel pissed!'

I found enough Coca-Cola to go round the guests of honour who were smiling broadly at the scene and talking to people through their interpreter.

'Got any dried mint?' asked one wild-eyed young climber, and I should have known better than to let him have some: it was the beginning of the magic mushroom season. But I was busy being the successful hostess and guided him to where Joe kept his selection of teas. Some time later I noticed two of the Japanese men and one of Alex's superiors from the British Mountaineering Council sipping from bowls Joe had brought back from Tokyo.

'What are they drinking?' I asked the interpreter, as nonchalantly as I could. He glanced over.

'Green tea,' he said. 'Someone's got a pot of it going in the kitchen.'

Joe was leaning against the stove, rosy-cheeked and smiling.

'Here you are,' he said, putting an arm around me. 'Stop flashing by and stay with me for a minute.'

'Joe,' I hissed urgently, 'two of the Japanese men and a bloke from the BMC are in there drinking magic mushroom tea and they probably don't know what it is.'

The BMC man appeared at my elbow.

'Great tea,' he bawled, 'any more left?'

The yellow pot was hoisted aloft and passed over heads towards him. I grabbed it.

'You'd better not drink this,' I said firmly.

'Now, now,' he coaxed, reclaiming the pot, 'I was drinking green tea before you were born,' and with an exaggerated wink he turned and marched back into the living room.

'Don't worry,' laughed Joe, 'it will be something for them to talk about when they get home.'

. I never found out if they knew what they were drinking, but legend has it that later that night, back in Manchester, an elderly couple were alarmed to see a minibus park in their driveway and disgorge twelve young Orientals led by an Englishman who, key in hand, strode purposefully towards the wrong front door.

I fell more and more in love with Joe, yet beneath the headiness and happiness of that state an unseen menace lay coiled; from time to time it would stir, as if to remind me that it held the power to fling me out of my previously unscathed existence, and that I should be watchful of its awakening. No bereavement or illness or major crisis had marred the passage into my twenties, I was childless and not responsible for anyone except myself. Going through school and university in the 1960s and '70s had been carefree, without the blight of unemployment or the pressures of extreme materialism. There had been a series of boyfriends and a few heartbreaks, but nothing and no one had touched my innermost core of feeling or threatened to wipe away the foundations of happiness. Life was light, I worked as a teacher, I took time out to travel, with my parents' help I bought a house and a car. But the sense that something was not really in place kept me from feeling settled and I searched haphazardly through people, places and experiences without knowing exactly what I was looking for. When Joe came into my life the feeling of arrival was overwhelmingly strong. I had applied for two different jobs when we first met, one for a posting in Ecuador, the other for a new position working with Vietnamese refugees in Manchester. The possible choice presented me with a dilemma. I had longed to return to South America, yet cringed from the thought of being uprooted and thrown onto my own resources with no support system; in England I was having fun, I had my own place and good friends. The decision was made for me; the British Council informed me that the position in Ecuador no longer needed to be filled as a resignation had been withdrawn, and days later Manchester offered me the job with refugees, which I took. By this time I had been mulling over whether or not to start a relationship with Joe. At the bottom of my heart, despite all the procrastinations, I knew it would be impossible to refuse him. Perhaps I held back at first because I guessed that the lessons ahead would be hard ones. And they were, right from the beginning. I was in love with a man who courted death, whose life made more sense to him if he pushed at its limits. It was not the fact that he climbed: it could have been anything that held an element of danger. If he had sailed, no doubt he would have chosen long, solitary and difficult voyages; if the country went to war he would opt for perilous missions. It was his nature: Joe did not want an easy life, though he often claimed to envy those people who could relax and be at peace with what and where they were. Which was how I felt, finally, with him. But along with that peace came the unseen menace, dormant but stirring.

'Climbing isn't as dangerous as everyone makes it out to be,' he said once. 'I could just as easily be killed crossing the road.'

But he knew, and so did I, that the stakes he faced were much, much higher.

It was rare that we were able to spend a whole, uninterrupted weekend together, but in mid-September, four weeks after his return from K2, we got away to the Lake District and spent two nights alone in a cottage, without a telephone. Joe's post-K2 tiredness caught up with him once he relaxed, and he was asleep by nine o'clock on the first evening. When he finally woke up, twelve hours later, he was astounded.

'I normally only do that on expeditions. Did I miss anything last night?'

On the Sunday I persuaded him to hike, something he usually vehemently refused to do in England.

'It took us nine days to walk out of K2 Base Camp and that was a forced march to beat the birth of Dick's baby,' he protested. 'I thought you brought me here for a rest – can't we stay in bed and read the papers?'

'Oh, come on, Joe. It's such a lovely day.'

'All right, then, but nothing too strenuous.'

We drove to the Duddon valley, parked in the village of Seathwaite and walked up to the crag above.

'I might as well climb for a while,' said Joe, and he gazed up at the rock wall, pointing out the different routes that he could take to scale it. Some looked easy, with hand and footholds visible from where we stood, but others, like the narrow vertical crag that Joe chose, seemed impossible to me. He set off, in jeans and trainers, without ropes, pegs or any of the usual protection, and overtook others on the crag who clanked as they moved, weighed down by all their hardware. I took photographs of him: how easy he makes it look, I thought. One slip and so much would change.

. As we headed back down the hill Joe said that he wanted to visit a couple who lived in the village. Their son, with three of his companions, had died in a fall in the Himalayas some years before. Joe and Pete were on the same mountain at the time and they went up to bury the bodies in crevasses. We were walking along a sunny, windy path as he told me the story. His eyes were hidden by sunglasses and his face was set.

'It was awful. I dreaded reaching them and having to decide what to do. But I can't be a mountaineer and then turn away from the possible consequences when they happen.'

He described examining the bodies and then using ropes to lower them into the mountain grave.

'Why not just leave them?' I asked, wishing I hadn't when he replied, 'Because of the birds.'

We were nearly at the village. Despite the sun and our brisk walking, I felt chilled and my head swam with images of snow and broken bodies and yawning crevasses. He broke the silence between us.

'I think it means a lot to these folk that I keep in touch. It seems to give them a link to their son. If it were me, I'd appreciate someone doing the same for my parents.'

As we stopped to pass through a gate I put my arms around him and pressed my face against his neck.

'Oh, Joe . . .'

There was nothing else to say. How could I put into words the fear that some day it could be him? What point would there be in even trying? His body was tense and after a few moments he gently moved me away and we walked to the house. The couple were delighted to see him. We sat in a tranquil, wood-lined room and they gave us slices of cake, and tea in delicate china cups. Next to me on a window-sill, photographs of their son and his wife peeped out from between potted plants and flowers. They talked and smiled and a clock ticked when the conversation paused. Sadness hung in the air and was harder to bear, somehow, because of their quiet dignity. Joe answered their questions about his future plans and they showed no disapproval that he was still climbing, but bade him to take care.

We drove away in silence. I leaned my head against the seat and shut my eyes tight, closing out the softening colours of late afternoon, hoping that the menace would cease its stirring, curl up quietly again and leave me in peace. It could be him one day. It could be him. There was too much tension in the car, I had to break it.

'Those people. They're lovely. It was good of you to go.'

For a few seconds there was no reply, and then, 'You probably think I'm hardened to such things, Maria, but really I'm not, it's always difficult.' He paused. 'Sometimes I wonder why I can't be content with Sunday rock-climbs like all those blokes on the crag this afternoon.'

I reached over to him, wanting to ease the strain we both felt. 'Perhaps we could arrange for a frontal lobotomy, Joe.'

He laughed.

'D'you think that would do it?'

The summer of 1980 stretched into late September, fine warm days with no hint of the impending winter. Joe ate huge amounts of food but his weight gain was slow and he looked constantly tired. The next expedition was looming: in December, as part of a team of eight climbers, he was to make a winter attempt on the West Ridge of Everest. No oxygen would be used and the climb would be undertaken in punishing weather conditions of extremely low temperatures and high winds. I strove to understand his motives for such a venture, and sought to hide the panic I felt at what seemed to be a high-risk undertaking. Joe gave the impression of having no qualms, except for a fear that he would not have fully regained his strength by the time they departed for Nepal.

The brush with death on K2, rather than weakening his drive to tackle big mountains, had confirmed his growing conviction that climbing was his main focus. There was an emotional change, too. Little by little he was resolving his past love affair; I sensed his pain and longed to talk to him about it, but the rules had been silently laid down from the beginning. One word from me on the subject and he would close up, tight as an oyster-shell. Although he never spoke of it, I sensed an acceptance in him of what had been and what could never be.

The progress of our relationship was speeded up by the pressures upon it and we grew increasingly close, yet, even more than at the beginning, Joe withheld a part of himself, the part he needed to preserve for the mountains. I tried to understand by imagining it was I who was the mountaineer: feeling as I did about him, loving him so fiercely, I could not conceive of putting myself deliberately at risk, and I could never contemplate leaving on a dangerous venture. If he allowed his heart to be as open as mine was, then he would cease to climb. When I looked at it that way, I understood him far better than I could understand the men who had wives and children, who had made definite commitments and yet still left their families in order to go on expeditions from which there was a chance they might not return.

The preparations for the trip moved into gear in synchronicity with the climbing party season, and I saw a good deal of the 'British Everest in Winter Expedition' team at social events. It seemed strange to imagine this group of attractive and spirited men on the side of the world's highest mountain at the worst time of year; looked at in logical terms it was plainly ridiculous. And yet I knew that part of what made them so attractive was their striving towards goals that most ordinary mortals would not even contemplate. People were beginning to ask me how I coped with loving a man who was so often away, engaged in such a dangerous activity, and I never really knew what to reply, where to begin. Perhaps the answer was that the intensity of everything made me feel totally alive. And I did not want him to change: his vivacity, determination and courage, his firm grasping of every second that life had to offer, were important among the qualities that continued to draw me to him.

Early in November we went to a party in Buxton. As neither of us felt like staying sober in order to drive home, Joe piled a foam mattress, sheets, pillows and a duvet into the back of his estate car. The first time I had seen him do this, the comfort he managed to create in the vehicle amazed me: it became a snug double bed on wheels.

'I spend enough of my life in sleeping-bags. There's no way you'd get me into one in England,' he would say.

The party was large and lively and most of the Everest team was there. As usual Joe and I went our separate ways, checking in with each other from time to time. I loved the moments when we caught each other's eyes across a room or through a doorway, the look registering that, although physically apart, we were very much together. I was in the kitchen, chatting to a girlfriend, when he came up to me with a worried expression.

'Carolyn Estcourt is here,' he said. 'I never really talked to her after Nick was killed and I've always felt bad about it. Do you think I should talk to her now, about Nick I mean? Is it too late?'

It was not really a question but a request for affirmation and support. I took his hand and we pushed our way through the hallway and into the front room of the house. Joe crouched next to Carolyn's armchair and I sat in a sofa opposite, between two of the team who were sharing an enormous joint and a bottle of whisky. I chatted and joked with them, keeping a surreptitious eye on the conversation across the room. Carolyn leaned over towards Joe, her face drawn, listening intently. His fingers wound tightly around a beer can and he seemed to be pausing for thought between sentences. I began to feel detached, as if observing them on film. Joe looks thin and pale and tired, I thought, and he is losing a lot of hair. Carolyn was talking and she cried a little. Two years, I thought, Nick has been dead for two years; I wonder what it is like for her now? Perhaps I should say something to her tonight, but what? I had had too much to drink, suddenly I felt maudlin and afraid, seeing myself in that chair instead of Carolyn, with another man speaking to me. They stood up and left the room and presently Joe returned.

'She's gone home,' he said. 'But we were both glad to have finally talked about it.'

It was hard to believe he was really leaving again, despite all the frantic meetings for packing and organizing. I had no idea of how much gear was needed for an expedition: equipment, tents, sleeping-bags, clothes, food, medical supplies, books, alcohol; mounds and mounds of boxes and crates were amassed at the Sheffield home of one of the team. It all had to be transported to London, flown to Katmandu and then onto a small airstrip from where it would be carried by porters to Base Camp. I sat in the room where most of the baggage was being sorted, watching the doctor on the team try to put all the medicines into some semblance of order. The mulled wine that someone handed me was a reminder that Christmas was only weeks away. The climbers scurried in and out, arriving with some boxes and leaving with others, arguing over how much of this or that really needed to be taken. Another of the girlfriends was there, busily integrated into the activity and seemingly knowledgeable about all aspects of the trip. She made me feel superfluous, and I had not even properly absorbed the name of the route that they would climb the mountain by.

'I prefer you that way,' Joe told me later. 'You're not a climber, so why pretend to be one. I'm glad you remain so separate from it all.'

My only real involvement was to remind him to keep up with the five-mile runs that were his main training for the expedition. Whenever he could, he also tried to do a little rock-climbing, and once, earlier that autumn, I had joined him. Joe had pointed out our route up the crag which was to be his warm-up for more difficult climbs and, he promised, little more than a vertical scramble. Secured firmly to the end of his rope, I was delighted to find myself moving easily up the rock, and I enjoyed stretching between hand and footholds. He shouted down instructions and encouragement until the slight overhang he scaled took him out of sight and earshot. The rope stayed taut and I continued confidently upwards, feeling pleased with myself. I was actually climbing! But the overhang proved too much for me. I stared up at it for a long time, fruitlessly searching for what looked like an easy way over. I felt frustrated and ridiculous, stuck to the rock face like a giant fly. Despite myself, I looked down at the ground, thirty feet below. My legs began to shake and my hands were cold and cramped. Suddenly the rope jerked and I was pulled up, arms and legs flailing and too surprised to protest. Joe came into sight, only feet away at the top of the crag. His lips moved in apology, and I noticed their blue tinge.

'Sorry, but I was freezing in the wind up here. How d'you like it? That overhang was harder than it looked. Want to try another one?'

I certainly did not.

'Most girls sit at the bottom of the crag and watch their blokes climb,' he had teased, as I scurried back to the warmth of the car.

His role of finding money for the expedition had again cast Joe into dealings with the media, a world he took to readily. The more publicity they got, the easier it would be to attract sponsors. I watched him on the TV screen being interviewed by newscasters and listened to his voice on morning radio as I drove to work; the man who had landed in the centre of my life was becoming public property.

This time, I had decided, I would say goodbye to him at the airport. We went down to London two days before the flight.

Joe had sponsors to see and a function to attend at 10 Downing Street. The King and Queen of Nepal were in town and a token mountaineer was needed to complete the reception dinner.

'Bonington's not available, Boardman and Scott are away, I think they scraped around the bottom of the barrel and came up with me!' he laughed. We stayed with the Clarkes in their Islington house: Charlie, a mountaineer and a neurologist with an extra interest in the treatment of frostbite, and Ruth, a psychiatrist whose reputation as a witty, outrageous and outspoken woman was widespread. Both were renowned for their immense hospitality to their friends, the climbers amongst whom would inevitably end up in the spare bedroom on the way to and from expeditions.

Through a squeaky wrought-iron gate and into a huge kitchen where overexcited dogs, children on rollerskates and startled cats careered towards us in welcome.

'Joe!' screamed Ruth. 'Darling! This is marvellous! Get down, dogs! And you're Maria. I'm so glad to meet you at last. They've all told me about you.'

'Wait till you meet Maria,' is what they had said, 'she's a match for Joe, a frightening woman.'

'Frightening?' I said. 'I hate being thought of as frightening.'

'Oh, no!' said Ruth, 'You shouldn't. It's the highest form of praise, you know.'

During those two days Joe rushed around making last-minute commitments with a newspaper and a television company. I looked at him over the Clarkes' dinner table, the night before the Downing Street reception.

'Joe, you need a haircut.'

'What!' he spluttered. 'Why?'

His curls had grown awry over the past three months, giving him a startled, eccentric appearance which I liked but thought the Queen of Nepal might not.

'And what about a suit?' chipped in Charlie, with a sidelong smile to me. 'No doubt you've got it all pressed and ready?'

Ruth's hairdresser fitted him into her morning appointments and while he was there a friend of Charlie's arrived with a suit which, he assured me, would fit Joe. I was sitting at the kitchen table crayoning with little Naomi, the youngest Clarke, when he slipped in through the front door and scurried upstairs, hoping not to be noticed.

'The suit's on the bed,' I called.

Ten minutes later he came sheepishly downstairs. The hair-dresser had taken him at his word: 'It's got three months to grow back, you might as well cut lots off.' His head seemed shrunken, an effect perhaps accentuated by the suit which was at least a size too big. He stood in the kitchen, gazing helplessly at the trouser legs buckling over his shoes, and pushing back a sleeve which reached almost to his knuckles to glance worriedly at the time.

'Er, well, what do you think?' he asked.

I teetered between great tenderness and a fit of laughter. He looked so vulnerable, years rolled away and he was a little boy on his way to church in new clothes he could grow into. Naomi thought differently.

'Why are you dressed up like a tramp, Joe?' she inquired innocently. We both roared then and I hugged him.

'Don't crease the suit!' he exclaimed. 'I'm late, I've got to go, but I'm holding you responsible for this!'

The farewells never got any easier: there was always that wrenching in the gut when he walked away and three months of uncertainty stretched ahead like a tunnel with no light at the end. Driving away from the airport the next day, I took a wrong exit and found myself on the motorway to Reading instead of heading north. It hardly seemed to matter, and it was thirty miles before I pulled myself together and began to think about how I could get back onto the right road.

FOUR

The winter of 1980 to 1981 was severe in Britain. My house had no central heating and sometimes I would wake up shivering, taking a few seconds to remember where Joe was, and then huddle in bed, trying to imagine the conditions he was enduring.

'In my tent at night it is −20 Centigrade,' he wrote from Everest Base Camp. 'On the mountain it is −30 to −40 degrees, but it is when the wind blows that we really feel it. Himalayan winter climbing is awful.'

I had again arranged to take leave from my job while Joe was on the expedition, and I returned to California for the month of December, waitressing over the Christmas period as well as travelling around and visiting friends. The different environment was absorbing and fun but worry remained, lurking always on the edges of my thoughts.

A man came into the restaurant one night in tears, and announced that John Lennon had been shot dead in New York. Like almost everyone else of the Beatle generation I was shocked and saddened, and I longed to share the feeling with Joe. That he was so far away and so out of contact was frustrating. It would be three weeks before the letter I wrote late that night reached him. Sometimes letters took even longer: the six-seater plane carrying the mail to the airstrip at 11,000 feet was often forced by weather to turn back and, if it did land, delivery then depended on the mail runners who took the letters up to Base Camp.

It was good to have the opportunity to go to the States and do something so different, but really I was just marking time in Joe's absence. If he had been in England, I would not have wanted to go away. There was the real difference between us: with or without me he would leave on expeditions; it made no difference to him.

'I'm sorry that the couple of days in London were a bit hectic and

42

the panic about nearly missing the plane made the parting so hurried,' he wrote in his first letter. 'I know you were pretty gripped over the last couple of weeks and I probably didn't pay much attention to it. I've really got to slow myself down a bit. I find myself out here and wonder how I got here, and all that I've passed through in the last few months. I know you'll find it hard over the coming months and I don't know what to say. I've never really thought about being alone on a trip – it's all so demanding and it must be difficult to accept such absorption.'

Back in England after my working holiday, I settled into a different job. Government cutbacks had forced the reception centre to close down after only a year. I had been relocated to assist refugee families in settling into the houses that had been found for them, and to monitor the progress of the children in their new classrooms. I worked alone, driving around between homes and schools. The Vietnamese people were welcoming and their courage inspired me, but I missed the closer contact I had had with my colleagues in the reception centre, and the chance to mull over daily concerns with them. Time began to drag by. There were five weeks when no letter or card came from Joe, and I turned to the support system of the other girlfriends and wives, some of whom had years of experience in this waiting game. They could interpret such silences more optimistically than I, and I listened gratefully to their theories until several letters, held up somewhere in the complicated postal links between Nepal and Manchester, arrived all at once.

Finally, in February, the message we had all been waiting for came through and was quickly spread among us – the men were on their way home, unsuccessful in their attempt to climb Everest but alive and well. Joe's arrival date in London fell during my half-term break and I drove his car down to meet him. One of his brothers was also at the airport and together we watched the passengers from the Delhi flight emerge from customs, expecting a familiar face to appear at any second. After half an hour we began to think up theories. Their luggage was being carefully checked, there was a press conference we didn't know about. The airline would not release a passenger list, and an hour later I was in a panic.

'There's bound to be a simple explanation,' said Joe's brother for the umpteenth time. 'They must have missed the plane.'

My name was paged and I rushed to an information desk.

'We've been calling you for a while, didn't you hear?' said the girl. She handed me a slip of paper. Joe and the team had been held up. They were coming in on the next flight, the following day.

I woke in the early hours of the morning and lay in the dark imagining Joe suspended somewhere over Asia or Europe, perhaps dozing in the aeroplane seat or drinking and chatting to the person next to him. He had left for Everest looking tired and still under-weight, not fully recovered from the ordeal on K2 and in no way ready to tackle the world's highest mountain. But his letters had been full of determination to press on despite the appalling cold, the bad weather, and the illness that had been rife amongst the team.

'If we do get a chance to go for the top, and it may be possible for only two to go, it will be a long, hard haul in bitter cold, but I'd love to have the chance.'

The letter had been dated January 23rd, and now, at the end of February, I was relieved that he had not had that opportunity. He would soon be climbing again in China, but until then I had a reprieve, a chance to relax and let go of fear for a while.

Sitting in the arrivals lounge, I prepared myself mentally for seeing Joe. After the months of intense cold, high winds and altitude he would be thin, debilitated and withdrawn. This time I would not be shocked and I was ready for a period of adjustment when he would be unable to make love to me and his sleep would be disturbed and fitful. The first passengers came through and nervousness sent me rushing to the washroom. Minutes later he appeared, loping along, scanning the faces that surrounded the barrier. His hair was long and unruly again, but his cheeks were rosy and his weight up to normal. He looked relaxed and healthy and his eyes had their familiar twinkle as he walked towards me. We kissed briefly and shyly, and hugged.

'You look so well!' I laughed, leaning back to check that he was actually there with me. 'Now own up, where have you really been?'

It was a different Joe who had come home this time. He was passionate from the start, talkative and eager to tell stories of the trip. Trekking from Base Camp to the landing-strip and spending some days in Katmandu and Delhi had allowed him to relax, to eat well and get some sun. The previous months had been arduous, physically and mentally demanding, but this time he had faced no personal abyss.

From Everest he had written to me about his plans for when he returned.

44

'If we get up this mountain I'll have the option of writing a book, which would be great, but I don't think too much about it as I feel one should make decisions about climbing a mountain on the circumstances contained in the climb itself and on no other factors, and I wouldn't want to feel urged on by something like a book.'

He was also hoping to make changes in his business and to buy a house: the time between the end of this expedition and the beginning of the next was obviously going to be full.

For the first two days he rushed around London again, making and settling deals. The book contract was secured, despite the expedition not having reached the top of the mountain, and Joe set his own deadline – which was to be just before he left on the next expedition to Mount Kongur in China, only twelve weeks away.

Late on his second night back we drove up to my house in Manchester. It was a more comfortable option than his cold, unaired flat; I had stocked up the fridge ready for his return and we had the place to ourselves.

'What about all this stuff?' inquired Joe. The car was full of expensive climbing and photographic equipment, as well as rolls of precious film. 'Will it be safe out here in the car?'

'No, let's bring it in,' I said.

My terraced house was one of only twelve on a quiet cul-de-sac opposite a tiny park, and there had been a recent spate of break-ins.

In the hallway he searched through a pile of luggage and pulled out a heavy, brown-papered parcel; he placed it next to the bottle of wine and glasses that I was setting out on the living-room table.

'Is that for me?' I asked.

He rarely handed a present to me directly, but tended to leave it somewhere until I noticed. I unwrapped the carved wooden statuette of a Hindu god, mysterious and powerful.

'Oh, Joe, it's so beautiful . . .' Tears pricked my eyes but he didn't leave time for sentiment.

'And I thought this might come in useful,' he said casually, producing from behind his back a plaited leather horse-whip, six feet long, black and evil.

'*Joe Tasker*, you've got a sick mind!'

'Well, if that's all the thanks I get!'

We tumbled, laughing, into each other's arms and the whip stayed where it had been thrown, on the living-room floor.

His body clock was not adjusted yet: by 4 a.m. he was wide awake.

'I'm going downstairs to start on my book,' he said, slipping out of bed. 'Stay here, I'll be back.'

I slept deeply in his absence. By the time he returned and wrapped himself around me, a dim, wintry light was filtering through the curtains, enough for me to make out the lines of his features and the expression in his eyes as we began to make love. Footsteps sounded suddenly in the room below us and came quickly and heavily up the stairs and along the landing.

'Is someone in there?' demanded a deep, masculine voice.

Joe's face above me was an accusing question mark. I had no idea what was going on; several people had keys to the house but this made no sense. It took me a few seconds to retort.

'Who the hell are you?'

'This is the police, madam. Please come downstairs immediately.'

We were out of bed in a flurry of duvet and sheets. I put my head around the curtain – a squad-car was parked outside and a policeman's eyes met mine. He said something into a radio.

'What on earth . . .' I began, and then panic hit me. Two weeks before, a card had arrived from California with no return address; when I opened it a small plastic envelope of marijuana fell out. 'To celebrate Joe's safe return,' the greeting read, and I stashed it away, not daring to tempt fate by sampling it before he was back. It was sitting in a box on a shelf, in the room below.

'Joe, I think this is a bust. What am I going to do – that dope is on the shelf.'

He was already on his way out of the door, pulling a sweater over his head.

'They've no right to come in here without a warrant. You've got nothing to worry about. Stay here for a few minutes while I talk to them.'

A muffled exchange was audible from below me as I put on a dressing gown and found my glasses. In the bathroom I could not manage my contact lenses: my hands trembled at the thought of headlines in the local newspapers and the recriminations of my employers. Joe had his back to me when I opened the door into the living room; his arms were crossed and he was leaning back in a relaxed stance. The policeman stood opposite him.

'Good morning, madam. Sorry about this disturbance.'

Joe turned and took my arm.

'There's been an attempted break-in, Maria.'

I looked around, confused. At the far end of the long room, by

46

the fire, papers and books lay scattered about; there was a wine glass, a mug, a teapot and an open briefcase. Of course, Joe had been working down here. The television was in its usual place, and the stereo; my eyes automatically covered these things. I had been burgled before.

'Oh, no, your luggage.'

. Untidy piles of boxes and bags were spread between the room and the hallway.

'It's all right,' Joe assured me, 'nothing's been touched.'

He went to put the kettle on, as the policeman began to explain.

'We received a call from your neighbour at 6 a.m. to say she had noticed that, although the curtains were drawn, the back window of your living room was open, and she presumed you were still away because your car was not outside.'

I mentally took back all my grumblings about the nosy lady next door. She was right, my car was at Joe's shop, where I had picked up his.

'We arrived at 6.05,' he continued, 'and entered the house by way of the open window, noticing a footprint on the sill outside and the plant pots that had been moved aside for ease of entry. Hearing noises from the room above,' Joe's face popped round the entrance to the kitchen and he winked at me behind the constable's back, 'and presuming them to be caused by the intruder, we proceeded upstairs. Mr Tasker has been explaining the situation here this morning, his recent return from the Himalayas and so on, and we presume that he unwittingly disturbed the intruder, probably when he first got up.'

'I wondered why it seemed so draughty in here,' called Joe from the kitchen.

In the middle of the room, five feet from where the policeman stood, lay the horse-whip, uncoiled and impossible to overlook. His eyes drifted over to it just once as he made his report, and then back to me, standing before him in a full-length and very sensible candlewick dressing gown, my eyes wide behind metal-rimmed National Health spectacles. He was well trained, his face gave no hint of his thoughts. Joe came in with a tray of tea and we sat down, joined by the squad-car driver, to fill out a statement. The two policemen were across the table from us; on a shelf in the alcove behind them, level with their shoulders, I could see the box containing the marijuana. I kept glancing at it, beset by a ridiculous fear that they would somehow realize its contents, as if it would begin to jump and jiggle about and turn itself in. What with that, and the whip lying there, and the fact that yet another burglar had picked out my house, I was extremely agitated. I wanted to put the whip away somewhere, but that would only confirm the suspicions that no doubt they already had. I wanted to grab the box and sidle out of the room with it, unnoticed, but that seemed impossible. Most of all, I wanted the policemen to leave so that I could collect my thoughts.

'Well, madam, the CID will be round to see you later this morning.' Mentally I breathed out: they were finished.

'Do you by any chance know Chris Bonington?' he continued, turning to Joe.

Here we go, I thought, and went to make fresh tea. An hour later, having extracted a promise from Joe to give a slide show for a police benefit fund, the two men left with assurances that they would keep an eye on my house. I collapsed at the table, weak with relief.

'Well!' said Joe, coming in from the hall after seeing them to the door. 'Who needs to go to Everest for excitement!'

The dawn raids to the fridge for chilled white wine went on for a couple of days. I was forever amazed how Joe and his mates could indulge in drinking sessions straight after arduous expeditions; even more puzzling was their apparent lack of training before setting off again. Most of them seemed to rely on weekend rock-climbs, and the hikes to and from the crags, to keep themselves in shape. But Joe had less and less time for even these, and his running had practically ceased.

'I'm still fit from the last trip,' he would say, 'but I need psychological training.'

This usually referred to the last-minute parties and binges which were an accepted part of each expedition. Joe had written from Katmandu, just as they were about to set off for Base Camp, describing their final fling before beginning the serious business of the trip.

'I meant to write last night but we got completely wasted on some whisky. We finally collapsed into our beds at 9.30 p.m. and it felt like 4.30 in the morning. Our star of the evening (can you guess who it was?) ended up puking up over a wall onto a dog which was eating up some of his earlier offerings.'

It was not the image that most people held of mountaineers, I was sure. These lads did fit the stereotype to some degree: they were fit, strong, determined, often bearded and usually dressed in comfortable outdoor clothes. But some of them also had a remarkable capacity for enjoyment, as if the danger inherent in their sport made them anxious to savour fully all of life's pleasures.

'Don't worry, I'm not turning into an alcoholic,' said Joe that morning, explaining the wine glass alongside the mug of tea. 'We did a lot of drinking at the embassy on the way back and I'm readjusting.'

Increasingly he enjoyed the time spent at my house, and my group of female friends intrigued and delighted him. Joe loved the company of women and flirtatious teasing was his forte. Sometimes, when I felt he went too far and disregarded my feelings, he would say, 'I'm only playing. I'm not after her. If I was I wouldn't be so provocative. I wasn't like that with you at first, was I?'

In ordinary conversation he had a knack of focusing intently on whoever he was talking to, making them feel very important. This had drawn me to him initially and it was not lost on other women. Jealousy crept in, as Joe's world expanded and became more public. Fame and power are aphrodisiacs, that I already knew, and so, I began to realize, are courage and risk-taking. Most of us would not dare to tackle a high and remote mountain and we are drawn to those who do. They play out our fears and let us exercise our fascination with that edge between existence and death; we can read their articles and books or watch the films and slide shows, and be thrilled and horrified from the safety of our own unthreatened lives. Joe received more and more invitations to give lectures or interviews. I often accompanied him to these and frequently watched in dismay as women were openly fascinated by what he did, and therefore by him. Of course he enjoyed it, and even when he didn't, he could not be offhand: dealing with a public was becoming part of his business.

'Just because I'm friendly doesn't mean I'm after them,' he would repeat defensively, if I expressed disquiet. My insecurity was something he found hard to understand. 'I can't be rude; how would you react if you were in my place?'

I had imagined myself prepared for a relationship with a mountaineer, yet it was more demanding than I had expected. I felt that I was sharing him – with the mountains, with the media, with his business concerns – and that I had no right to complain or ask for more time. But it had been my choice, after all; Joe had certainly not talked me into anything. And, I asked myself, would I prefer a safe, secure and predictable love affair with a man who worked nine to five? Obviously not, for it was surely no accident of fate that I had fallen for such a man as Joe.

The list of Joe's possible expeditions stretched well into the future, as permission to climb the mountains had to be applied for long before the event. Mount Kongur and the East-North-East Ridge of Everest – these were certain and had been marked in his diary for some time. The first mention of Mount Kongur had been made the previous August, after a party for the Japanese climbers.

'I think I'm going to be invited on Bonington's trip to China,' Joe had said in the bathroom, as he wiped away toothpaste from around his mouth. 'Al mentioned it. He's coming round tomorrow to show some slides.'

Al Rouse and Chris Bonington had just come back from a reconnaissance trip in China, which had recently begun to open its doors to the West, and they had negotiated permission for the unclimbed Mount Kongur during the following year. Joe and I had still been getting used to each other after his long absence on K2. He was beginning to look and act normally again, he was leaving for the Everest in Winter climb within twelve weeks and yet there he was thinking ahead to another expedition almost a year away. The prospect had sent my mind into a spin, but he had obviously been undaunted.

'It's not official yet, but I'd love to go.'

Al's slides, the next day, had been stunning. The pictures of the people in that remote, north-eastern corner of China had fascinated me, but Joe had been eager to see the mountain, a virgin peak; he and Al had gazed at images of it taken from different angles and with a variety of lenses, and had talked routes and strategies for hours.

Eight months late, and six weeks after the end of the Everest in Winter trip, the British Mount Kongur Expedition to China began to take on massively glittering proportions. For the first time Joe was not consumed with worry about finding money for a trip, as the whole venture was being sponsored by Jardine, Matheson & Co., the huge multinational company based in Hong Kong. Four doctors were going to Base Camp to conduct scientific tests on the mountaineers and a film was to be made of the climb. It was a prestigious affair, generously funded and, as the first British mountaineering expedition to China, well publicized. I was beginning to enjoy the razzmatazz of publicity and functions, and I went everywhere that I could with Joe.

He, even more than I, relished switching lifestyles to foray into the worlds of the landed gentry and the upper classes. He possessed a remarkable ease with people from all walks of life. When he left the rarefied atmosphere of the Jesuit seminary he had worked as a dustman before going to university. Perhaps the adjustments he must have been forced into then gave him the naturalness that I always admired. It did not matter who he was with – one of his nine brothers or sisters, the lady from the corner shop, an influential sponsor or the Prime Minister – Joe was simply Joe, without pretence but with a knack of saying the right thing at the right time. My aplomb was less polished than his, though, and I was more prone to social gaffes, forgetting an influential VIP's name on more than one occasion.

When I was invited with Joe to 10 Downing Street for a reception in honour of the Kongur expedition, I decided to have my hair done for the occasion. I emerged from the fashionable London salon with an alarming creation that drew stares on the tube. Joe liked it and insisted I should not wash it out. We were the first guests to arrive that evening; I could sense Joe's suppressed laughter as Mr Thatcher shook my hand and gazed at my head in open astonishment.

From the way the climbers talked about it, the Kongur expedition was going to be less arduous and shorter than most.

'Just a stroll,' predicted Al Rouse.

'I certainly hope so,' said Joe. 'I could do with a holiday.'

Since that first night back in Manchester he had worked hard on his book and had completed a first draft in just over a month. But he had refused to let me see any of the writing, which disappointed and offended me a little. Once I peeked over his shoulder while he typed, and he was cross.

'I haven't got long to write this, Maria. I can't afford to be influenced by what anyone else thinks.'

He put the finishing touches to the book on the way to Kongur, posting the amendments and extra material to his publisher from China.

I was slightly more relaxed about this trip; all the publicity and fuss, and the presence of the doctors and company trekkers who were going along to Base Camp seemed to me, quite illogically, to lessen the dangers. 'Great date to fly,' said Joe on the way to the airport. It was May 13th. 'I'm glad it's not a Friday.'

Summer was on the way, our relationship was at its happiest and most secure and I felt prepared for another separation. But at the moment of departure all the façades of safety I had mentally thrown around Joe fell away, the fears rose to the surface and reality hit me as brutally as always. When the goodbyes were over I had breakfast in the airport restaurant with the other wives and girlfriends.

'Will you be meeting him here when he gets back?' asked one.

Maybe it was because of some deep-seated superstition, but I found that I could not answer her.

I arrived back in Manchester later that day to find that the spring blossoms had started to fall from the tree outside my house. I pressed one of the pink flowers and slipped it inside my first letter to Joe.

By early June I had still not heard anything from him. There was a climbing party being held in Buxton and I drove over.

'Hey, we got a card from your bloke!' shouted someone at me across the hubbub.

'Joe?'

The man looked embarrassed.

'How many blokes have you got? Have I said something wrong?'

That innocent piece of news caused me much unhappiness over the next few days. Another person rang to say that she, too, had received a card. Thrust back into a familiar and upleasant vacuum – no contact, no news – I could only guess at why he had written to others before me. Joe always had a long list of people to whom to send cards from each trip, and logically I knew that he had begun that process earlier than usual. But mail took on such an important role during the expeditions that an incident like this would send me into an emotional maelstrom. A letter eventually arrived. Nothing was amiss, and I vowed to be more relaxed about the irregularity of mail in future.

'Because daylight hours are so long (it's light until nearly 11 p.m.), I don't feel fully occupied. I'm looking forward to getting up the mountain this time and getting back home.'

He wrote that after several weeks on Kongur. Though he was committed to reaching the summit, his usual unbending determination seemed to be less apparent on this trip. And I was feeling differently, too. I had drifted into an almost dreamlike state, blocking out thoughts of disaster more effectively than ever before.

52

At work I had too much free time – the number of Vietnamese refugees being allowed into Britain had been drastically cut, and the ones I was helping to resettle were adapting quickly to their new environment. An ex-boyfriend came to visit me, and the weekend we spent together left me with no guilt: there was little emotion between us, only some comfort and the ease of familiarity. While he was still in the house I received a letter from Joe, yet even the irony of that did not touch me. Despite the steady stream of information about the expedition that Jardine, Matheson was sending, I felt increasingly distant from Joe. He had been away on expeditions for eight of the sixteen months that we had been lovers. This was taking its toll on me, and by late June I had begun to feel as if we were inhabiting different planets.

I had a growing friendship to buoy me: Sarah Richard had moved into a neighbour's house a few months before I met Joe, and we had felt a strong and immediate connection. As time went by, we discovered common interests and an increasing enjoyment in each other's company. While Joe was away in China, my ex-lodger, Alex, returned from one of his trips, met Sarah through me and they quickly fell in love. I have a photograph somewhere of the three of us sitting in the park opposite the house, Sarah and I watching Alex unravel a pile of climbing ropes that had been sitting in the back of his car. A lovely sunny afternoon, we look young and colourful and carefree. Alex was planning his next trip – he was also going to China. Now that Sarah had a mountaineering boyfriend too, our mutual understanding deepened. As we talked about the two men and our relationships with them, I gradually began to click back into a more realistic state of mind, and to think about Joe coming home.

The school summer holidays would be underway by the time Joe returned, but I had nothing planned except to spend a lot of time in Derbyshire with him. Catriona, who had moved to London, phoned to say she had a last-minute booking for a holiday in Corsica and asked me to join her. The dates coincided with the final two weeks of the expedition.

'Get your body brown and sexy, ready for that wee man,' she said.

It seemed like sound advice. I envisaged returning, tanned and refreshed, a few days before Joe came home.

On one of the last days of the school term, the telephone brought me running downstairs at 6 a.m. Silence at the other end was broken by crackles and whistles. I held my breath: according to my calculations they should have been going for the summit around then.

'Maria Coffey?' The accent was heavy. 'Call from Beijing. Hold the line please.'

Joe's voice ebbed and flowed over thousands of miles. They had climbed the mountain sooner than expected; he would be home within a week.

I picked him up at his literary agent's flat early on a warm July morning, as he was breakfasting with the team and various dignitaries who were gathered to welcome and congratulate them. It seemed to take us ages to get across the room to each other.

'You look like a beautiful willow,' he said, giving me a pungent kiss. For the climbers it was night-time and they were drinking wine with their bacon and eggs. We sat together on a sunny window-sill as Sir Douglas Busk, the Chairman of the Mount Everest Foundation, made a speech. Joe had an arm around me, we held hands and I felt ridiculously happy. The Jardine Matheson limousines which had brought them from the airport stood outside, gleaming in the sunlight next to my battered VW Beetle. Pete was coming with us as far as his mother's house in Manchester.

'Back to reality, mate,' laughed Joe as they stuffed gear into every nook and cranny of the tiny car.

On the motorway I told him of my holiday plans.

'Oh,' he said. 'Can't you cancel?'

Pete's face in the rear-view mirror broke into a huge grin. Here was fuel for a fire. He leaned forward.

'Ever heard of double standards, Tasker?'

I was very tempted to call it off but it was too late for refunds and I was loathe to let Catriona down. And a part of me said, go, you're always talking about independence, now act upon it. Joe took us to the airport. He stood and watched, his face tense, until I was sucked behind the security-check screen. It was the only time that I was the one to go away.

Corsica was awful. Too hot, too crowded, too commercial: we were there at the wrong time of year. Fourteen days felt like forever. Back in England Joe was calling in to see friends of mine.

'Lost, lonely and wistful,' said one. 'Did him the world of good.'

That reunion was the best.

'I had no idea of what it was like to be the one left behind,' he admitted.

'I missed you so much, Joe,' I told him.

And he, unprecedentedly, replied, 'I've missed you, too.'

A card he wrote on his way back to England had arrived at my house while I was away.

'We have now reached Hong Kong,' it said, 'and the only dangers we face are alcohol and sunburn.'

. He was relaxed after the Kongur trip. The climb was less straightforward than anticipated but conditions had been generally good and the team had obviously had a fine time in Hong Kong on the way back, as they talked more of that than of their experiences on the mountain. Seven months stretched ahead of us before the next trip, 'the big one', to the north side of Everest. He would be in England over Christmas and New Year, and for my thirtieth birthday the following February. It was to be our longest period of time together.

'I'm going to Pakistan on Saturday,' he announced one Monday morning in late August.

My face, as usual, gave everything away.

'Cheer up!' he laughed. 'It's only for a week's conference. I'll be back the following Friday.'

But he did not phone from the airport on Friday night, as he had promised. I checked to see that his flight had arrived and, early the next morning, drove to his house. He was surprised to see me.

'We got in late,' he said, in reply to my questions, 'so I drove straight here. I didn't want to wake you in the middle of the night.'

His usual warmth was missing: he avoided my eyes and drew back from my embraces. I went for a riding lesson and thought it over. Intuition told me that he had had an affair. But I was afraid to confront him. Did I really want to know about it? And what right did I have to complain, anyway? He might simply turn the question onto me. I viewed my own unfaithfulness as a harmless fling that had nothing to do with my love for Joe, so why should I presume his to be different?

When I walked through the back door into the kitchen, I felt, for the first time ever, unwelcome in his house. I expressed this.

'What do you expect?' he replied coldly. 'You turned up here this morning with no warning. I've got a week's work to catch up on.'

'You've always got work to catch up on,' I challenged. 'There's something else. What is it? What happened at the conference?'

He looked directly at me for the first time that day.

'I know it's my fault that we're apart a lot, but that's how it is.

Have I ever cross-examined you about your activities while I'm on trips?'

We held each other's gaze for a moment, then both turned away to do something else. I ran a bath, stripped off my riding gear and lay brooding in the hot water. Joe's office was across the small landing. I could hear him typing. The telephone rang, and his muffled tones reached me through the wall. The door opened, and he perched on the edge of the bath.

'I'll wash your back,' he said.

We made up then, but the conversation in the kitchen was never continued.

Early in September he breezed into the house with, 'Good news and bad news, which d'you want first?'

I opted for the good.

'After Everest I'll be home for six months.'

'Great. And the bad news?'

'Ah. You might not be thrilled about this one. After that, back to K 2 for a winter ascent. We just got the permission. Me and Pete. I'm not sure who else will be coming yet. I'd like to ask Dick.'

If any mountain was going to claim him, I was sure it would be K 2. Going back for a third try, and in the winter, seemed to be pushing luck way too far. But there was no point in dwelling on it; the event was a year away and, like him, I was learning to live from expedition to expedition. 'When you come back in one piece from Everest,' I said quite calmly, 'then I'll start worrying about what you've just told me.'

FIVE

By the autumn of 1981 the plans for the Everest expedition were in top gear and the team was meeting frequently. Chris Bonington, Pete Boardman, Dick Renshaw, Joe Tasker: between them they had a formidable amount of experience in difficult, high-altitude climbing, yet their venture, the East-North-East Ridge without oxygen, seemed audacious in its scale and its level of danger. Charlie Clarke, the doctor on the trip, was to conduct experiments on the physiological effects of altitude, and Adrian Gordon, who lived in Hong Kong, was the Base Camp manager. They were there primarily for support and organization, and not to act as back-up climbers. It was a tiny team, preparing to tackle a giant.

I had my own logistical problems. A government grant was allowing me to plan renovations to my house that would make it impossible for me to live there while the work was in progress. Since early September I had been mulling over what to do when the time came to move out, and my pride forbade me from prompting Joe into suggesting the obvious solution. We met Pete Boardman for a drink one evening in the pub that was local to his Derbyshire house. He and his wife Hilary were firmly based in Switzerland but kept on their 'English Base Camp', finding friends to look after it for them.

'Do you know anyone who would like to live in our place, rent free, from the beginning of next month?' he asked me. 'They'd just have to pay bills and let me and Hilary stay whenever we're back here.'

'4 Greenfield', as they called it, was halfway between my office in Manchester and the house Joe had bought in Derbyshire. Pete looked quizzically from me to Joe when I explained my predicament, but he made no comment.

'Just for a few months?' was all he said. 'Well, that seems all right. We could ask around for someone else to take it over from you.'

We had already invited him for dinner the following evening.

'How about you two discussing this tomorrow night?' interjected Joe, and the subject was dropped.

'Why don't you move in with me?' he asked on the way home. 'It seems silly to do anything else. You spend such a lot of time there anyway.'

I accepted, without probing for the reason behind his sudden offer, and moved in with him almost immediately.

There was work going on at his place, too – each day Steve the builder would arrive and start to hammer and drill. A new staircase emerged, a floor was laid, all the old carpets were thrown out. We walked on silk rugs thrown over smooth, black, plaster-dusted asphalt. When I returned from visits to the construction site which my house had become, Joe would say, 'I bet this is just what you need.' Yet it was warm and comfortable and homely.

Joe's publishers had offered him another book contract and he had accepted. Some friends of his who lived nearby gave him the use of a study to write in and he went there whenever he could. Once again I was not allowed to see the manuscript but this time he talked to me about its progress. The book was to be an account of his climbing career up to the second attempt on K2; he was reliving painful experiences and delving into his deepest feelings about mountaineering. Insecurities over the quality of his writing and the reactions he would encounter from fellow climbers constantly beleaguered him. His first book, *Everest the Cruel Way*, an account of the Everest in Winter expedition, had been recently published and was proving controversial amongst the climbing community. Joe's outspokenness brought him critics and he was more sensitive to this than most people realized. But he ploughed on with *Savage Arena*, grimly determined to finish it before leaving for Everest.

'I'll wash up!' he would insist, eagerly and most uncharacteristically, when by so doing he could delay the moment of setting off for a day of solitary writing.

'This is the last book I'll ever write,' he said once, after an eight-hour stint at the typewriter. 'It's too lonely and too heartsearching.'

There was a short pause.

'I wonder if I could write a novel. A best-seller – that would really piss old Boardman off!'

Undercurrents of rivalry and unresolved dispute ran between him and Pete Boardman, whose prize-winning book about their ascent of Changabang, *The Shining Mountain*, had included some of Joe's material. The blurb on *Everest the Cruel Way* described Joe as co-author of Pete's book, and this was not well received. Pete's mother had been on the telephone in a quiet fury.

'Typical of Boardman, a true mummy's boy,' said Joe vindictively.

'They have every right to complain,' I countered. 'If you were piqued about Pete not giving you enough credit you should have sorted it out back then and not used your book to try to settle the score.'

'Well, okay, it was a Freudian slip, perhaps. But Pete should still have phoned me up before his mother. We are mates, after all.'

Pete was a frequent visitor to Joe's house, but always alone; while he commuted to England for expedition meetings, lectures or work on his books, Hilary usually stayed in Switzerland, busy with her job at a hospital. The only chance I had had to meet her was at their wedding, shortly after the K2 expedition, but my brother got married on the same day so I had not been able to accompany Joe. We were eventually introduced at the Downing Street reception in honour of the Mount Kongur ascent. I had heard a lot about her. 'Formidable,' was Joe's description, but he said that about me, too. Hilary was small, conventionally dressed, and her long, brown hair framed a bright and confident smile. Beneath my own astonishing hairdo, I was nervous. She shook my hand firmly and I sensed a quiet assurance about her. We exchanged a few words before the mêlée of the party swept us apart, unaware of how important we were to become to each other.

Joe and Pete were long-standing climbing partners; they had been together on four Himalayan expeditions and had shared in success and tragedy. The rivalry between them led to constant bantering, but it was a tension and a teasing that rested on the security of friendship bonded by experience. An implicit trust in each other's ability in the mountains made them happier climbing together than with anyone else. In their determined and unswerving commitment to mountaineering they were alike, but in every other respect they seemed opposites. Pete was a broadly-built, darkly handsome man whose eyes and jaw were softened by flesh, giving him a gentle, boyish look. A rigorous training schedule kept him in shape for his expeditions. He had impeccable manners and was considerate and quietly charming, especially around women. These qualities infuriated Joe, as did Pete's open devotion to Hilary.

'He's such a *good* boy!' he would mock.

'When Joe phoned us, Pete would turn up our stereo so that it sounded less domestic in the flat,' Hilary told me, much later on. 'There was always a kind of friendly tension between me and Joe, as if he was vying with me for Pete's time.'

She stopped for a second to think.

'He was *jealous!*'

They seemed to me to be inside-out versions of each other. Pete's soft, romantic exterior concealed a well of strength and determination, and Joe was a gentle, warm and vulnerable man beneath the hard shell that he presented to the world. It was comfortable to be around them; whether they were teasing each other, bickering or working as a team, the spirit of shared experience and common acceptance always shone through. The three of us drove back from London one day, the morning after an expedition meeting at Charlie and Ruth Clarke's house. Joe had dug out an old snow-leopard coat that I had once bought in a jumble sale, and he persuaded me to wear it to the meeting, producing the desired reaction from Pete.

'How could you *wear* such a thing . . . how can you bear to even *own* it?'

His face was a picture of open horror. Such easy shockability delighted Joe and as the evening turned into a drinking session he had begun to surpass himself, becoming increasingly outrageous, iconoclastic, and flirtatious with the women. Pete scolded him roundly on my behalf over breakfast and his penitence was a surprise to everyone. Joe was now slumped in the back of the car with a request for quiet, mellow music, while I drove and chatted to Pete. He was talking about the signs of ageing.

'I've got deep lines on my face. It must be the altitude. It doesn't seem to affect Al Rouse or Dick Renshawe, they still look really young. But as for that old piece of withered parchment on the back seat . . .'

I glanced back; Joe was chuckling and smiling in amusement at Pete. It was a warm and somehow very intimate moment between them, the banter revealing a deep affection.

Our lives were merging and the relationship was taking on a pattern which I could see stretching ahead. There were sticking points, not least of which was that, unlike Joe, I was moving

60

towards the desire for a full–blown commitment. Though being single suited me, I did harbour a secret wish eventually to marry him. I was not broody, but sometimes I had little fantasies about being pregnant with his child. The reality of having a mountaineer's baby was something, however, that I saw with clear and untinted eyes, and I wondered at the strain that women with families were under when the men went on expeditions. We should have been talking about all of this, but we never did. Climbing was Joe's focus. He wanted to tackle bigger and more difficult challenges for as long as he was able. My desires were one-sided, there seemed little point in expressing them and, though I would hardly admit it to myself, I believed they might frighten him away. I tended to have conversations on the subject with girlfriends, frequently getting things out of proportion. Insecurities and worries would buzz around my head, but I was optimistic despite them. We would work things out, given time. We had to; I loved him as I had loved no one before, it was as simple as that.

And there was a general settling taking place: Alex and Sarah began living together in Derbyshire. Other people we knew moved close by. Friendships, loves and daily lives were inter-weaving, the future looked bright and I was lulled into a sense of security.

Late one Friday night towards the end of 1981, the phone call came from Julie. Al Harris, the most irrepressible member of the North Wales rock-climbing scene, the catalyst for countless wild events and the man who had introduced me to Joe, had fulfilled his prophecy of dying young.

'It will be falling off a route or in some horrendous car crash,' he used to say. And it had been the latter, on his way to a party, speeding round a blind bend. Joe and I clung together and talked until the early hours about our lost friend, shaken by the awareness of life's fragility that a sudden death brings.

The funeral, in Llanberis, was a huge gathering; two people flew in from New York, others had driven hundreds of miles. In the pub afterwards there was drunkenness and abandonment, just as Al would have wanted.

'You could almost feel him there, grinning at us all,' said Joe as we drove away.

An image of Julie's face stayed with me: her laughter swept away by pain, and eyes that seemed hardly to focus on the friends who came to gently speak to her.

Perhaps it was just coincidence, but Al's death seemed to trigger off a series of fatalities which almost wiped out a generation of top British mountaineers. It went on for years; it is still happening, of course; the mountains continue to claim lives, but I eventually stepped away from the scene, unable to take any more. And by then, many of the young climbers who had been my friends and acquaintances were gone.

Pressures built steadily around us: the expedition preparations were gaining momentum and Joe was feverishly working on his book. I had begun a new job with a schools-based Curriculum Development agency, which involved an initial ten-month training programme. I was driving fifty miles each day to and from work, stopping off en route to check the progress on my renovations. Sometimes, when I simply could not face the journey to Derbyshire, or if the weather was too bad, I would stay with my brother and his family in Manchester, and occasionally Joe joined me there. It was a taxing lifestyle and our relationship had become a pendulum of highs and lows. One evening, just before Christmas, I sat by the fire writing cards and wrapping presents while Joe talked on the telephone in his upstairs office. The room looked blitzed: open trunks on the floor spewed out climbing gear and clothing, plaster was chipped away from the walls at ground level ready for damp-proofing. But it was the temporary chaos of a home being improved, all the familiar things were still there, the cane furniture, the rugs, the books and stereo and television, and the atmosphere was friendly and warm. Halfway through addressing an envelope I stopped and put down the pen, overwhelmed by the strength of feeling that had suddenly crystallized in me. Home and dry, I thought; I had no wish to be anywhere or with anyone else. Joe came in, he was wearing the funny furry boots that he always took to Base Camp.

'I'm very happy,' I told him. He wound his arms around my waist, leaned back slightly and smiled at me.

'You're lovely,' he said.

Simple words, made almost unnecessary by the feeling that flowed between us.

But such harmony and peace could suddenly transform into tension, usually when my insecurities surfaced and caused Joe to draw away. I felt threatened on so many sides. His climbing and the burgeoning career that went with it absorbed him. Life had taken on a vicarious quality for me; my work and my own travelling paled into mundanity and insignificance alongside the brilliance of his adventures, and I began to feel boring. Joe tried to reassure me: he valued the fact that I had an existence outside the sphere of mountaineering to which he could turn for respite.

'I like it when people ask you something about climbing and your face goes all blank, and then you tell them off for presuming you should know,' he said. 'It would be awful if you echoed my opinions just for the sake of it.'

Such hardheadedness on my part was deliberate. I was striving to hold on to my own identity as a person who could be interesting and of value in her own right. Joe's reassurances were not enough. At parties, meals and receptions, the conversation would take on a now familiar cadence.

'Oh, you're Joe's girlfriend, lovely to meet you. What is he going to climb next? When is the book due for publication? I heard him on the radio, he was marvellous,' and so on.

And I would smile and respond with the pride and love that I did feel for the man, but, inside, a part of me was withering away. Of course these people did not want to hear about my teaching job or my petty day-to-day concerns, and I could not blame them. We were meeting because of Joe's remarkable talents, and not because of anything that I had achieved.

There were some prestigious lectures on the Mount Kongur expedition. For one of these I drove down to London with Joe and Pete, to the Queen Elizabeth Hall. The lecture was to be about the ascent of Mount Kongur and the medical tests carried out at Base Camp; all the climbers and doctors were taking part and it was to be a lengthy affair. Before it began, a reception was held in a function room beneath the auditorium. Catriona had come along, and I stood with her amidst cultured voices and expensive clothes, lifting drinks from the trays that waitresses manoeuvred through the crowd. A Lord and Lady came to greet me, and the television journalist with them shook my hand. Catriona was flabbergasted: this was a side of the climbing world that she had never seen. We caught glimpses of the mountaineers between all the people: Joe, Pete, Chris Bonington and Al Rouse. Their beards and casual attire marked them out and were permissible because of their achievements. Joe hardly spoke to me during the reception. There were others he had to attend to, people from the sponsoring company and the literary and media worlds. Despite the hubbub around me, I felt empty. I was not where I wanted to be – at Joe's side, involved and needed in this part of his life – but standing apart, observing him from a distance.

He came over to me.

'We have to go. You can watch the lecture down here on video and carry on drinking. I'll be back as soon as I can.'

But I wanted to feel the atmosphere of the hall and I followed him upstairs. Crowds of people streamed through the doorways and into the foyer – it was to be a full house. No wonder he's nervous, I thought. For the first time the implications of Joe as a public figure hit me fully. All those hundreds of people would be looking at his slides and listening to what he had to say. He would make them laugh and think, they would buy posters and books afterwards, and perhaps on the way home they would talk about him and his experiences.

'See you later,' he said, and hurried off, looking preoccupied and worried.

Perhaps it was that preoccupation that brought us problems, or, at least, the way I dealt with it. There were many occasions when I felt far removed from him, superfluous and uninvolved with his concerns. Work took him away more and more: lectures, meetings with publishers and the media. It all seemed so glamorous and I felt I had little to offer in comparison. For one whole week he was driving around the country on business.

'Wish I was home,' he said on the phone. 'I need to be getting on with my book.'

And what about me, said a little voice inside, but I stayed silent. The day he was due back was an awful one for me, a morning with truculent students followed by an afternoon of interminable and boring meetings. And then the long drive to Derbyshire through heavy Friday-night traffic, punctuated with a couple of stops for weekend shopping, queueing up in supermarkets and struggling to the car with heavy plastic bags. It was dark and raining when I got to the house but the lights were on. Steve the builder and Joe were in the kitchen, drinking beer and laughing.

'I'm telling him about this TV thing I did today,' said Joe as he greeted me.

He had just driven up from Southampton where he had recorded a programme for children's television, yet he seemed far more relaxed than I was after my journey from Manchester. I began unpacking carrier bags and pushing things into the fridge and cupboards.

'And then that bird, the big blonde one, she got me to sit in this mock bathroom with her, we perched on the edge of the tub and we each had a telephone and kids rang in and asked me questions. She was good, teasing and joking but prompting me at the same time. Really professional.'

I poured myself a drink and walked through to the living room. Joe appeared in the doorway.

'What's wrong? Why don't you bring your drink through and come and talk to Steve?'

I didn't even look up.

'It's been a hard day, Joe. I don't feel like hearing about you and big blonde birds.'

He was usually adroit at controlling his feelings, but not on this occasion.

'*You've* had a hard day?' he exploded. 'I don't suppose anybody else in this house has?'

From the kitchen Steve called, 'See you Monday,' and we heard the sound of the door closing behind him.

'Well, great,' Joe continued angrily. 'I invite Steve for a drink and you arrive in a sulk and poison the atmosphere.'

I did not know what to say. I had so looked forward to spending the weekend with Joe and it had begun like this. He echoed my thoughts.

'It took bloody hours to drive up from Southampton, and I was really looking forward to getting here and seeing you and telling you all about the programme. And then you get jealous and uptight because I mention a big blonde. I didn't even fancy her, if that's any consolation.'

I looked into my drink, confused. Jealousy had been consuming me lately, and I found it impossible to control or conceal. His words had summed up a picture in my mind of a vivacious, interesting and attractive woman snuggled close to him as the TV cameras ran, and I felt hatred for her and resentment towards Joe. It was awful, it was destructive, and there seemed nothing I could do about it. When I eventually spoke my voice was small and strained.

'Sometimes . . . I feel so dull . . . next to you. My job isn't great. I'm not fulfilled by it and I'm not central to your life.'

I stopped; there was so much more to say but I was not courageous enough to continue. If I told him everything in my heart, surely he would flee. It was a mistake I made frequently during those months. Joe softened; he sat next to me and stroked my hair.

'The way you came into the middle of that story, it must have been awful. I'd have felt the same, if it was the other way round. You are interesting, Maria, and so is your job. But you have to believe that yourself. I can't do it for you.'

He spent the weekend writing but took time off on Sunday morning so that we could have some leisurely hours together. Inevitably, perhaps, we had another row. Joe was furious.

'I've got so little spare time, this sort of thing is a waste.'

Frustration washed through me.

'Arguing is a normal and healthy part of a relationship. You need time for that as much as everything else.'

Joe had a strong sense of justice: if he believed he was right he would defend himself to the hilt, and when he realized his own error he would accept it and try to make amends. Our reconciliation on that Sunday morning was a powerful one, healing the rifts of the past two days. Yet even then, with his eyes full of intimacy and love, I felt that he was looking through me, beyond me to some distant place. His mind was always so busy and, I knew, never solely on me.

Maybe it was because we were closer and I was more in touch with his thoughts than before, but it seemed to me that Joe had a deep concern about the forthcoming trip to Everest. He spent hours one night chipping plaster away from a wall in the kitchen to expose the bare stone, and eventually sat down exhausted, covered in dust. I smiled, it was odd to see him in workman's clothes, a boiler suit and big boots.

'It'll look great when it's finished,' he said, 'but I hope I'm not wasting my time.'

My smile faded. I knew what he meant, though neither of us followed up his train of thought. Years later a friend who had just returned from another attempt on the East-North-East Ridge of Everest spoke to me about Joe's expedition in 1982.

'What they took on was vast, just that small team without oxygen,' he said. 'We thought of them a lot when we were up there. We were so many more in number, it amazed us how much further than us they got on the mountain. But what they tried to do, it was quixotic, totally quixotic.'

Tilting at windmills. The picture flashed before me. Trying for near-impossible dreams, driven on by the tiny chance of success that made the gamble worthwhile. Weeks before he left, we attended an Alpine Club function where there were many elderly and distinguished climbers, men and women, pioneers of mountaineering in the Alps. Joe was talking about one of them, a man he considered a hero.

'Where is he?' I asked. 'Point him out.'

He scanned the heads.

'Over there. The one with grey hair and a suit.'

I looked; almost all the men in that room had grey hair and suits, and we began to laugh. Later, as we huddled against the wind on a London street and watched out for a taxi, Joe suddenly said, 'You know, I hope I end up like that, meeting my old climbing mates in the Alpine Club, swigging at gin and tonics, and chatting to the new young mountaineers.'

Oh yes, I thought, I hope for that too.

As the days ticked by, the expedition departure date loomed larger, the deadline for his book approached and the tension between us mounted. Joe was becoming exhausted. Sometimes he would come into the house, flop onto the sofa in his overcoat and fall instantly asleep.

'I need to go on this trip for a rest,' he'd say.

He dozed off in the dentist's waiting room and even under the barber's scissors. I was finding his preoccupations harder to bear than ever. The closer we came to his leaving, the busier he became and the more I wanted to spend time with him. It was a formula which did not work out and he resented the pressure he felt from me.

'Why can't you just relax?' he said one night. 'All this questioning I feel coming from you about whether or not I want you with me and if it's all right that you're living here, it's really wearing me down. Just let things be and then we can both rest.'

My attempts to suppress my feelings for him and my fears for his safety on Everest were doing exactly the opposite of what I wanted. They were driving him away. It became almost unbearable: I was holding so much in, and it was doing our relationship no good at all. Lack of time increased the pressure: he would soon be gone again for another three-month stint. One night, after a meal, I finally let go. Sitting across from him at the kitchen table I began to talk, at first hesitantly, until the words held back for too long started to flow out under their own momentum. And suddenly it was easy, and it felt free and natural, to be expressing love and worries and future dreams. I told him I loved him, and that I felt an emotional bonding that was strong and enduring. I told him I felt we should begin to live together on a more permanent footing when he returned from his expedition, or at least make moves in that direction, that it seemed to me a logical step in our relationship. I expressed the worry building up in me about the trip to Everest, and how hard it was for me when he was away, despite all my defences. There was more. I can't remember it all but I spoke for what seemed like a long time. Joe listened, his blue eyes tired, concern furrowing his forehead. He took my hands in his and shook his head.

'Maria, I'm not ready for this. There's so much I have to do, that I want to do, and I need to feel free. The climbing – it's not fair for me to expect anyone to have to accept all that – you're here with me because you want to be. I can't take on the responsibility of making demands on you. I value you enormously but I can't commit myself.' He paused. 'It's just not possible . . . how could I?'

So there it was. I had known all along, of course. The mountains came first. He was impelled to continue along the road towards more challenging climbs. Sometimes he bemoaned the loss of simplicity in his life. A climb was no longer a pure act but was engaged with sponsorship, newspapers, television, books, films, the whole media machinery. But there was no turning back for him, and his relationships, however dear, had to fit in or be left behind.

I cried then, and Joe's words, as so often before, were, 'I don't know what to say.' Nothing was resolved, but something between us was freed by that conversation. The problems that had been locked away and festering in my mind were at last out in the open and it was a starting point from which we could begin to work them out. I promised to express my thoughts more often without fear of the consequences.

'If I can only guess at what's going on in there it makes it really hard for me to react,' said Joe, tapping my head.

But for now everything was put on a back-burner until we had more time, until he returned from Everest. Then he would be home for six months, before leaving again to attempt K2 in winter. We opened up to each other once more and our last days together were tender and happy.

The team gathered in London on February 28th, the night before the flight to Hong Kong, which was the first leg of the journey into Tibet. Chris's wife Wendy, a veteran of these separations, stayed in the peace of their Lakeland home and Hilary had said goodbye to Pete in Switzerland. Dick Renshaw, his girlfriend Jan and their little boy joined Chris, Pete, Joe and me for a meal at Charlie and Ruth's house. There was no need to discuss the tension we all felt on that final evening, for we shared an understanding of the seriousness of the venture that was to begin the following day. As always in the Clarke household, an abundance of excellent food and wine was accompanied by much good-natured bantering, warmth and laughter. But this occasion had an edge to it, a sense of strain that came from the subliminal awareness that this could possibly be the last time we would all be together.

I lay in Joe's arms later, too tense to sleep.

'Close your eyes,' he whispered, and he stroked my eyelids with his fingertips. 'I used to do this to my little brothers and sisters when I was putting them to bed. It always seemed to work.'

The tenderness made me cry.

In the morning Joe and I went for breakfast at a large hotel in central London. I couldn't eat much, my stomach felt tight and knotted. Driving across the flyover towards Heathrow, I watched the planes glinting in the sunlight as they rose rapidly or circled slowly down through the hazy blue sky, and I reminded myself that in just twelve weeks I would be back on this same road, on my way to welcome him home. I had lots to do, a newly renovated house to decorate. The time would pass quickly.

Joe held me tightly whenever the flurry of checking in baggage and posing for photographs allowed. And I held tight to my feelings, wanting this to be a calm goodbye, wanting to face him without fearful tears. But as the escalator took us to where the rest of the team were being hurried through passport control, I broke down. Joe cradled me in his arms.

'You keep busy,' he said gently. 'Get all that wallpapering and painting done for when I get home – then you can do mine.'

Teasing me to ease the pain of the moment of separation. I laughed, but my inner terrors were suddenly exposed and raw and the tears kept coming. He had to go.

'Don't fret, Maria, I'll be all right.'

Just before he disappeared through the doorway he turned back towards me; one hand held a passport, the other steadied the bag of camera equipment slung over his shoulder. In that last long look, concern and love and regret seemed to pass across his eyes. As I blew a kiss he was suddenly gone. I never saw him again.

PART TWO

. . . Long, long must be our parting;
I was not destined to tell you thoughts.
I stood on tiptoe gazing into the distance,
Interminably gazing at the road that had taken you.
With thoughts of you my mind is obsessed;
In my dreams I see the light of your face.
Now you are started on your long journey,
Each day brings you further from me.
Oh, that I had a bird's wings
And high flying could follow you . . .

from *Chinese Poems*, Arthur Waley, 1968

SIX

'I told you before,' Alex had said. 'There's a one in ten chance of getting chopped on a high–altitude expedition. Sure you want to get involved with a mountaineer?'

His bluntness made me wince.

'Too late, Alex,' I had replied. 'I already am.'

Two years later, I was becoming adept at blocking out the bald truth of that statistic. Sometimes it came through, piercing my defences and reminding me of the menace that now underpinned my life. Pictures would flash before me: being called into an office at work for a phone call, empty and reclusive nights at my house, a memorial service. But I would dismiss these, telling myself that I was exorcising the fear by making it material.

Everyone had such respect for Joe and Pete as a team. Other climbers would praise their safety in the mountains, their skill and good judgement, their apparent invincibility. They had both survived so many expeditions, so many tests of endurance and skill, and had always come home. The weight of Jardine Matheson's backing, the slickness of their organization and advertising, seemed to put the whole venture on Everest less at risk. I allowed these façades of security to overshadow my awareness that Joe was facing a huge task, and that he was prepared to push at limits, both his own and those of the mountain. Even during the final weeks of the 1982 expedition, when we were receiving only obscure messages, sent down from the mountain by mail-runner and telexed to Jardine's London office, I kept the fears suppressed.

Joe had returned from Kongur enthusing about *The Right Stuff*, an account by Tom Wolfe of the American space programme and the training of its test pilots and astronauts. He saw parallels between the gladiatorial nature of the world described in the book and his own sport, both of which are most newsworthy when a

73

tragic accident occurs. Just before he left for Everest I began to read it.

'You might find parts of it upsetting,' he warned.

An image from the book lodged in my mind. The dark-suited chaplain of the airbase compound walks towards the front door of a house. A woman, turning her car into the driveway, sees him from behind and is instantly numbed, having feared this sight for months, understanding its meaning, knowing that he has come to break bad news. I did not need to ask Joe: this was what he had been referring to.

My job and all the renovation and decoration at home kept me busy while he was away. It was a bustling, creative time and it was fun to see the house take on a new character. I thought of him constantly and wrote to him about what I was doing and about the Falklands War, which had broken out since his departure. One night I perched precariously on a ladder in the living room, scraping wallpaper from a difficult corner and half-watching 'News at Ten' on the television. A ship had left Portsmouth that day for the Falklands, with hundreds of young servicemen aboard. I stopped working, sat on a rung and looked intently at the images on the screen: women embraced husbands, lovers, sons, brothers; they cried and waved and blew kisses as the huge vessel moved away from the dockside to take its human cargo on a hazardous voyage. Viola's words, from two years before when Joe was in Nepal, suddenly came back.

'It's just like wartime.'

There was a sudden tension in my lower back. I shifted on the ladder and a strip of paper hanging from the wall grazed my arm. The newscaster's voice became a background noise and washed over me as I stared down at bare floorboards, only vaguely aware of the flickering screen across the room. A mental barrier had been penetrated and a nerve painfully touched.

'It's going to be all right,' I muttered to myself, and I jumped down, replaced the sound of the television with loud rock music and scraped away at wallpaper into the early hours of the morning.

While Joe was on Everest, Alex was away climbing a mountain in China. Sarah and I grew very close. We jogged together and attended the same yoga class. We talked endlessly. After parties and sessions in the Derbyshire pubs we recuperated at the little cabin she shared with Alex, and hiked in the surrounding hills. The spring was unseasonably sunny and warm and our skins began to lose their winter pallor. The two men were due home around the same time, in early to mid-June.

'Maybe we can bring about a reconciliation, Sarah.'

We sat outside the cabin by the stream, eating toast and reading the Sunday newspapers. It was the second weekend in May. A horse snorted in the adjoining field and walkers waved to us as they started out on a section of the Pennine Way that ran close by.

'I think it's more Joe than Alex, you know.'

'You're right. He can be really stubborn. The fact that Alex is my friend won't make him change his views. And he thinks that Alex is totally unworthy of you.'

Sarah laughed. There was no love lost between our boyfriends, especially in recent months. 'The problem is, Sarah, they're both so outspoken and so determined in their views. I can't be bothered with it all – I can't be doing with all these climbing politics.'

'Well, it's up to them to make friends. Anyway, Alex will only be home for twelve weeks before he goes to Annapurna. I'm worried about him.'

'He'll be all right.' I felt good about the future, for both of us. 'Everything looks bright, Sarah. There's plenty of happiness ahead.'

And so it seemed, on that gorgeous May morning. But, far away in Tibet, it was the last weekend of Joe's life. She was to remind me, in times to come, of my prediction.

It's strange how one can react almost neutrally at first to terrible news, as if the mind shifts gear to be able to absorb the facts. Hilary, in Switzerland, returned from work to find her friend Annie sitting outside the apartment, waiting for her. Annie did not need to speak.

'Peter's dead, isn't he?' said Hilary.

She bathed, changed, packed and flew to England within hours, only breaking down when she reached her mother-in-law's house.

Illness had forced Dick Renshaw to leave the Everest expedition, and he had been back in England for two weeks. The minor stroke he had suffered at altitude augured badly for his future in mountaineering. 'Try to cheer him up if you see him,' Joe had written. My chirpy, unsuspecting greeting when he arrived at the house on that hot afternoon, early in June, must have made it even harder for him to tell me. His words didn't pierce me at first. I poured wine and led him outside to the tiny, walled yard, away from the small gathering of family and friends who'd come to celebrate my new carpets. Earlier in the day, watching the carpet-fitter at work, the thought had flitted into my mind, 'What if he doesn't come home . . .' Because somewhere deep in my subconscious I knew, I had known for a while, I had dreamed of it. But allowing the knowledge to surface was unbearable, and I had chased that thought away like all the others, revelling instead in the transformation of my home, thinking of how Joe would love the luxury. An old green easy chair was in the yard, waiting to be carried back inside. I retreated into it, clutching the wine glass, as the meaning of what Dick was saying began to break through the shutters my mind had thrown up against his first words, 'I've got some tragic news.' All I heard now was that Joe and Pete had disappeared on the summit attempt, nothing else registered. They were lost, gone.

I wonder how I managed to sit upright, to hold the stem of the glass, to find words to ask Dick to leave me alone for a while. My mind seemed to slow to a stop, and yet I was suddenly intensely aware of tiny details: the petals of pansies moving in the breeze, warm air against the skin of my arm, hushed voices from within the house. A sheet on a washing line in a neighbour's garden billowed and flapped. Sarah appeared, a torn face in the doorway, her hand against her mouth. With her arms around me, the stillness began to shatter irreversibly, like a slow-motion picture of a windscreen hit by a stone. Tears welled up from somewhere deep inside me, and with them came the first shock waves of realization that he wasn't coming home. It must have been minutes since Dick had broken the news, but in my memory I sat suspended for a long time before breaking down, stunned by the unacceptable fact that the future I had looked to was wiped out, leaving only a black, infinite and terrifying abyss.

The big green chair stayed in my yard. I watched it through the kitchen window as the seasons changed, dusting it with leaves, covering it with snow, a friend who had helped me through a terrible time and whom I couldn't discard. A year passed before I could bear to let it be taken away. In those first days the chair was my refuge. I curled in it as people came and went with kind words and flowers, wine and embraces. An almost festive atmosphere developed, friends who had been out of contact met at my house, there would be periods of giddy laughter and I would slip into that same heightened awareness as when Dick first told me, observing as faces, objects and sounds took on a crystal clarity and then gradually faded back to normality.

Dick had left me earlier in the afternoon and gone to stay with old friends of his who lived nearby. I had barely spoken to him, after he told me. But suddenly I needed to talk and to listen, to find out more about what had happened. Sarah would drive me over. I washed my face and changed out of the sundress.

'You look lovely,' said Sarah. She seemed puzzled. 'I haven't seen that outfit before.'

The bright yellow mini-skirt and matching T-shirt showed off my tan. They were new clothes, bought especially to wear to the airport when Joe got home. I don't know what compelled me to put them on that night.

Dick spoke gently, telling me all he knew. Chris and Charlie were still on their way home, he had heard the news over the telephone, a call from Jardine Matheson. It was hard to absorb. His words seemed to drift past me, I couldn't catch them all.

'Twenty-seven thousand feet . . . rock pinnacles . . . fourteen hours climbing that day . . . perhaps a fall . . . a snow fluting could have collapsed . . . the Kangshung Face . . . a long fall.'

None of it made much sense. Other people came into the room, the conversation shifted. We talked about Joe as if we were reminiscing over an absent friend. Funny stories were told and we laughed.

It grew late. Dick and his hosts were tired, and Sarah wanted to drive me back to the house. I lingered, afraid to leave the friendly atmosphere and the aliveness of Joe that we had conjured up between us.

Sarah lay next to me on the living-room floor when I awoke and held me for a long time, until I began to calm, to breathe more easily and begin to speak. At 6 a.m. the temperature was in the high sixties. A hot and sunny day stretched ahead. Day one.

At night I slept on the living-room floor, unable to face my bed, and each morning I would have a few seconds of blessed forgetfulness before reality surfaced. Joe and Pete had disappeared. They were not coming home. It hit the television screens and was front-page news on Sunday. I went out and bought a copy of each newspaper. Walking to the shop seemed to take a long, long time. It was puzzling to see people cheerfully greeting one another and commenting on the lovely weather. I wandered round the grocery section first, putting coffee, milk, orange juice, bread and bacon into a wire basket. We always had big breakfasts at weekends; Joe liked the works. He would usually trade tasks with me: 'I'll go out and buy the stuff, and please notice that it's *raining*, if you'll cook it.'

The papers lay on the floor, beneath the racks of magazines. The *Sunday Times*, the *Observer*, the *Sunday Telegraph*, the *Mail*, the *Mirror*. A separate pile for each publication. Every copy was a fat bundle because of the weekend sections and the colour supplement tucked inside the folded pages. Joe and Pete's faces went in and out of focus. Black on white, blurring into grey.

'Need any help, love?'

The shopkeeper leaned over the counter, resting his weight on his forearms. I must have been standing and staring for a while. He was an amiable man and I went in there often, but at that moment I couldn't bear to meet his gaze. Gathering a copy of each newspaper I turned to him and tried to pay; the money was hard to understand — first I gave him too little and then far too much.

'Late night last night?'

I nodded and hurried out.

Sitting in the doorway to my yard, with the sun streaming in, I wept over the photographs. They gazed up from the page, hats shading their eyes, posing for an official picture on Mount Kongur, strong and healthy and alive. I understood the meaning of heartbreak that morning as the physical pain of Joe's loss seared through my body, doubling me up and making me clutch myself against the hurt. Those newspapers remained unopened and yellowing for three years until, before burning them, I looked into their pages and read of other events of that week in a world which, for me, had come to a halt.

Sarah stayed, day and night, for ten days. She was strongly supportive and our closeness drew her into my grief. It was as if our growing friendship had been a preparation for this. She cried in the face of my despair, unwittingly rehearsing for her own tragedy later that year.

'I've just heard from Alex,' she said gently one evening. 'He's on his way home. I'm sorry, Maria. I had to tell you.'

'No, no, I'm glad, Sarah. Christ, if anything had happened . . .'

The day before he flew into London she left my house.

'I must go to him. You have to begin to face this alone.'

And so it was. In the early days after the news broke I became like a small child again. Friends and family persuaded me to eat and to sleep; they provided for all my needs and allowed me to fall into my feelings with no consideration for anyone else. But after a while even the people who loved me the most had to draw away, to look back into their own lives and be reassured that all was well there. Those were hard times, when the attention ebbed and I began to understand that the strength to get through this ordeal had to come from within me; no one and nothing else could provide it. I asked an elderly friend, twice widowed, what I could do. 'Everyone has to find their own way, Maria,' she said. 'Grit your teeth and try to get on with things.'

It was sensible advice. The necessary daily rituals kept me functioning. Bathing, dressing, shopping, cooking, driving: I did them all with apparent calm. In conversation I would hear the ease with which my words flowed. But inside my head, while I did the chores and formed the sentences, I would be helpless and lost.

The Sunday after we had received the news of Joe and Pete's disappearance, Hilary had telephoned me from her mother-in-law's house in Manchester.

'We're strangers,' she said, 'but through all this we'll come to love each other.'

Sarah drove me over to where Hilary was staying. Through that night we talked, telling stories, connecting into each other, recreating the men and our lives with them. In the morning, sitting in the sunny, flower-filled garden, she suggested that we go to Everest Base Camp. It was more than a suggestion, it was a statement of firm decision.

'If you won't come I'll go alone.'

I thought about it for days. It was three months since I had seen Joe; he had been so far away and now he was so inconclusively gone. There was no hard fact of his death, only conjecture over what happened to him and Pete after their disappearance; no bodies had been recovered, no one could tell us about the last hours of their lives. Perhaps going to the mountain would help me to ritualize his death, to understand and accept it. But I knew it was something that Joe might not have wanted me to do, and this held me back from a decision. He had never approved of wives or girlfriends going along on expeditions because, he said, it caused tensions and a diversion of energies. Should I now step into a part of his life that he had kept private from me? For Hilary it was different. She and Pete had climbed together and he had involved her in his expeditions, sending her carbon copies of his daily diary. Theirs had been a remarkably close relationship, a first and an ultimate falling in love, and their marriage was free of mistrust, doubt or fear. Going to Everest was the only thing that Hilary could do, she had to draw as physically close to Pete as possible. His last letters to her had been full of longing for home, he was tiring of the strain and separation of expeditions. And they had desperately wanted a family. There had been a sense of resolution between them of which I now felt deeply and painfully envious. We had needed more time, Joe and I, and his death left me in limbo with much unsaid and unanswered. Despair was heaped on top of grief, I felt emotionally dispossessed and cheated of a future which was only just unfolding. I finally decided to go to Everest, but for reasons different from Hilary's. She went there for Pete; I went for myself, to reach towards the beginnings of resolution in my relationship with Joe and to find an acceptance of his death.

Days after the news broke, letters began to arrive. They came from relatives, close friends, acquaintances, colleagues and people I had never met. Some were apologetic, wondering if to send condolences was the right thing to do: 'If this is a blunder, please forgive it.'

It is not easy to put words down on paper in such circumstances – that I remembered from the time I tried, and failed, to write to Carolyn Estcourt after Nick's death. But now, when someone I know is bereaved I make myself send a note, because the comfort those messages gave me was immense. It didn't matter how long or short they were – one card simply read 'Thinking of you' – they reassured me that I was not alone, that people shared in my grief. For some the expressions of sympathy took courage.

'It is almost exactly four years ago that Nick was killed,' wrote Carolyn. 'I always feel rather tense and depressed about this time and I was really shocked to hear the news of Pete and Joe. The disbelief is the instant reaction, followed by hoping that it is not true . . . Please call or phone at any time. When the general furore has died down you may really be in need of the support of someone who has been through it all. I cannot pretend to have really recovered myself but have learnt to control it somewhat.'

Alex's ex-girlfriend once said, 'If he survives,' when talking to me about their relationship, and I had been shocked by her honesty. Now she wrote, 'Somehow I used to think it could never happen to the men we loved.' Not everyone had heard about the tragedy so quickly. Al and Adrian Burgess, close friends of Joe's who had been on the Everest in Winter expedition with him, were in the Himalayas. It was Lorna, Adrian's wife, who wrote.

'We have recently arrived back in Srinigar after seven weeks of trekking in the remote valleys of Ladakh and Lanskar. News is so irregular and outdated there. In Leh, we heard a rumour that Bonington's team had encountered trouble. Then Uschi and Reinhold Messner brought us news from a Peking press release that Joe and Pete had disappeared. All of us, Uschi, Reinhold, Alan, Adrian and I sat quietly for a few shattered moments. So close to home. But it is funny how one's mind protects itself. We let ourselves question the reliability of the second-hand news source. For the climbers, perhaps it was an unsettling moment. How could two of the best climbers in the world simply have disappeared? For me, and I suspect for Uschi, it was a confrontation with a threat that lurks constantly in my life. Uschi's first question to me was whether Joe and Pete had families. I mentioned you, and Pete's wife whom I've never met. Someday I may be forced to find in myself the strength which I hope you are finding now.'

The letters made me cry, but I was so glad when they arrived. Replying to each one gave me some purpose for a little while.

'He was like a relation,' one of Chris Bonington's sons wrote. And, in a poignant postcript, 'I hope this stops Dad climbing.'

It had not occurred to me before, but I found that our society expects the period of public mourning over the death of a loved one to be short. After my initial and acceptable outward show of emotion, there was a well-meaning but firm pressure from many quarters to 'put on a brave face', and I found myself doing just that, time and time again. Unconstrained grief is discomforting for the onlooker, it is too forceful a reminder of the fragility of life. I envied the rituals surrounding death in other cultures, the weeping and wailing at the graveside, the wearing of black clothes for a pre-scribed time. Denied such props, I swung in the other direction. I wore bright clothes and was calm and strong in public, and everyone said how well I was coping. It was in private that I frequently fell apart. But there were friends who listened, with patience, for years to come while the healing took place. Among them, three were the most important. With Hilary and Julie, and later that year with Sarah, I shared the common experience of losing a lover or a husband at a young age, and explanations of emotions were unnecessary, for each of us understood what the others were going through.

One day drifted into another and I spent more and more time alone in the house. Life began to focus around my living-room table, where I would read, talk on the telephone and write. Two weeks after hearing of Joe and Pete's disappearance I began a journal, and it was a necessary and valuable release, a receptacle for the feelings with which I could no longer burden those around me. By early August, when Hilary called me from Switzerland, the pages of the book were full. The first entry begins, 'Sunday night . . . tried to look at the date but it doesn't seem right to do so now.' The passage of time was painful at first, because each minute that ticked by brought me closer to realizing that I was indeed awake and not deep in some nightmare-ridden sleep.

Chris returned to England on June 10th, and he and Wendy drove down to see me a few days later. They had already visited Joe's family in the North-East, and Pete's mother and Hilary on the way into Manchester. It must have been so hard for him, for both of them.

'Waiting for Chris and Wendy,' the journal reads, 'I am gripped by a strange stillness, it is physical, I feel it in my chest. All is heightened again . . . What happened to Joe and Pete? Did they tumble down, roped together, one pulling the other? Were they hit by rocks, ice, snow? Did they fall asleep clutching each other? Hilary feels it is the last. I hope they are holding each other, not broken and apart. I think of Joe's face, frozen, iced, set . . . I still can't believe he won't walk in and hold me, and we can tell each other how we've suffered in our own ways . . . I mourn for his future as well as mine. For him, still so much more to do yet . . . Snatched from life. Will they ever be found? I think Chris is here. I'm afraid.'

It was a gentle meeting. We spoke for a while and then walked out into the summer evening to find somewhere to eat. Inexplicably, I led the way to the Italian restaurant which was a favourite of Joe's. Later, when they had left and I was alone in the quiet of the house, I wrote, 'I'm hoping for numbness again . . . Chris cried when he recounted how he felt he should have gone up to look for them, but was unable. Wendy, so quiet, concerned, a beautiful spirit . . . I need to go and cry.'

And, some days later, 'How can he be a memory, I still feel his presence . . . If he was home now everything would be so different. It would have been this weekend, I'm sure, if they'd been successful on the attempt. Exciting, loving, sexual. Instead, this loss, the glass of wine, the ivory telephone on the brown chenille tablecloth. A turning point. Life will never be the same.'

Separate memorial services were held. Joe's was first, a Catholic Mass in his parents' town, with a gathering in a marquee behind their house afterwards. People milled about outside the church before the service began, greeting each other and chatting. Climbers' deaths always bring their friends together. At one of the later 'wakes' it occurred to me that there were folk there I had not encountered since the last funeral. Hilary linked an arm through mine.

'Well, they've got five more minutes to turn up.'

A popular film at the time showed a man racing into his own memorial service, dirty, dishevelled and most definitely alive. We laughed, but I was rigid with tension. The church was full, people stood at the back and along the sides. Priests and a bishop concelebrated Mass. From my front pew I felt the air stirred by their movements about the altar and heard the swish of the vestments. It was a long service. The congregation stood, sat, knelt, stood again. Prayers were chanted in harmony, bells tinkled shrilly and the Eucharist was held aloft to receive the Body and Blood of Christ. For me there was no meaning or relation in this to the fact of Joe lying frozen on a Himalayan mountain. As the faithful moved forwards and lined up in the aisle, I remembered my First Communion. Seven years old, excited and nervous, like a child-bride in the white dress and veil. Light–headed because of the fast since the night before, and looking forward to the celebration breakfast afterwards. Praying that I would not be sick or swoon, as I had heard of other girls doing in previous years. 'If you don't feel well, take deep breaths,' my mother had told me. Closing my eyes, I could hear the taffeta rustle around me again and catch the scent of my posy. Lily of the valley. Tiny white flowers nestling in long, ridged, dark green leaves.

I sat back on the pew, suddenly nauseous and sweating. How much longer? It would be as terrible to faint now as all those years ago; I must take control. Breathe deeply. One of the priests, who had taught Joe in the seminary began to speak of Joe's life. He asked for prayers for those in sorrow and read a list of names. Mine was not included. People stood up around me. It was over. Ruth Clarke leaned forward and clasped my shoulder. I sat for a while, gazing at the empty altar, delaying what was to come next. There was a rustle behind me and two bright eyes beneath a mop of corkscrew curls appeared. Little Naomi Clarke.

'I've been hiding,' she said solemnly.

She took my hand and we walked out of the church together. Joe's mother and father, with some of his sisters and brothers, were in the vestibule, shaking hands with all of the congregation as they left. Naomi and I were almost the last. The air, as I stepped outside and inhaled sharply, was cool and damp.

A well-dressed woman approached me. I remembered her face from one of the pre- or post-Kongur receptions.

'Maria, my dear. I didn't know you had a little girl.'

Naomi looked up, puzzled.

'Does she think you're my mummy?'

They both walked away, the kind woman retreating with unnecessary apologies and Naomi skipping off to find her sister. There were people everywhere; Joe's father was giving directions to the house. An invisible bubble separated me from the activity, the conversations, the smiles and condolences. I had no desire to break through the membrane and join in. What I did want, more than anything else, was to be lifted bodily from where I stood, like Our Lady ascending into heaven, and be carried up and away until the church, the crowd, the reality of it all, were no more than tiny dots on the edges of my vision and my memory.

I almost arrived late at Pete's memorial service: a traffic jam held me immobile for half an hour in sight of the church. There was a gathering afterwards at '4 Greenfield', the Derbyshire house that was now Hilary's alone.

A little group of us stood drinking white wine out on the sloping front lawn: Sarah, Alex, Tim, Doug Scott, myself.

'Come down to my car,' said Tim.

I followed him, unquestioning. We sat in the front seat and he filled his pipe, a traditional 'man and his dog' type of pipe, with a mixture of tobacco and hash. When I first met Tim the brilliance of his mind and his unrelenting wit had astounded me, and as time went on so did his capacity for drugs, alcohol, hot food and a minimum of sleep. Smoke gathered around our heads and then funnelled towards the window that he opened.

'How're you doing, Coffey?'

He didn't look at me as he asked, but concentrated instead on refilling the pipe. I smiled. He could appear and sound quite fearsome, but there was much kindness beneath his gruff and often sarcastic exterior.

'Oh. All right.'

'The memorials are over now.' He stopped to strike a match and then inhaled deeply, holding the smoke in his lungs for a few seconds. 'Joe wouldn't have wanted you to mourn too much. You know what he would have wanted, don't you?'

'Tim, please, I . . .'

'Imagine you were the one who'd died.' Swivelling in the seat, he faced me now. 'Can you see Tasker in a black armband for long? Not fucking likely. He'd have got on with his life. And that's what he'd have wanted you to do.'

'Well, it wasn't me that died. Why the hell should I behave like he would have done?'

My anger came more from weariness than anything else. I had little energy left for self-defence. There was no resentment towards Tim, though. He was a good friend who cared about me, and I valued that.

'It's easy for you to say that, Tim. You don't know how it really feels.'

He gave a short, throaty laugh.

'Of course I do. I've *seen* people die. A mate of mine fell off a route and landed at my fucking feet.'

'It's not the same. That wasn't your lover you saw die. And at least you were there with him.'

'Listen, Coffey, I'm not trying to give you a hard time. But Joe was doing what he liked best when he got the chop. And if he was resurrected tomorrow he'd soon be in the mountains again. You won't be doing him any favours by long-term lamentations. Or yourself. Anyway, kid,' he squeezed my hand, 'let's go and do some drinking. But remember what I said.'

I did. Barely three months later he took me to one side in a pub and told me that his doctors had diagnosed cancer of the bowel. Of course he had suspected as much, the day of Pete's memorial.

'I envy them,' he said. 'I'd rather get the chop on a mountain. Any time.'

He lived for almost two more pain-filled years. I was in France when he died. A friend rang to tell me. There was a huge thunderstorm that night and it felt as if Tim were filling the elements, venting all the energy that his illness had robbed him off.

It was all very well to have decided to go to Everest, but that was only a halfway point. Somehow I had to find money to pay for the trip.

'It won't be cheap,' Hilary had warned, and she was right. In 1982, China's continuing 'closed doors' policy on Tibet severely restricted the number of tourists, and those who were allowed in paid highly for the privilege. To reach Everest we would require truck, yak and porter hire, the services of an interpreter and a liaison officer, several nights' accommodation in Lhasa and other Tibetan cities, and all of this added up to thousands of pounds. I had no savings to draw upon; it seemed like a financial impossibility.

'I really want to go.'

Sarah and I sat drinking wine and discussing the problem on a warm evening at the end of June.

'Then you must.'

'But how? I don't want to borrow from my family and the bank wouldn't give an overdraft of that size.'

'What about the house?'

'The house? Do you mean sell it?'

'No. I don't know what I mean. But there must be a way.'

Of course, the house. I had lost all interest in it, and its peaceful new interior seemed pointless now. But the renovations had increased its value, although the mortgage had already been extended once to pay for my share of the work. Still, it was worth a try.

I had to steel myself to go into the Alliance Building Society office in Manchester. The apprehension was worse than when I had gone to the doctor to get leave from work just after Joe's disappearance. Trying to explain to him what I needed and why had reduced me to tears. He had been kind and had quickly written a note.

'The patient is suffering from reactive depression and requires two weeks' rest,' it had said.

This was going to be more complicated. A young, pretty and efficient girl sat me down at her desk.

'I wondered if it's possible to get another extension on a mortgage – when it's not for home improvement.' My voice sounded very feeble.

'Yes.' She drew out the word. 'It is possible, although the interest rate is higher. What would you intend to use the loan for?'

I took a deep breath. There was no point talking around it, I might as well tell her.

'My boyfriend was on a mountaineering expedition to Everest.

He disappeared. I want to go out there. It's very expensive. That's why I need a loan.'

The remainder of the breath came out. I couldn't say, 'He died.' It was two years before I could say that.

Her gaze dropped from me to the pen she held poised above a 'Request for a Further Advancement' form.

'I'm really sorry.' She swallowed and looked up. 'I saw it on the news. You'll have to apply directly to our Head Office. I'll telephone them. I'm sure it will be possible. I'll need to take your name and some other details . . .'

Back on the noisy, traffic-jammed street I felt elated with relief. And not just because it seemed I would get a loan. She had been kind and sympathetic and unintrusive. I had dreaded the interview so much, yet it was already over and she had made it as easy for me as possible.

Head Office were equally accommodating, and the cash came through within a month. The next hurdle was to gain permission to enter Tibet and, in particular, the remote areas around Everest. This procedure, if permission was granted at all, usually took months, and we wanted to go before the winter closed off the region. Help came from Jardine Matheson; with their intervention, doors of bureaucracy swung magically open, and by the end of July the permits were stamped into our passports. The company made all the arrangements for us, negotiating on our behalf via telex with the Chinese Mountaineering Association. The initial cost was a staggering fifteen thousand pounds, plus air fares, but through the hard work of Jardines this was eventually halved.

Although I was due to start working with the Curriculum Development Agency, my employers granted me leave of absence during the first month of the next academic year so that I could make the journey. I had been mentally 'away' from work since early June, but I received a constant stream of support from colleagues who eased me through the final weeks of term.

Only a few people knew of my plans to go to Tibet with Hilary. I guessed that there would be much opposition to the idea, and I had no wish to explain my reasons or justify motives. Gradually it leaked out, and my suspicions were proved correct. Reactions ranged across concern, incredulity and unease at what some thought a ghoulish venture. Prominent among the critics were my climber friends, of whom Alex was the most outspoken. 'You're daft,' he said. 'Joe wouldn't have wanted you to go, it's a creepy idea. And you're being ripped off by the Chinese . . .' And so it went on.

For many climbers I think Hilary and I represented a reality which they preferred to turn away from. They had spouses, lovers, families who would suffer if they died in the mountains. It seemed that by going to Everest we were somehow stepping into their arena and bringing with us tangible proof of the pain they risked inflicting by indulging in such a dangerous sport. I avoided discussing the issue: we were not trying to convey a message, but were simply doing what we could to cope with the reality we had found ourselves in. The surviving members of the Everest expedition gave us whole-hearted support. They were devastated by Joe and Pete's disappearance, and with them we could share our bewilderment and grief. They and their families became valued friends, always at the end of the telephone when we needed to talk, opening their homes to us and doing all they could to help in the planning of the journey.

My parents were terrified for my safety in Tibet, but they never tried to dissuade me from going. Witnessing my hurt was so hard for them, they felt helpless and reached out with comfort whenever they could. My family, Sarah, my friends and the community of the climbing world, they all pulled me through those early days.

SEVEN

Everything had irrevocably changed for me on that June day in 1982. A few days before Joe's departure for Everest in February I had turned thirty, an event which lacked the significance usually associated with new-decade birthdays. We had had a party in my house, the rooms were still cleared of furniture and music bounced around the bare walls and floors.

'This is the big three-oh. How does it feel?' friends asked. But everything felt just as it had the day before.

That was no longer true. With the news of Joe's disappearance a certain lightness, a carefree spirit untouched by real sorrow, left me, and I was made older by grief. The bathroom mirror on that first evening reflected a tanned body, still clad in the skimpy sundress I had put on in the innocence of the morning, and above it a face that was drawn, ravaged by tears and suddenly, to my eyes, aged.

The future was terrifying. Friends rallied round, telling me how strong I was, but I felt alone, adrift and afraid. Sometimes the preparations for Tibet would bring bouts of positive hopefulness, but then I would remember that I had to return and face my life again and a dark depression would descend. I was drinking too much, sleeping irregularly and, with the onset of the school vacation, slipping into lethargy. It was Hilary who roused me from this state. She telephoned from Leysin, in Switzerland, early in August.

'You must come here. You need some experience at altitude. Martin and Jane are driving over at the weekend and they have room for you – phone them up.'

She was right, of course, and within days I found myself in the Swiss Alps.

Leysin is a picturesque village clinging to the south-facing side of a valley and peopled, alongside its Swiss inhabitants, by a multi-national crowd of skiers, climbers and general good-timers. At the hub of the activity is the Club Vagabond, run by a Canadian couple, Dave and Joanne. Joanne was joining us for the first leg of my 'training', a hike up the 10,000 feet Dent du Midi, with an overnight stop at a mountain hut. I gazed at the peak, its sharp, toothlike formation easy to pick out from the stunning mountain range which was the view from Hilary's apartment. Despite my links with the world of mountaineering I normally took little exercise, apart from the occasional jog, and I didn't feel confident about the endurance test ahead.

Hilary surveyed my clothes: the jeans, T-shirt and trainers I stood in, and the assortment of summer garments in my rucksack. She began rummaging through a wardrobe and drawers, and pulled out knee-length britches which were too big for her, and cotton shirts, thermal underwear, woollen socks and raingear, which had been Pete's. When I had tried it all on, she and Joanne agreed that I at least *looked* prepared for the Alps.

The sight of family groups trekking the same path as us on the following day reassured me that the Dent du Midi was less formidable than it had seemed from a distance. In three hours we reached the hut, a large, log-built structure set in flowering pastures and backdropped by mountains. Hut mores were strict. Outdoor shoes had to be exchanged at the door for wooden clogs, wire baskets hung from the ceiling for food storage and climbing hardware was put in cupboards set into the wall. As soon as we arrived Hilary raced upstairs to the communal bedroom. A long wooden shelf, covered with mattresses, ran along two of the walls and she made a quick survey for any unreserved spots near the windows. We were out of luck and I realized the implications of this later on when I tried to sleep amidst a sea of snoring bodies, away from any fresh air. It was to be a dawn start so we turned in early, leaving our clothes at hand and ready for a quick and efficient get-away in the morning. I lay awake for a while, listening to voices in the dining room beneath me and the clump of clogs on the wooden floor. The door creaked opened, light flooded in and was quickly closed out again. Dark shapes moved around the room, illuminated now and then by the flash of a head-torch. Someone was rustling around, settling down inside a sleeping-bag, sighing and yawning. Snuffled breathing turned gradually into a snore. I remembered Hilary's advice: 'Try not to be awake when the snorers start up,' and realized that I had left it too late.

Joe Tasker. *(photo Chris Bonington)*

Left Joe asleep at the end of a party. *(Sarah Richard)*
Right Joe rock–climbing in England. *(Mountain Magazine)*

Joe making an attempt on the summit of Mount Kongur, 27 June 1981. *(Pete Boardman)*

At Base Camp, Mount Kongur. *(Chris Bonington)*

Joe and Pete Boardman on K2. *(CB)*

The British team on the fatal Everest expedition, summer 1982, *l. to r.* Chris Bonington, Charlie Clarke, Adrian Gordon, Joe, Pete Boardman, Dick Renshaw. *(CB)*

Joe and Pete in a relaxed mood on an approach march. *(CB)*

A snow cave on the North-East ascent – one of the last photos of Joe, with Dick Renshaw. *(CB)*

Left Hilary Boardman and Maria in Leysin, Switzerland, celebrating after their excursion into the Swiss Alps. *(Marie-Noelle Kingsley)*
Right Maria on the journey into Tibet. *(Hilary Boardman)*

Maria with Tibetan villagers in the Kharta Valley. *(HB)*

Left The roof of the Sera Monastery. *(HB)*
Right Zhiang with prayer flags. *(HB)*

Left A statue of Buddha at the Sera Monastery. *(HB)*
Right Golden figures at the Jokhang Temple. *(HB)*

Left Trekking through the Kharta Valley. *(HB)*   *Right* Tibetan villagers in the Kharta Valley, with a woman and child hiding from the camera. *(HB)*

The ruins of the Rongbuk Monastery, with Everest in the background. *(HB)*

Left The last snapshot Joe sent to Maria from Everest Base Camp.
Right The granite slab commemorating Joe and Pete. *(Charles Clark)*

The East-North-East Ridge of Everest, from the Rongbuk Glacier. *(HB)*

Breakfast was bread, jam and huge bowls of hot chocolate. Hilary was gradually instructing me.

'The body needs more fluid at altitude, so drink lots. You must remember that in Tibet.'

In dawn light we left the Alpine fields and began to hike up through a grey, barren, moonlike landscape, scrambling the final section to the rocky pinnacles at the summit. I breathed deeply, glad to be there in the clear morning light.

'Hilary, what is *that*?' I asked, as clouds cleared to reveal a huge massif nearby.

'Le Grand Combin,' she replied. 'It's the second highest peak in the Alps. Funny, Pete and I never got around to climbing it.'

Racing down from the summit, they taught me to scree-run.

'Bend your knees, relax, *go for it!* It's good practice for when you learn to ski!'

We gulped beer in the sunshine, gathered our belongings together and trekked back to the car for the drive to Leysin. Over pre-dinner drinks in the Vagabond bar Hilary went into a huddle with some men I recognized as instructors from the International School of Mountaineering, the ISM, of which Pete had been director. At least two of them had been at his memorial service. She seemed diminutive next to the strongly-built mountain guides; her head craned upwards as she talked and they bent down to listen and reply. Perched on a nearby bar stool, I relished my new sense of well-being, muscles relaxed after exertion and skin warm with sunburn. A few more jaunts like this, I thought, sipping a gin and tonic, and I would really fitten up. Hilary returned.

'Before dinner we'd better go over to Guy's house,' she said. 'His feet are the same size as yours and you can borrow boots, crampons and gaiters from him. He's got an ice axe you can use as well. I've got everything else we need.'

I looked at her blankly, the glass poised midway to my open mouth. 'ISM are setting off tomorrow to do Le Grand Combin,' she continued, 'and we can go along with them.'

Blankness turned into panic. The image of that huge, snow-covered mountain loomed before me. How was I ever going to 'do' anything on that?

'But . . . Hilary . . .'

'Now don't worry, it'll be all right. I'll look after you.'

Weakly I reminded myself that she was, after all, an experienced mountaineer, before taking a large gulp of my drink.

We met the ISM group at Le Grand St Bernard Pass. Ten clients and two guides, midway through a seven-day course, with the rock-climbing section behind them and now about to tackle mountaineering. They all seemed fit, strong and capable, and must have wondered about the new arrival who had trouble fastening her boots and complained about the weight of her pack. It was a long hike to the mountain hut and I quickly became the runt of the group, stumbling along on aching feet behind the firm strides of the others, and too engrossed in trying to keep up to take in the loveliness of my surroundings. After four hours of this, as I was about to surrender to tiredness, Hilary appeared on a rock step and shouted to me that I was nearly at the hut.

'If she's just saying that . . .' I muttered furiously to myself, but when my head drew level with her feet I saw it. Sitting on the wooden steps I eased my grateful feet out of the unfamiliar boots and took in the surroundings. Ahead of me stood the outhouse, a small stone building with no door, so that its occupant could appreciate the breath-taking view of rocky crags, valley pastures and snow-capped peaks. I regretted not being able to whistle.

The hut was tiny, just two rooms. Downstairs the space held a kitchen area, a dining table and, suspended above, a double bed that was lowered at night. Up a very narrow, winding staircase were two rows of bunks and a sleeping cupboard for the hut guardian, crammed with his belongings. While we ate, packed in around the table, I wondered about the small, gruff man who cared for the hut and speculated on what route may have led him to such a strange and singular life, its bouts of feverish activity when people arrived at the hut contrasting with the utter peace and solitude that would be his when we left.

Again we prepared for the morning but now it was more complicated. Each of us left a pile of climbing hardware downstairs – helmets, harnesses, karabiners, ice axes, ropes, crampons, boots – then squeezed into the tiny sleeping-space, hectically arranging clothes, rucksacks, sleeping-bags and head-torches before settling down. Hilary set the alarm for 3 a.m., explaining that we had to get as far up the route as possible before the sun warmed the snow and made it unstable. There seemed little point in reacting to this unsettling piece of news; the next day was charted out and I could not resist its course.

'Pity Joe can't see me,' I mumbled to her in the dark. 'Sometimes he'd get me out of bed by tipping up one end of it – he'd never believe this.'

'You never know,' she whispered. 'He's probably having a good laugh about it with Pete!'

After what seemed like only minutes of sleep the strident alarm jerked me awake and I joined in the flurry of dressing. Head-torches revealed flashes of blue and red thermal wear. Little was said, but the space was filled with shufflings, zippings, occasional grunts and the rustle of sleeping-bags being pushed into stuff-sacks, the small nylon bags that miraculously swallowed up large amounts of fabric and down. Outside, after the rapid consumption of fried eggs and bread and several cups of tea, the cold air stung my face and I found myself in the middle of the night, being helped to don unfamiliar harness and gaiters. We crunched off over frozen stones, away from the warmth and light of the hut.

'When we get onto the snow slope we'll stop and rope up,' said Hilary, 'and I'll show you how to fasten your crampons onto your boots.'

I looked up and breathed deeply. What has brought me here, I wondered. The night, pure and crystal clear, had a surreal quality. Stars filled the sky, and high clouds scudded across a half-moon. Little pools of light ahead of me in the darkness moved slowly upwards: the leading group had begun the ascent. Hilary roped me to her, and crouched at my feet to deal with the crampons.

'These are easy to fit on, not fiddly like mine.'

She straightened up, checked the rope at my waist, smiled.

'There you are, little Maria, a real mountaineer. Joe would be proud!'

'He'd think I'd lost my marbles, more like.'

Our pace was slow and steady. I put my feet where hers had been and followed her instructions exactly. Move in long zig-zags like this, change the axe from hand to hand to keep it uphill, stop and knock snow off the crampons like so. It all seemed inevitable, something not chosen but there for me to do without question. I became completely absorbed and fell into a laboured rhythm of breathing, movement and little thought.

As the sky was lightening we reached a rock band that was clear of snow. I teetered clumsily over it in the crampons.

'Look back,' said Hilary.

'Amazing,' I whispered, gazing down at the steepness of the slope we had climbed.

'See what you can do?' she laughed.

When dawn came we stood and rested and watched on a high ridge; so began a day of breath-taking beauty amid a world of snow, ice, blue sky, sunshine and the gradual revealing of the mysteries of mountains. A day when I felt alive and strong and happy for the first time in weeks. Below us, the valley side swept cleanly down to the glacier, and snow crystals caught the rays of the rising sun; above, white peaks began to gleam and harden against the sky. The air was cold, still, perfect. I thought of Joe, of what had driven him to embrace hardship and deprivation in his sport. Maybe it was that the further he explored his limits in the mountains, the harder he pushed himself, the greater were the rewards of moments such as this, I thought, as I looked behind at where I had climbed and ahead to where I was to go.

It was decided that Hilary and I, while keeping in view of the rest of the group, would continue to climb alone. Throughout that day the rope was my true lifeline, and in her I placed implicit faith and trust. Undreamed of things became a matter of course, a necessary part of passing through the mountain environment. I clung to a small ice wall, attached only by the points of my crampons and the ice axe, and at the bottom as I leapt across the yawning bergschrund where the glacier parts from the valley headwall, I had a memory flash of my schoolgirl diagrams of that very formation. Hilary pointed out the telltale grey lines of covered crevasses and I learned what distance we needed to stay apart in case one of us should fall in.

A loud crack rang out as we began the ascent of a long slope, and one of the cornices, the overhanging masses of snow and ice high above, that Hilary had been cautiously eyeing, tumbled down, breaking into football-sized chunks of ice and following the curve of the slope towards us.

'Crouch!' yelled Hilary. 'Dig in the axe to the hilt!' and we dodged the balls as they whistled past.

'We have to move fast up this slope,' she said when it was over. 'There are more cornices up there. Keep up with me. If another one falls off, do exactly what I tell you.'

Adrenalin pushed me on, my movements became coordinated and efficient, hidden reserves of strength and determination were coming through. I felt joyous, glad and grateful to be alive, the threat of the loosening cornices above only heightening my aware-ness of life and its sweetness. It was like breaking through a cloud cover to discover a bright sky and sunshine above, a sudden realization that happiness was possible.

By midday we stood at the summit of Le Grand Combin, the perfect weather rewarding us with a 360 degree vista of Alpine peaks. I was light-headed with altitude, with exertion, with the thrill of achievement. But there was no time for lingering; we had to reach another valley, a different hut, and had a long afternoon ahead, so after a quick lunch we began our descent. The route down led across a narrow, vertical ice wall, beneath which the slope fell away steeply for hundreds of feet. There was a ledge, just wide enough for one crampon. I had to walk along it: the fact seemed to stand in front of me, mocking. For the first time that day fear overtook me. I could not move. Hilary's calm, confident voice came from behind.

'You came across this on the way up, Maria, but you were focused upwards and didn't notice. Don't worry, I've got you firmly anchored here with my ice axe. If you slip – but you won't – I'll have you securely, I'll just pull you up. That's it, off you go, don't worry, I've got you . . .' she talked me through fifteen uncertain steps across the ledge.

'Hilary, it's all ice here. I can't protect you!'

While I was still searching for somewhere to anchor the axe she came across, sure in her movements.

Our little expedition went on for two more days. I learned, absorbed, pushed myself, and it was only on the final afternoon that exhaustion began to take over. Staggering through thigh-deep snow and afraid of the electrical storm that was raising the hairs on my neck, I dreamed of rest, of dry clothes and food. That night, in the Vagabond bar, I felt I deserved the congratulations for my efforts. Hilary was already planning the next jaunt and, despite my tiredness, I knew I would not protest this time. Someone asked what I had found hardest over the past few days. There was no hesitation in my reply: 'The ice wall.' It must have been the gin which made Hilary confess. She told me that she had watched my shaky progress across that perilous ledge in fear; there was nowhere for her to drive in her axe and secure me and no other way down the mountain, so she had done the only thing possible in allowing me to believe I was safe. Her voice, calmly encouraging me, had given no hint of what she must have felt, knowing that if I slipped we would both have a long and serious fall.

I gazed at her, taking in her words. Incredulity mingled with strong feelings of respect, trust and affection. That day on Le Grand Combin sealed the bond that had been growing between us. We were ready to go together to Tibet.

EIGHT

'Take this with you.'

A simple yellow card with the words 'Considering how dangerous everything is, nothing is really very frightening.'

I hugged her.

'Thank you for coming, Claire.'

She had left her husband and children for a night and driven down to be with me when I set off from Manchester.

'Of course I had to be here. This is a crossroad in your life.'

Claire, my friend since the first day at university. We had been through adventurous, formative times together, and although our lives had curved off in different directions we were still touchstones for one another. The guard walked down the platform shutting the doors with loud bangs.

'Time to go, ladies! Climb aboard!'

I opened the window and leaned out. Claire grasped my hands as the train jerked and began to move. Her eyes were alight and full of tears. 'Write *everything* down, Maria.'

It was August 30th, six months to the day since Joe and Pete had left for Everest. I looked out at the orderliness of surburbia flashing by and leaned back against the headrest.

'Two gin and tonics, please.'

The man pushing the trolley gave Hilary her change, put down plastic cups and miniature bottles and grinned at us. Please don't ask what the celebration is, I pleaded silently. Hilary raised her glass.

'Here's to Peter and Joe: I wonder if they know we're on our way.'

The alcohol eased my headache. Friends had called round the night before and a little party developed. There was an air of expectancy, a tension that made everyone drink too much and talk

97

about ridiculous, irrelevant things. As people left I saw them to the front door and accepted their anxious wishes of good luck. Alex and Sarah were there, and within the week he was setting off on expedition to Annapurna. We were close friends, but I found it hard to talk to him. Their relationship, the love that was obvious between them, and the fact of what he was about to do were all too hurtful to dwell upon. Sarah was quiet and thoughtful that evening, concentrating on Alex. Our farewell was almost nonchalant.

'Make sure you come back safely,' I told Alex.

'Don't let Hilary talk you into doing anything else ridiculous,' he replied.

It had been 5 a.m. before I fell into a fitful sleep. Four hours later I was awake, full of nervous energy and frantically packing as the telephone rang and rang. To be finally travelling was a relief, but there was none of the usual thrill and anticipation of embarking on a long journey; instead I felt dulled and resentful at having to go through all this.

Memories flooded in at Heathrow Airport. Joe's arm around me as he talked to a reporter, his hand creeping up under my sweater and making me squirm and giggle when it was my turn to answer questions. Saying goodbye, stroking the soft skin on his cheeks where the beard ended, just before we moved apart and he walked away. I phoned my mother.

'I'm going to Mass every day until I hear that you're safely home,' she said.

Her voice was high and trembling with concern and love, and I gave in to the tears I had been holding back all morning.

We saw Le Grand Combin from the plane. I wanted to shout to everyone aboard, 'Hey, I stood on the top of that!' but I kept it to myself and felt a warm glow of pride. Now and then Hilary and I talked. She told me of flying to England after getting the news of Pete's disappearance. Annie Haston, who was also the widow of a climber, took her to the airport and had to verify that the unrecognizable scribble on the cheque was, in fact, Hilary's signature. The stewardesses were gentle and sensitive and did not press food or drink on her. She had to change planes and from the transit lounge she telephoned her parents, to tell them. All of that and alone; I shuddered to think of it. I had been surrounded and cushioned by people and still it had been unbearable. She described a torch-lit ski descent with Pete in Leysin and dancing afterwards in the Club Vagabond, giddy on wine and fresh air and love.

'We were bouncing off the walls. We could have been the only two people there.'

Time was suspended, we sped through space, across continents, 620 miles an hour. Images on the cinema screen flickered, mouths moved soundlessly and people around me laughed at what they heard through the headphones. I was grateful for the elderly man in the next seat who neither spoke nor glanced in my direction. Passengers craned for a glimpse of Hong Kong as we approached, but I couldn't bear to look, I didn't want to leave the plane, I wanted to spin back, back to a reality that I did not yet believe was irrevocably over. Suddenly I focused on the high, narrow, tightly-packed buildings of the city and we were down.

A sleek limousine, courtesy of Jardine Matheson, slid us through streets teaming with people and traffic to our hotel. It was late morning; I curled up in a foetal ball in bed, my body as confused and tired as my mind. Maybe sleep would restore everything, maybe when I awoke the world would be understandable again.

'Get *up*!' shouted Hilary from the shower, 'I've just worked out how much this is costing us a day!' and she quoted a figure so horrendously high that I was rapidly propelled out of bed.

Dazed and jet-lagged, we plunged into the smart central area of Hong Kong. Shop windows displayed expensive goods, symbols of affluence and ease. Chic women in designer clothes and with immaculate hair, make-up and nails passed us, leaving aromas of perfume in their wake. We seemed to be the only people sauntering along. Everyone else was purposeful and in a hurry.

'Let's go down here.'

I followed Hilary along a cobbled alley and suddenly, around a corner, a few feet away from the rich and Westernized Hong Kong, we entered another, remote world. Double front doors were opened wide to reveal small shops, pungent with unknown smells, whose wares spilled out onto the street: baskets and sacks crammed with snake-skins, mysterious dried leaves and fungi, beans and dried fish. Market stalls, vendors and customers pressed together in a tight maze of colour; bleeding animal carcasses hung above head level on display. Men wearing only shorts and a glaze of sweat pushed past us as they ran down the street to unknown destinations, and bicycles careered by. Beggars crouched in corners, hands outstretched. High above this buzz of activity the balconies of apartments were festooned with hanging plants, and shuttered windows opened into dark interiors revealing glimpses of people moving busily about their lives. For a short while the mental struggles that Hilary and I were going through stood in proper perspective. Time slipped by, we found ourselves staggering with tiredness and, re-emerging into the Western world a few streets away, we began to search for a taxi.

In the hotel restaurant that evening I watched a beautiful Chinese girl and an American man at the next table. They leaned towards each other and spoke in low, intimate tones. She laughed out loud at something he said, throwing her head back, and he reached over to stroke her exposed neck. Since Joe's death I had felt totally numbed about men, and sex was an abstract idea. I was glad of this, I did not want my body to re-awaken and make demands, but watching the couple stirred up memories of loving times and made my heart ache. Lying in bed, waiting for the sedative to take effect, I remembered Claire's words at the station in Manchester, the day before and half a world away . . . 'a crossroad'. A thread in my life had been severed and I wanted to find a way to mend it, so that I could feel happy and whole once more.

'You must ensure something positive emerges from all this,' my brother John had said, days after we heard of the tragedy. His words and Claire's swirled around my head as the pill began to drift me away. I stood poised on that crossroad between the past and the future, with no idea which direction to take.

Our plane tickets into China were waiting for us in Jardine Matheson's plush headquarters. As we were shown around the offices and conference rooms a feeling began to creep over me, one which came back again and during the coming month, that I was following in Joe's last footsteps. Sitting in the deep leather armchairs, walking on the roof and taking in the panoramic view of Hong Kong, I could feel his imprint: I pictured him laughing, talking and enjoying the comfort of the surroundings. The feeling intensified later that evening when the company held a party for us. We were both nervous as a limousine whisked us up through the expensive heights of the city to a large and palatial house. The Everest team had taken along a group of company employees as trekkers during the early part of the expedition, and these people were now gathered to meet us on the eve of our departure. They were full of stories of Joe, Pete and the others, including accounts of the reception that had been given for them just before they left for Tibet. As the evening wore on, I imagined the scene that would have been enacted had they all returned from the climb, an evening of laughter instead of memories and strain. We gave presents of Joe's and Pete's new books, both published posthumously. A man handed me some snapshots. He cleared his throat nervously.

'I thought . . . these are some I took of Joe . . . I wondered if you might like them.'

Joe in a transit lounge in China, wearing the hat I gave him, looking tired but relaxed. Getting out the words to give my thanks was hard; the gesture was simple yet it meant a lot to me.

'It seemed . . . it was the least I could do,' he said.

The customs official at Canton Airport stood behind the wooden trestle table looking quizzically through my rucksack. His uniform, a regulation grey, hung loosely on his body. First impressions of China swam before me as I picked up the bags and walked away from him: huge bamboos in an interior courtyard, sunlight shafting onto a wicker bench, a sudden drabness after the colour of Hong Kong, the sparseness of floor coverings and furniture. A mural ran along a wall, a long poem illustrated with paintings of mountains, rivers, soldiers. It began:

The Red Army fears not the trials of a distant march;
To them a thousand mountains, ten thousand rivers are
    nothing.

I made a silent wish for the same tenacity in the days ahead. In the high-ceilinged, sunlit airport restaurant waitresses huddled by a white-clothed table and smiled curiously at us. We pointed hopefully at the menu and were soon served with a lunch of rice, meat fried in batter and, to finish, soup.

Sitting on the tiled floor of the departure lounge waiting for the flight to Chengdu, I surveyed the three Swiss men who had joined us for the journey into Tibet. The Chinese government had charged a lump sum for the cost of permission, transportation, guide, interpreter and accommodation, and our party was allowed to be up to five in number. A friend of Hilary's was with us, along with two of his friends, and their aim was to reconnoitre for possible guided tours in the Everest area. Denny was a firm, solid character, in middle age and extremely fit. As a mountain guide and ski instructor he had known Pete well, and only months before he had dug Hilary out of the avalanche which had engulfed them when they were heli-skiing together. The tall, thin, rather rakish Pierre, in his mid-thirties, was a travel agent who was full of nervous tension and always concerned about flights, dates, itineraries. And finally, quiet and dreamy Jacques, fifty years old and anxious that his physical prowess might not match up to the demands of the mountain. We had asked them along on the journey because we needed to split the costs five ways, and for them it was a good deal because all of the usual problems of gaining permission to enter Tibet had been bypassed. I had no wish to socialize with them or to share any of the usual camaraderie of travelling companions. I was sunk into my own thoughts, quietly trying to soak in some trace of the man I had lost and to look at the places he had seen during the final part of his life. For Denny, Pierre and Jacques, Hilary and I must have made strange fellow-travellers, as foreign as the soil we were now on. Tensions arose: they wanted to make changes to the itinerary that we, because of our emotional investment in the journey, could not agree to. But it is of no use to dwell on the disagreements, and for this reason our fellow-trekkers will not figure largely in the story ahead.

As I watched them, the three men were in heated dispute with airport officials, as their papers appeared to contain no permission for Chengdu. The argument was finally resolved and we filed up the steps of the small turboprop and into its wallpapered interior. A stewardess issued fans and everyone began to wave them, swishing warm air around the cabin. I wiped my face and neck with a hot towel and stole glances at the other passengers, still not quite believing I was actually in China. In front of me sat a young soldier in a green uniform, its stiff collar bearing a red star. His hair was newly clipped, high above his ears, giving the back of his head a vulnerable look. He turned, his dark Mongolian eyes registering surprise at my European features emerging from the steaming towel, and we smiled shyly at each other.

There was a stop-over at Choggin. Inside the drab transit lounge, ochre walls were lined with wooden benches that creaked under the weight of the people who filled them. Fans turned slowly on the ceiling in a vain attempt to aerate the humid and overcrowded room. A man sat clutching a basket out of which stared five dried geese, complete with beaks and eyes and looking shrivelled and surprised. I went in search of a ladies' room and was intrigued by the precarious arrangement I found. A ceramic riverbed had been built into the floor, and above it were wooden stalls with stable doors. There were no seats, simply a handhold and places for the feet to guide one's perilous balancing act above the stream of running water. I feared for the old lady who had made shaky progress into the stall next to mine, but she shuffled out again, unscathed.

By mid-afternoon we were in Chengdu, part of the press of people trying to squeeze through the small, wrought-iron exit gate. Ahead of me was the man with the geese; he held the basket high to save it from the crush and the birds' heads bobbed about atop their long necks. Waiting at the gate were the Chinese officials who would accompany us to the mountain and back. Zhiang, the liaison officer whose job it was to guide us through the maze of bureaucracy that the journey entailed, spoke no English, but the interpreter, Dong, made gracious introductions. His medium height, slight build and Western clothes were in sharp contrast to Zhiang's tall, muscular, army-uniformed frame.

On the long drive to the hotel we passed through a farming area. Irrigation ditches were dug along the roadside and above these rice was spread out to dry, dotted here and there with small bundles of hay. Farm labourers, their eyes shaded by large coolie hats, went by on bicycles or bent over in the paddy fields, ankle-deep in water. Some sat outside a house, the brown of its thatched roof contrasting with the green fields. I pressed against the window of the minibus, trying to soak it all in.

The hotel was large and faceless. I opened the window-shutters of our room and looked out over the concrete city and the cyclists and pedestrians in loose cotton clothing of the regulation blues, greys, greens and browns. Chengdu is reputed to have only ten days of sunshine a year, and this was not one of them. There was a knock at the door and Hilary opened it to a tiny woman pushing a large wheeled urn. She indicated the hot-water flask between the two beds, wanting to replenish it. A tin of jasmin tea was on the tray beside the flask, along with two delicate lidded mugs painted with Chinese characters. We sipped the scented brew, a toast to our first night in China.

Downstairs in the vast dining room, Dong outlined the finalized version of our itinerary. The circular table had a revolving centre-piece holding the most choice dishes, and as he talked we reached forward with chopsticks and transferred delicate morsels from the plates to our individual bowls. The exact nature of some of the food was uncertain, but I didn't want to interrupt Dong to inquire.

'Tomorrow morning we fly to Lhasa and spend two nights there.

Then a truck will take us to the head of the Kharta Valley on the eastern side of Everest. This will take four days and we will stay in official rest houses on the way. In the Kharta Valley, and during the trek up to the Karma Valley, we will camp. It is forty-five miles up the valley – with yaks and porters, there and back should take us six days.'

Joe and Pete had not been to Kharta. Our purpose on that side of the mountain was to see the Kangshung Face, at the head of the Karma Valley, down which, it was conjectured, they had fallen to their deaths. To reach it we would have to trek, with yaks and porters, for several days.

'From Kharta the truck will drive us the hundred miles to the north side of the mountain, to the Base Camp area in the Rongbuk Valley. It will take most of a day to get there. We will spend six days in that area before returning directly to Lhasa.'

During those six days Hilary and I hoped to reach Camp Three, Advance Base Camp, on Joe and Pete's route, at 21,000 feet. The main problem with this itinerary was the shortage of time for altitude acclimatization. Lhasa was at 12,000 feet, Base Camp in the Rongbuk Valley at 17,000 feet. We just had to wait and see how our bodies would react.

Before bed I explored the hotel, getting lost in the maze of corridors, lifts and stairs. To my surprise I found a bar on the roof where I drank a hot chocolate, watching the mix of Chinese and foreign guests. The tourist shop on the ground floor was still open and I stocked up with American candies for the trip.

Hilary and I were the first of our group to be up and ready in the morning, and at 5 a.m. we sat on wicker chairs in the dark, humid warmth of the hotel porch, talking to a kindly Chinese man who was also on his way to Lhasa where he worked as a travel agent. Driving out of town down the wide, tree-lined boulevard, our minibus passed joggers exercising in the hour before dawn, young men clad only in loose cotton trousers, their sweating torsos reflecting the streetlamps and headlights. As I leaned to look out at them I woke Hilary, who had dropped off to sleep against my shoulder. She rubbed her eyes and peered at the runners.

'They must be late for work,' she mumbled, before her head nodded and settled back against me.

A crowd of people, clad in green and brown cottons, waited in the airport departure lounge for the same flight as us. One woman had a baby on her back in a wicker basket; sitting next to her, his feet not reaching the floor, was a little boy in a miniature army uniform who regarded us solemnly, his peaked cap pulled to one side of his head. Our group was ushered past the other travellers and into a side room where breakfast was spread across a white-clothed table. Cakes, spam, hard-boiled eggs, peanuts in aniseed oil, rice, weak milky coffee; it was hard on our Western stomachs at 6 a.m.

We flew for three hours, over a vast range of peaks that reached 23,000 feet, across the high Tibetan plateau and along the Brahma-putra Valley. Hilary took photographs but I sat still, gazing through the window down to 'the greatest infinity on earth'* and feeling emotion rise in me. It spilled over into tears as I stepped down from the Ilyshin 18 onto the landing-strip, breathing the rarefied air and seeing the intensely blue sky of this country that, six months before, I believed I would never visit.

*Heinrich Harrer, *Return to Tibet* (London, 1984)

NINE

Lhasa was two hours away by minibus along a dusty road, through brilliant light and a landscape of intense and sharply defined colours. Rolling brown hills were the backdrop to a lake of bluest water, and the hues of a newly renovated Buddha shone where the image had been hewn into a rock face. But Lhasa itself, on first impressions, lacked colour. Grey, squat buildings, their corrugated-iron rooves glinting in the sunlight, were laid out along concrete streets down which young Chinese soldiers sauntered or cycled. There seemed little evidence of the fabled ancient city which existed until the Chinese invasion in the 1950s. Then the Potala came into view, the exiled Dalai Lama's palace, a vast architectural wonder shimmering on a hill, the most awe-inspiring building I have ever seen. I craned my neck to keep sight of it as the bus left the city limits, took us along arbutus-lined roads past a gravel works where lorries backed from a gate and belched exhaust fumes, and finally drew up inside the large compound of the 'Guest House', the barracks where all foreign visitors stayed. Someone had been gardening: colourful flowers broke through the dusty soil and brightened the entrance to the reception desk and the communal dining hall. Joe and Pete had stayed here, too: their expedition stickers were on the glass doors.

Hilary and I shared a room which opened out onto a courtyard of sun-yellowed grass and a view to the steep and rocky hillside behind. There was a rudimentary bathroom four doors away with sporadic running water, two toilets and a trough-like basin. Our beds were narrow, high and hard, and piled with eiderdowns for the cold nights. We left our luggage on the polished wooden floor and returned to the dining hall for lunch. Sunshine streamed through the windows of the high-ceilinged room, which reminded me of a school hall. At the tables sat other tourists, mostly elderly Americans or Germans.

'I don't want to talk to anyone here,' said Hilary firmly, and I understood her reticence. It was not easy for us to explain to strangers the reason for our presence in Tibet. But, as food was being served, a face familiar to me from photographs was suddenly at our table. Pertemba, a Sherpa guide, had stood with Pete Boardman on the summit of Everest in 1975 after an ascent by the South-West Ridge. Hilary had met him in Nepal and, later, during his visit to England. He greeted her now with tears shining in his eyes. The news of Pete's death had only recently reached him. We had heard he would be in the Rongbuk Valley around the same time as us, leading a small trekking group, but this meeting in Lhasa was unexpected and Hilary was visibly shaken. They withdrew to another table to talk, and after lunch I joined them. Pertemba gave us the feeling that he totally understood the motives behind our journey, and, like Hilary, he did not accept the theory that Joe and Pete had fallen to their deaths down the Kangshung Face.

'I would have known if Pete had died violently,' said Hilary. 'I would have sensed it.'

Pertemba nodded; perhaps they fell asleep, totally exhausted, and simply did not wake up.

I listened, but my mind that afternoon could not dwell on death. I was concerned with re-creation, with trying to picture Joe sitting in this dining room, relaxing and laughing after a meal. There was comfort in this but also a growing tension. Each day now was bringing me physically closer to the place, and therefore also to the fact, of his death. Reaching Everest was our goal, but we could not stay there for long; soon I would have to turn away from the mountain and accept that I was leaving him behind me.

Hilary and I rested in our room after lunch, silently wrapped in separate thoughts and tired by the sudden increase in altitude. But we roused ourselves: our time in Lhasa was limited and we decided to visit the old part of the city. Dong and Zhiang drove us back along the grey roads to the edge of the Parkhor, a market street encircling the sacred Jokhang Temple.

'We will wait here for you,' said Dong. 'Please return in two hours.'

'Why don't you come with us?' I asked, unthinking.

'No, no, we wait here. Two hours, please.'

Later, when I saw the remains of monasteries that the Red Guards had ripped apart, the machine-gun bullet-holes strafed across what was left of the walls, I began to see why Dong and Zhiang hung back. Whatever the rights and wrongs of their recent history, the Tibetans understandably resented the presence of Chinese, particularly those in uniform, in the parts of their world that they had managed to salvage from the horrors of the Cultural Revolution.

The Parkhor had obviously escaped the worst of the ravages, for it gave me a strong and immediate sense of old Tibet. Once again, as in Hong Kong, we slipped quickly from one world into another, and my first impression of Lhasa, its military-camp atmosphere, dissolved away. Makeshift stalls of wood and canvas stood on sunlit cobbles. The houses that lined the street were constructed of timber and roughly hewn white-washed boulders held together with clay. Their upper storeys seemed to overhang precariously, tipping forward with bright red and blue window-shutters, colourful flower-boxes and fluttering prayer-flags. Some houses had shops on the street level, their doorways opening into dark, cool interiors. Market vendors called to us and poked out their tongues in the traditional greeting as we wandered along looking at the jewellery, the blocks of tea, the rancid yak butter and the sacks of barley flour. One stall was simply a large rug spread on the ground, round which members of the Khampa tribe, from eastern Tibet, bargained intensely over turquoise bracelets and brass cymbals. They were beautiful, impressive men with sharp, fierce features and long, black, ribbon-braided hair, and they paid us no heed as we stopped in our tracks to gaze at them. As the only tourists in the market place that afternoon, however, we did attract a lot of attention. An old man with a long white beard stopped and regarded me in amazement. He encircled one of my thin wrists with his fingers and poked gently at my upper arm, obviously intrigued by the lack of muscle. Turning his attention to Hilary, he compared her strong arms with mine and then went on his way, wreathed in smiles of sheer amusement. Two Buddhist nuns in brown robes came by, their shorn heads covered by white headdresses with starched, wing-like pieces protruding at ear level. They seemed delighted by the sight of us and laughed merrily, especially when a little girl ran by and smacked me playfully on the bottom.

Bicycles were the only vehicles in the street, and the tinkling of their bells was a continuous background noise. The cyclists wove between the shoppers and browsers, there was no pushing or shoving and a feeling of gentleness and ease pervaded. After the uniformity of dress in China, these people were full of visual contrasts. The myriad colours of waistcoats, aprons, headscarves, belts and hats were layered with dust and dirt but still bright against the black or brown cloth of their dresses, loose trousers and shirts. Turquoise encased in silver adorned ears and wrists. And wide, generous smiles opened up across stolid features to express amusement and delight: smiles which cheered me throughout the journey and caused me to marvel at the enduring spirit of the Tibetans despite their poverty and their tortuous history.

Hilary began to feel dehydrated from heat and altitude, so we looked for somewhere to buy a drink. The first shop doorway round which we put our heads opened onto a room full of leather hides hanging from low ceiling beams. Men working at wooden benches laughed and beckoned to us to enter. Our next try was more successful and we walked into a cool, dim room and across a stone floor polished by years of footsteps. The walls of the shop were of darkly-stained wood, and the place was empty except for a counter at one end. On this far wall shelves reached to the ceiling and held row after row of bottles filled with mysterious, brightly-coloured liquids. We spoke not one word of Tibetan between us and the shopkeeper laughed as we hummed, hawed and finally pointed to a bottle containing a thick, yellow liquid which looked like concentrated fruit cordial. The light outside made us squint so we found a wooden bench in the shade of a tree and settled down to investigate our purchase. A shaven-headed monk sat nearby and his saffron robes reflected the liquid that we sniffed at and sipped cautiously. He watched our investigations with open curiosity. Whatever was in the bottle may have been a fruit drink, but it definitely had a strong alcoholic content.

'Do Tibetan monks drink alcohol, Hilary?'

'I wouldn't have thought so. Shall we . . . ?'

'Let's offer it to him. He can only refuse.'

He enfolded the recapped bottle within his robes in a swift, smooth motion, chuckling with glee. While Hilary went off in search of a tap I took out my camera, but the monk shook his head and turned his face away. Within minutes a group of children had formed round the bench, gesticulating excitedly for me to take their photographs. I did so and they held out their hands, not, as I first presumed, for money, but for the Polaroid pictures they were expecting to see emerge from the camera. I was sorry to disappoint them and felt suddenly ashamed to be a tourist.

The Jokhang Temple, a shrine of great holiness, stands at the centre of the Parkhor. Pilgrims were circling the temple clockwise, spinning brass and wooden prayer-wheels and sending out incantations on the wind with each revolution. The more devout measured the distance by prostrating themselves full-length on the ground. A hollow-faced young man, clad in loose sacking, prayed loudly as he repeatedly threw himself down and drew himself up again to his full height. The wooden slats tied to his hands and knees for protection made loud slaps as he hit the cobbles. The small boy with him was going through the same ritual of devotion, and from their weariness and dirt-smeared skin it seemed that they were nearing the end of a long journey. An old man sat on the cobbles near the temple, his eyes shut and his head moving to the rhythm of his chanting and clapping. Other pilgrims stood against the wall turning prayer-beads through their fingers. And there were beggars; one woman bared sagging, wrinkled breasts and held aloft a baby's bottle, while at her side a child held a newborn baby. Close to the temple the sense of devotion heightened and the crowd increased, streaming through the two large entrance pillars, across flagstones hollowed out in places by hundreds of years of prostrations. There was a huge prayer wheel and I waited in turn to spin it, sending its hundreds of carved incantations out onto the breeze. Prayers for Joe and Pete, I thought. We could not go in – it was time for us to return to the minibus. Drawing reluctantly away from the milling devotees we retraced our steps through the market place, past the grisly meat stalls where the red of the flesh and the dripping blood were intensely bright in the afternoon sun, and back into modern-day Lhasa.

It had been a wondrous afternoon, and my senses felt assaulted by the array of sights, sounds, smells and colours. But the new experiences had been poignant. At every turn I had imagined Joe, visualized him filming in the market place and laughing as children crowded around him. The stages of grief are well understood, and I knew that I was going through the 'searching' process, seeking out a lost mate in a place I knew he had been, re-creating him, not yet fully accepting that he was dead. But knowing it did nothing to alleviate the hurt.

Back at the Guest House we washed our hair at the tap in the courtyard. Sitting on the step with our heads wrapped in towels, we enjoyed the last of the day's warmth in that sheltered spot and wrote postcards. Beyond Lhasa there would be no communication with home.

'What are you going to tell people?' asked Hilary.

'Weather great, food Chinese, wish you were here.'

She threw a damp towel at me. In truth, it was hard composing the postcards. Briefly I described my impressions of Lhasa and my feelings about the next stage of the journey. There were many people who would want to hear from us, who had helped us in various ways over the past months and who would appreciate a card from Lhasa; it was worth the effort.

Sitting up in bed after dinner, Hilary read aloud from Pete's diary the account of his visit to the Parkhor: it was a strange echo of our afternoon. My head ached and my fingers were tingling, both the effects of suddenly arriving at 12,000 feet from sea level. I reached for the sedatives, anxious to sleep, and stepped outside into the courtyard to gaze at the stars appearing in the sky above Lhasa, until the cold and the effects of the drug sent me to bed.

TEN

Pete's diary recorded that he and Joe had walked from the Guest House to the lake behind the Potala before dawn one day, to photograph the sunrise. Hilary had asked Dong over dinner if we could do the same, but he and Zhiang had organized a day of tightly-scheduled sightseeing which they did not want us to miss.

After breakfast the next morning, we all set off for the Sera Monastery aboard a minibus. As the Potala came into sight Zhiang said something to the driver, and we swung off the highway and onto a side road. Dong turned round.

'This is a quick way to the lake.'

It was just as Pete had described it in his diary, totally still and perfectly reflecting the splendour of the palace. A mist hung about the Potala, increasing its aura of mystery. I felt that it could vanish into thin air at any moment. Groups of Chinese soldiers, off-duty but still in uniform, horsed about on the lakeshore and took photographs of each other against the awesome backdrop.

At Sera, Dong and Zhiang once again hung back and we entered the courtyard of the monastery without them. Stone steps led up and into a great dark hall supported by carved wooden pillars and festooned with *thankas*, long strips of intricately-painted silk that were suspended from the ceiling and reached almost to floor level. Shafts of sunlight, alive with dust motes, pierced the gloom, and the air was thick with the smell of rancid yak-butter candles and burning juniper twigs. The religious paintings on the walls had recently been renovated and their reds, blues, greens and golds stood out brightly in the dim light, unlike the grease- and smoke-darkened colours of the *thankas* and the entrance pillars. Along the walls stood large, peaceful, golden Buddhas, representations of past incarnations of the Dalai Lama. At the back of the spacious hall were a series of small, windowless rooms, illuminated by candle-wicks that floated in vats of the strongly pungent yak butter. Statues of spirits, some welcoming and benign, others darkly fearsome, were crowded together in the gloomy interiors and threw long and flickering shadows on the walls. A rope slung between posts guided the progress of pilgrims past these deities and I joined the shuffling press of people, moving slowly along amidst a murmuring of prayers. Now and then there would be a halt, bumping us all together, as someone reached forward with a gift to add to the white scarves, money, jewellery and photographs of the Dalai Lama with which the altars were festooned. I was conscious of being a curious tourist, and of the wealth displayed by my clothes, my watch and the camera hanging from my neck, but the people around me did not seem to notice. With bowed head and clasped hands, I reached back to a Catholic childhood to find expression of my respect for their devotion.

Later that day, in the Drepung Monastery, the absence of pil-grims gave me the feeling that we were in a museum, and a scattering of monks was the only indication that the building housed a religious community. I broke off from our group and went alone up flights of narrow stairs, along a dark and low-ceilinged corridor and onto the flat roof. Sunshine burst through the opened door and made me fumble for my glacier glasses. On the edge of the parapet was a row of golden figures, guarding the building against intrusion. I approached them slowly, trying to recall why they seemed so familiar. And then the memory washed over me: Derbyshire; logs crackling in the fireplace; our heads bent together over photographs. A February night, six months before. Joe and I had looked at this rooftop together then: there had been a picture of it in one of his books on Tibet. Leaning against a wall, looking past the statues to the tin rooftops of Lhasa reflecting the sunlight, I wondered if he had climbed up to this roof, too, and if perhaps he had remembered that same night. A low chanting began and broke into my reverie. At a nearby altar an elderly monk was prostrating himself before the Buddha. My presence seemed not to disturb him, yet minutes later he was angrily gesticulating at the two young Chinese soldiers who walked past, obviously upset by this physical representation of the force which had attempted to desecrate his faith.

Hours slid by, and the effort of trying to absorb so much was exhausting. It was early evening before we returned to the Guest

House. I was sleepily finishing dinner when two men came to the table and introduced themselves.

'We are journalists, from Holland,' said one. 'I believe you are the wives of the two British men who disappeared on Everest.'

My head snapped up. I was suddenly awake. Some of the reporting in British newspapers about Joe and Pete had left me wary of the press.

'We are covering the Dutch ascent of the North Col. We have just returned from Rongbuk. You are leaving for there tomorrow?'

Hilary had told me about the team of Dutch climbers with whom we would be sharing the Base Camp. She and Pete had been friendly with two of them in Europe, and she was looking forward to a reunion.

'No. We're going to Kharta first.' Hilary looked tense. 'Why are you in Lhasa?'

'There has been an accident,' said the man. 'An avalanche. A climber is badly hurt and we are here to send a report back to our newspaper in Holland.'

Her face was already pale.

'Who?'

The journalist paused.

'Eelco Dyke – you know him?'

Listening to the account of what had befallen Hilary's friend, a cold, eerie feeling crept over me. I had the sensation of picking up some residual echo from the walls of the spacious dining hall, some remnant of conversations that the survivors of Joe and Pete's team must have had there, in that same room, on their way home after the disappearance. Leaving her deep in conversation with the two men, I wandered back to our room and fell into a disturbed sleep. In my dream Joe was alive, he was with me in my Manchester house and we were eating a meal together. It was so realistic and normal that I awoke in confusion and had a few seconds of mental struggle before I remembered where I was and why. It was not a good start to the day, and I could barely hold back my tears over breakfast.

The truck that would take us to Everest was parked outside the dining hall. Tele, our driver, was busy warming up the engine, checking the numerous tyres and loading gear onto the back. It was a big, lumbering workhorse of a vehicle; wooden slats along the sides rattled, and chains hanging down from the hinged rear flap clanged as we bumped along unpaved roads. It belched out exhaust fumes, stirred up clouds of dust and shook every bone of its passengers' bodies, but it proved to be totally reliable. Tele was a tiny, birdlike man whose skinny legs would scramble in and out of the truck at great speed. He barely reached above the steering-wheel, and it was a wonder to me that he drove the heavy beast with such surety. He had a wide, gap-toothed smile and usually wore a woolly hat but no socks, a fact which bothered me throughout the trip. Dong suggested that Hilary and I sit in the driver's cab but we declined, wanting the panoramic views from the open back of the truck, and prepared to accept the choking dust and chill winds that went with them. Zhiang joined Tele, and the rest of us settled down amidst the piles of gear, following Dong's instructions to pad ourselves against the bouncing of the truck. We were sweating inside salopettes and down jackets, but soon we would need the protection of these as the altitude increased and the temperature dropped.

We rumbled through the streets of Lhasa and onto the Friendship Highway, past the Buddha cut into the rock and across the long bridge spanning the Brahmaputra River. It was a gradual climb through a barren landscape of brown and purple hills and a vast expanse of space, sky and intense light. The road led over a series of passes and between these we crossed plateaux, each higher than the last. At Khamba La Pass dozens of squares of white cloth, each with a holy inscription, were tied to sticks held in place by a small cairn. The little flags flapped wildly in the wind at 15,700 feet, sending prayers onto the air currents. I cut a piece from my long silk scarf and tied it to one of the sticks, then stood back to watch how the wind whipped my little flag about, and how its colours were bright against the blue of the sky. Joe used to wind that scarf around his neck when he was rock-climbing in England; sometimes a corner would work loose and the wind would blow it against his face as he stood at the bottom of the crag squinting up at the route. At every prayer-flag cairn that we passed I left a piece of that scarf, feeling impelled to do so without really knowing why. Perhaps it was a ritual of mourning, or a gesture of my attempt to accept Joe as part of Tibet.

The road skirted Yamrock Lake for thirty miles, and every few hundred yards birds rose from the rushes on the shore in a frenzy of flapping wings and startled cries. When the lake was out of sight behind us on the dusty plateau, we stopped at a petrol station. It was a rudimentary affair, a low clay building with the tank on the roof and pipes that ran inside, through measuring cylinders by the counter and out of the wall to the yard. There were no pumps: the drivers filled up their own cans with petrol and decanted these into the tanks of their vehicles. A young Tibetan girl sat behind the counter, calculating the cost of each transaction and taking money from the customers. Despite the overpowering fumes she smiled cheerfully. While I held a funnel for Tele, Zhiang helped him to pour the petrol until the truck's large tank overflowed, and we found room for the reserve cans in the back. The smell of petrol mingled with the dust as we drew away, making us cough and cover our mouths with scarves.

I hunched in the back of the truck, withdrawing from my companions and the surrounding landscape, and letting jumbled thoughts of the past fall around my mind. The bumpy road, the rattling vehicle and the lashing of wind and dust all faded into fantasies of being in Joe's car, driving to the pub on Saturday nights, watching his profile in the light of the dashboard as we talked and laughed. Easy, uncomplicated music playing on the tape deck, music that matched the sweeping lines of the Derbyshire Dales and the winding, unlit roads. Parking next to a stone wall and walking arm in arm down the steep hill. Up the steps and into the warmth and light of the crowded bar, where friends with flushed faces greeted us and offered drinks. A long, long way from this rutted and potholed road in Tibet. Resentment welled up. I was too young to be going through this, everything had been cut short just as it was beginning. Joe's talents had been flourishing, there had been so much more for him to do. And all those lost opportunities, the conversations and the times together that I had looked forward to and which now were never to be. Regret: it was such a hopeless feeling.

Behind my closed eyes was a screen across which memories flitted, going in and out of focus. One took shape: leaving the airport after Joe flew to Hong Kong, and driving his car back up to Derbyshire, to the factory which had bought out part of his business and which now housed his shop. One of the secretaries took the keys from me.

'I'll pick the car up just before he gets back,' I said numbly.

'Now don't go running off on any holidays after this expedition,' she told me, with mock sternness. 'We all felt so sorry for him the last time.' Joe was popular with the girls there, sent them cards from his trips and joined in with their Christmas parties.

'No,' I replied, 'I won't. I won't do that again.'

It was not until I was reversing my little Beetle out of the factory yard that the anger hit me. Why should I have felt so guilty when she said that? Why had I needed to reassure her that I would be there for him when he returned? What the hell did she or any of the other girls know about life with such a man, anyway? He breezed into the office, flirted with them all, impressed them with his ease and friendliness and brought a touch of glamour and excitement into their lives. But what did they know of the stress and the fear that I lived with, or of the jealousies and insecurities that plagued me? Could they handle such a relationship? Had they thought of that when they tut-tutted about my going to Corsica so soon after his return from Kongur? I almost turned the car around and marched back into the office to confront her. But the innocence of her remark dawned on me as I drove away. There was no reason why she or anyone else should understand the complexities of loving a man like Joe; I certainly had had precious little idea at the beginning.

A tingling in my cheeks and the soles of my feet brought me out of the daydream and back to the truck. I wiggled my toes inside my boots and looked up. The road was dog-legging steeply, giving wide-angled views back across the valleys and plains. Two boys waved from a sulphur pool set against a rock face. On the Kharo La Pass, at 17,000 feet, the road ran close to the jumbled crevasses of a glacier and we could see up to the place where it originated, on the mountain which rose up another 4,000 feet. The altitude was making my palms tingle, too. I rubbed my hands together and scolded myself for the slip into maudlin thoughts, for it was a privilege to be in that high, wild place and have all senses intact to appreciate it.

Midway down the other side of the Kharo La Pass we stopped for a lunch of tinned meat, biscuits and lychees beside a mountain stream. I wandered along it to find a private spot. When I returned, with my face washed clean of dust, Tele handed me a posy of wild flowers. Hilary had one, too.

'He rushed around looking specially for the flowers he wanted,' she said.

Far away, on a hillock that rose sharply from the plateau, the outline of Gyantse's ancient fortress was etched against the sky in the clear afternoon light. The sight was entrancing and grew gradually closer and larger until finally we skirted the city, the third largest in Tibet. The walls of the fortress were like giant bared teeth, high above us. The truck trundled on, Gyantse began to recede and the light of the afternoon softened towards evening. A farmer in a dusty hamlet paused in his work to wave. I plugged into my Walkman, to a tape called 'China', and for a while my sadness and concerns ebbed away and were lost in the beauty of the Tibetan plateau.

Twelve hours after leaving Lhasa we drew into the military camp at Xigaze and fell out of the truck, dusty and aching. It was already dark and we were ushered straight into a dimly-lit dining room where one table was laid with a meal of rice, meat and dried fish. Relieved that the constant motion of the day had finally stopped, we ate everything and slaked our thirsts with cup after cup of green tea. The stars were out by the time we left the dining room, and the air was sharply cold. Our room had an Everest sticker on the door.

'Maybe Pete and Joe slept here,' Hilary wondered aloud.

The large, speckled mirror reflected two dusty, dishevelled figures; we cleaned up using the wash-stand and jugs of cold water before crawling beneath the eiderdowns. It was good to be stretched out in bed, to relax tired muscles and rest aching bones. My mind would not calm down, though: it continued to spin. I was beginning to think of Joe on the mountain, to visualize where he lay and what he looked like. Not knowing what had happened to him was hard to bear and made acceptance of his death more difficult. Some little part of me still harboured the hope that they would miraculously appear. For weeks after first hearing of his disappearance I would step towards the ringing telephone, unable to suppress a thought of 'maybe'. One afternoon I stood in a greengrocer's in Manchester, waiting to buy fruit and listening absently to the news on the radio behind the counter. The last item came on, an 'interest story' before the weather.

'The mountaineer who was pronounced missing presumed dead after falling from a Himalayan mountain has turned up in a Nepalese village, alive and well.'

As his name was announced and the accident he had survived described, I left the shop, empty-handed and in tears. It could not have been Joe or Pete, it was far too late, and yet those first few seconds had brought me a flash of impossible but undeniable hope, and I felt crushed and cruelly tricked. Chris Bonington had told me that the chances of anyone surviving a fall down the Kangshung Face were almost negligible. He had also explained that if something had happened to hinder their progress near the summit of Everest – an injury perhaps – they wouldn't have survived for long as at that altitude, especially without an oxygen supply, the body rapidly deteriorates. So there was no hope. And yet, deep in my psyche, I was clinging to one final, disintegrating straw. Which was why approaching the mountain was difficult: I sensed that being there, seeing with my own eyes the enormity of the challenge which Joe had taken on, would force me to begin to accept and to let go.

By 6 a.m. I was wide awake again and tense. Hilary stirred in the bed across from me. Our friendship was growing, accelerated by the experiences we were sharing. There was already a remarkable ease between us and we were tuning into each other's thoughts.

'We're going to see them today, Maria,' she mumbled sleepily, and I knew what she meant.

ELEVEN

Xigaze, the second great city of Tibet, houses the Tashilumpo.
This beautiful monastery, with its gleaming golden roof, is
the seat of the reincarnate Panchen Lama and the home of an
increasing number of monks, including some novitiates. Inside its
large wooden gates is a small walled town with irregular flagstoned
streets winding through buildings and courtyards. The place had a
peaceful, self-contained atmosphere, but this was not enough to
banish the sense of emptiness and the echoes from the past which
seemed to resound through all the monasteries I visited in Tibet. At
least in the Tashilumpo the monks seemed to be purposefully
engaged in worship and work, and not just in showing tourists
round. I felt calm within those walls and moved about slowly,
taking in as best I could the images before me. Within a cavernous
hall, shafted with light from the high, narrow windows and hung
with huge *thankas*, yellow-swathed monks on rows of cushions
chanted and bowed their shaved heads towards an altar. Hundreds
of candles flickered around the huge Buddha, and the smell of
burning yak butter, juniper and incense was strong. Two young
men in brown robes walked among the rows carrying large brass
jugs and pouring tea from these into bowls at the feet of their elders.
The chanting echoed around the hall, insistent and intoned, until
somewhere out of sight a gong was loudly struck and caused a
sudden hush to fall. The monks sat still and silent as the low note of
the gong reverberated around the raftered ceiling high above.
Other tourists continued to walk around, pointing up to the silk
thankas with audible comments. I wanted to put a finger to my lips,
to signal them to be quiet. Perhaps it was the Catholicism I had been
born into which made me stand back in the shadows, thrilled by the
solemnity of the ceremony and reluctant to break the mystery of the
moment. Our guide, a tiny, elderly monk, shooed me down

the central aisle of the hall and into a room which held the tomb of the fourth Dalai Lama. It was a massive dome of mother of pearl, embedded with precious and semi-precious stones. Blatant wealth, when compared with the poverty of the Tibetans.

'I felt like this in the Vatican,' I whispered to Hilary. 'It's beautiful, but so confusing.'

'Let's go outside,' she said. 'I need some air.'

We slipped away and wandered into a small, sunken courtyard, bright with flowers and full of sunlight. A tethered goat chewed on a mound of vegetable peelings, and windows opened into spartan rooms.

'Perhaps those are living quarters,' I surmised. 'They remind me of the nuns' cells at my convent.'

'No wonder you and Joe get on,' she said. It was a long time before she could talk consistently of Pete and Joe in the past tense. 'You're both religious refugees.'

A young monk came out onto a balcony. He looked cross and waved us away. We hurried off to look for the guide, ashamed of our trespass.

Old and very precious texts were opened up for us in the library, the lives of Buddhist saints inscribed on thick pages bound in beautiful silk brocade. In a nearby room six monks sat on mats on the stone floor carving words on wooden blocks to be used for printing sutras, or prayers, in texts and on prayer-flags. One monk spied the book on Tibetan monasteries which Hilary had under her arm and indicated that he would like to see it. They all left their work and crowded excitedly around, pointing to photographs.

Two young novitiates chopped vegetables for a broth in the kitchen, and giggled when we put our heads around the door. Huge cast-iron pots and a sooty kettle steamed on stoves fired with brushwood and yak dung, large brass ladles and funnels hung on the wall.

I visited the clean, white-washed outhouse in the main courtyard. There were only a few flies to be swatted away from the hole in the floor. A monk walking by averted his eyes as I emerged and a tiny goat scampered along behind him.

In a small, incense-filled room above the courtyard, twenty elderly monks sat on colourful rugs and floor cushions, facing each other in two rows. Robed in red and wearing angular hats, each had arranged before him a bell, a set of small cymbals and a conch shell.

They were chanting, their upper bodies rocked to and fro slightly and they made strange hand movements as part of their prayer. One dipped a long-haired brush into a bowl and flicked the liquid around him. Suddenly, and in unison, they picked up the instruments: bells tinkled, air passed through a conch, the cymbals clashed and a low drum-beat sounded. Hairs rose on the back of my neck as the music rolled around the room and subsided once more into a low chant. Again I stood back, in a corner, humbled to be a witness to this ancient ritual. My stance had unconsciously become similar to Joe's – feet apart, arms across the chest, leaning slightly back – as if willing him to materialize and share the experience with me. The prayer was over; the room fell silent. There was only a shifting and rustling as the monks removed their hats, folded them flat and put them away inside silk envelopes. We left quietly, passed through the sunlit walls of the Tashilumpo and returned to the truck for the next part of our journey.

It was a long and beautiful drive, with no other traffic except for an occasional army truck. On the high, wide plains, white- and grey-walled villages would appear like tiny specks that grew and gradually took shape as we approached. A yak was tethered outside one, chewing contentedly against a backdrop of plateau, snow mountains and sky. Along steep valleys the road clung to purple and brown rock faces that displayed wind-eroded, fluted formations. Far below, irrigated farmland ran along the riverbanks in solid strips of green.

We stopped for lunch at a windswept pass where a few wild, long-haired yaks grazed hopefully among the rocks. One had a prayer-flag fluttering from its horns. Hilary wanted to photograph gear donated to us by a climbing equipment company and I herded up the animals to be in camera range. It was peaceful there: prayer-flags in the wind, the ponderous yaks and, beyond it all, snow mountains on the horizon.

On the other side of the pass the road dropped steeply and was flanked by precipitous terraces rising from a rushing, whitewater river. I stared intently: the feeling of *déjà vu* was overpowering. And then I remembered – Joe had filmed this stretch of road: it had been shown on BBC television. I imagined him leaning out from the Land-Rover, asking the driver to slow down, wondering how that piece of footage would turn out.

We rounded a bend and an impressive mountain range came into view, the peaks shrouded in cloud. Makalu, Lhotse, Nuptse – I heard the others identify them. Hilary clutched my arm and pointed.

'There it is, Maria.'

Above the clouds, impossibly high, was the summit of Everest. Denny banged on the roof of the driver's cab and we ground to a halt. With the engine cut, there was silence, save for the wind and the whirr and clicking of cameras. I gazed and gazed at the mountain, immense beyond my imaginings. I could pick out the ridge where Joe and Pete were last seen. The image blurred, tears were washing down my face and collecting in the jacket collar pulled tightly around my chin. A sense of desolation hit me hard. A man I loved, a man who shared my life for over two years, had perished on that mountain, almost at the highest point on earth. A cold, hard place, relentless and utterly remote. There was a 'flag' of snow blowing from the summit of Everest; I shivered, imagining the force and chill of the wind up there. So many people had said it, and of course I already knew: Joe had not wanted to die so young, but, if it was to be, he would have wished to end his life as he did, high in the Himalayas. There was a simplicity and a beauty in the manner of his death, no debilitating illness or sordid car accident but a strong and certain overwhelming by the forces of the mountain. As the truck started up I knelt on rucksacks against the cab, looking up at the ridge, drawn towards the sudden physical reality of Everest, as bewildered as a hurt child and in as much need of comfort. The road swung round, Everest went out of view and we began the approach to Xegur.

The ruins of Xegur's fortress stood above the town on a steep hill. In the courtyard of the large military encampment beds of dusty flowers were surrounded by an array of barracks and halls. Still dazed, I climbed down from the truck and turned to Hilary. Her face was tear-stained but she hugged me reassuringly.

'We're getting closer, Maria.'

As we moved further from Lhasa our accommodation became increasingly basic, and in Xegur the rooms and the food were very spartan. To improve the evening meal Denny shared out fruit-cake and whisky. My tears in the truck had released tension and left me tired and relaxed, and at 14,500 feet it took only a little alcohol to lift my spirits. When the sun went down the temperature dropped dramatically, and we all made our goodnights and set off from the dining hall for our bedrooms. I left on my socks and thermal underwear and curled under the heavy quilt trying to warm up.

'Will this keep you awake?' asked Hilary.

She was propped against pillows in her bed, reading from Pete's diary by candlelight.

'No, ummm,' I mumbled, floating away into a whisky-hazed tiredness. I awoke to hear her moving about in the dark.

'I'm walking up to the fortress to watch the sunrise,' she said. 'Pete did it and he says there is a complete view of Everest from up there. Come with me.'

'It's so cosy in here. Do I have to?'

'It's up to you, but I can't wait. There's not much time until dawn. Come on, you'll be sorry if you miss it.'

I forced myself up and was shocked awake by the cold air. Within minutes we had slipped out into the starry night and were through the encampment gates. It was intensely quiet; our figures cast moving moonshadows on the steep, flagged streets of the old town as we stepped softly between sandstone and clay walls surrounding the courtyards of the houses. Behind a large wooden gate a dog barked in alarm, a donkey joined in with loud braying and within seconds there was a deafening chorus of animal cries. We hurried along the steep lanes, giggling and nervous that the whole village might have been woken. The cacophony died to a hush, the animals settled again and silence crept back over the walls around us. But then another sound began, one that stopped us in our tracks and made us stare at one another in wonder. From somewhere among the low buildings the beautiful cadence of a monk's song rose up, a pure voice lifting on the air towards the approaching day.

At the outskirts of town we scrambled up the loose rocks of the steep hillside and along the remains of the fortress walls. It was hard work at that altitude and I pushed to keep pace with Hilary. Dawn began to break; we stopped and sat and watched as the massive outline of Everest appeared against the lightening sky, and the sun shimmered upwards and slowly bathed the whole mountain in an orange glow. There was none of the pain or bewilderment that I had felt in the truck on the previous afternoon. Everest on that cold, clear and lovely morning exuded a great peace and strength, and I breathed deeply, taking it in. As the mountain emerged into the day I acknowledged its power, the power that had claimed Joe and Pete. And I acknowledged it calmly, without bitterness, without anger. Something in me was changing, moving slowly forwards in pace with our journey. 'Everest' — it seemed too everyday a word to describe what we saw.

'Chomolungma,' I whispered to myself. 'I think I am beginning to accept.'

Shrill music blared from the loudspeakers of the military camp; the silence was shattered and our vigil broken. Sunrise had engrossed us, we were late and began to hurry down over rocks that were now red in the early morning sun. The village was awake and startled to see us. An old lady's skirts swept the ground as she hobbled along bent over a stick, and she jumped with fright as we passed. Our path was suddenly blocked by a snarling dog, and we watched with mixed feelings as its owner ran out of a house and whipped it into submission. We peeped into courtyards, curious to catch a glimpse of the villagers' early morning lives. A cow ruminated on a doorstep and the small girl playing beside it ran indoors at the sight of us.

Back inside the camp, the truck was ready to leave and the Swiss trekkers were pacing around it impatiently.

'Dong is angry,' said Jacques. 'He is waiting for you in the dining hall.'

The table had been cleared of everything except our share of breakfast – corned beef, rice and milky tea. Zhiang smiled as we hurried in.

'We didn't realize we'd be so late,' I said apologetically. 'We've been up to the fortress. Are you angry?'

'No,' said Dong. 'But I was worried. It's better if you let me know of your plans. Then, if there is a problem, I can help.'

We gulped down the food and drink, threw our packs onto the truck and set off for the Kharta Valley.

Nothing broke the monotony of the plain; the dirt road stretched ahead and disappeared into a point in the far distance. After an hour's drive a tiny dot came into sight and as we drew closer it became a small stone hut. A chain was hung across the road in front of it. We halted and two Chinese soldiers emerged and walked round to the back of the truck, looking at us and our luggage with unsmiling faces. Zhiang climbed down and followed them back into the hut with our papers.

'Exercise your legs,' said Dong. 'This will take some minutes.'

I examined the chain: it was welded to one post and padlocked to the other. A symbolic barrier, for a vehicle could simply leave the road and drive around it. Miles of flat, stony landscape stretched on all sides to the hills and mountains on the horizon. A wind raised the dust but there were no clouds in the sky. This was the road leading into the Kharta Valley – telephone wires stopped just up ahead and there were no other trucks in sight. We were only the fourth group of foreigners to be entering Kharta since the 1920s. I felt a thrill of excitement: this checkpoint symbolized for me the remoteness into which we were heading. The papers were in order and we were allowed through. As we drove away a guard carried the chain back to its post, padlocked it and closed the road behind us.

TWELVE

Zhiang climbed down from the truck with a wooden frame in his hand and beckoned to Hilary and me.

'It's a flower press,' explained Dong. 'He's a botany student and he would like you to help him collect some specimens.'

At six feet tall, broadly built, with closely-cropped hair and a huge neck the same width as his head, Zhiang was an imposing figure. I had no words to tease him about not looking like a botanist, but his sheepish grin indicated that he read my thoughts. On our first meeting I thought I picked up an air of indifference and abruptness from him but I was wrong, misreading what was simply an initial shyness. Without a common language, and despite his official position as liaison officer, he managed to convey warmth and affection towards us, as well as an understanding of our motives for the journey. We looked at the photographs he pointed to in his wild-flower book and helped him to search among the rocks and stony soil. The plants we found were tiny and delicate, true survivors on this high, weather–beaten plateau, and Zhiang's large, strong hands placed them gently into the press.

Across the Rongbuk River and up through steep and spectacular valleys, I listened to Vivaldi's *Four Seasons* on my Walkman, and the magnificence of the music and the surroundings merged, helping me to forget the discomfort of the rattling, bumpy truck. On the approach to the Kharta Valley trees appeared, a sudden springtime after the aridity we had become used to. The truck negotiated the narrow streets of an oasis-like village and branches plucked at our hats and sunglasses. We pulled off the road and onto a field of long, lush grass. Another checkpoint. A crowd of wild-looking children, dirty and barefoot, with matted, tangled hair and wide grins, gathered excitedly around. Denny handed out pencils and Pierre threw handfuls of sweets, causing a whirl of dust and flying feet and hands. These seemed gratuitously thoughtless acts on the part of the Swiss men, and I snapped at them irritably, but they ignored me and continued until Zhiang chased the children away.

A river flowed through the green valley floor and streams and waterfalls tumbled down the stony hillsides to meet it. The truck crossed a narrow, shaky and insubstantial bridge and came to the end of the track, a flat meadow next to the river.

'We camp here,' said Dong.

Watched by people from the nearby village we erected the tents. Four to sleep in and one large 'wigwam' for cooking and eating purposes. We were to wait at this site until the yaks and porters arrived for the trek up the Kharta Valley.

After three days of bone-rattling truck travel, exposed to wind, sun and dust, everyone was tired. My stomach was sick and I felt dispirited and depressed. Hilary was low too.

'My last fantasy is gone,' she said. 'I thought they might have been hanging around here in Kharta.'

A joke to mask her pain. Our Swiss companions were not faring too well, either. Denny suspected a hairline fracture in his leg from a particularly brutal bump against one of the petrol cans in the truck, and poor Jacques was continuing a battle with his intestines. It was a sorry crew that gathered in the big tent. Zhiang, assuming the role of chief cook, had prepared a delicious soup full of garlic to help us cope with the altitude, followed by 'boil in the bag' dinners on rice. I ate little and crawled off to the tent I shared with Hilary, feeling unwell and sorry for myself.

Hilary was up and out of our tent early the next day, but I stayed late in my sleeping-bag, lacking any impetus to move. My head felt heavy, stuffed full of conflicting memories that fanned out in every direction. The mornings were always the worst times for me, those minutes between waking and rising when there were no distractions and I was softened by sleep and at my most vulnerable. The only cure was to get up and start the day, to engage my mind with any activity, however mundane, and block out the flow of feelings. But sometimes, as on this morning, the thoughts poured in and overwhelmed me.

'Joseph would never have married while he was still climbing.'

One of his family said that to me, after the memorial service. Joe and I never discussed marriage; we had barely talked about love.

'Why do you need to hear the words?' he once challenged, in a voice tinged with resentment. 'Can't you tell how I feel about you by the way I look at you and touch you, by what I do? Surely actions mean much more?'

So only once did I tell him that I loved him, and now I regretted holding back so much.

'He kept you a secret from me for ages,' an old friend of his told me after Joe's disappearance. Oh, the hurt. He liked to store things up, to bring them out when he could surprise people. It was a mystery to him why Pete should send a copy of his daily expedition diary to Hilary.

'Diaries are supposed to be private – what's the point of keeping one if you're going to *show* it to someone?' Joe would ask incredulously.

We went to see a play about Burgess, Philby and Maclean.

'If I hadn't become a mountaineer I would have been a spy.' His eyes twinkled over a beer glass in the theatre bar.

'You've got to be joking, Joe!'

'No,' he insisted. 'All that tension, imagine the adrenalin! And so many secrets! I'd have been a good spy.'

The memory made me smile. I folded my arms behind my head and bent my knees to relieve the stomach cramps. Sunlight was filtering through the tent walls along with the sounds of breakfast, spoons clanking on plates, voices and laughter. No one ever knew all of Joe: he was a deeply private man, but I had wanted to understand him inside out. He railed at me sometimes for clinging.

'You get more of me than anyone else,' he said one day. 'Why isn't it enough?'

There was a moment then when the hard facts of our relationship had stood out quite clearly, and I knew the answer to his question. Loving him was not easy, the separations and fears were hard to bear and he never seemed to give me credit for coping with them. I broke the bitter silence.

'If it's so unsatisfactory for you Joe, then you should look elsewhere. There are plenty of eager women around.'

The words came out quietly and calmly and I knew I could go through with it, no matter how much it would hurt. His face changed, a panic came into his eyes.

'I want you with me,' he said. 'But it's better to expect nothing, and then everything you get is a bonus. It's the way I live now.'

Expect nothing . . . anger surged through me and a wave of nausea swept across my stomach. I sat up and hugged my knees, burying my face in the soft mounds of the down sleeping-bag.

'So bloody stupid . . . oh, Joe . . . for Christ's sake.'

Frustrated mutterings, emotions with nowhere to go.

Was this why I was in the tent feeling sick, while Hilary was eating breakfast? Because she understood the nature of her relationship, she knew Pete had loved her: these were concrete and longstanding facts, and not a quavering question-mark suspended forever in time and space?

My insecurities were there after Joe's death, as strongly as before. Those heart-stopping moments when he would walk into the house or I would catch his eye across a roomful of people, the total suffusion of feeling when I woke up in his arms – I knew, of course I knew, that they were shared moments, that he had felt them too, and now I wanted nothing so much in all my life as to have him next to me, to talk and talk and talk, to say all the unsaid things and never again to hold back a single word.

Hilary's head was framed in the tent doorway.

'Are you all right? We're walking to Yupa. You can come along later with Denny. Eat some breakfast, we can't have you getting any thinner!'

Get up and start the day, I urged myself. Outside the tent the sides of the steep, narrow valley were bathed in sunshine, and the freshness of the air made me feel grubby in comparison. I plunged my head into the cold river water and scrubbed shampoo into my scalp, trying to shock myself into a better frame of mind. Stones skittered around me and I squinted through soap suds at the flock of tiny Tibetan goats running by, like so many Yorkshire terriers with their long coats and short legs. The two young boys shepherding them squatted beside me, pressing their hands against their mouths in a vain attempt to restrain their astonished giggling. One reached up and poked a tentative finger into the soapy mass of hair stuck to my head. I smiled and wiped the suds from my eyes.

'Hello,' I said, sending them both into paroxysms of laughter. They watched, mesmerized, as I rinsed the soap out of my hair and rubbed in conditioner. Encouraged by my smiles, they reached for the bag of toiletries and huddled together over it. The contents were taken out one by one, laid on the grass and carefully examined. Soap in a box, toothpaste and toothbrush, a face cloth, a mirror and comb, creams and contact lens solutions – everything was touched, tasted and tried out. And then the prize, a shower cap I had brought, without knowing what I would do with it in Tibet, from the Hong Kong hotel. The smaller boy pulled it over his ears and jumped about, screaming with laughter and avoiding the grabbing hands of his companion. Suddenly they froze and swung their heads around in alarm: the goat herd was scattering along the valley. Without a look back they raced off, the younger of the two struggling to keep up with his companion and suddenly oblivious of the plastic, frilled, flower-embossed shower cap on his head.

'How's your stomach?' asked Dong in the food tent. 'Zhiang has made a rice pudding for you.'

I wanted to put my arms around both of them and hug them hard. Joe had been right, I was alive and healthy and everything else was a bonus.

Denny and I set off slowly towards Yupa, the first village along the valley on the same side of the river as our camp site. He winced with pain every time he put weight on his left leg, but refused to acknowledge it, telling me instead about his experiences in Nepal. On the outskirts of the village he pointed out the pile of stones that was the remains of a *mani* wall. Each stone was engraved with a holy inscription, and when the wall had been standing it had been used for prayer. During the Cultural Revolution the Chinese Red Guards had destroyed most objects and places of worship from prayer-wheels to monasteries to *mani* walls. But rebuilding had begun, and these stones had been heaped into a mound and were being used again for their original purpose. An old lady moved clockwise around the stones, spinning the prayer-wheel in her hands.

'*Om Mani Padme Hum*,' she chanted, 'Hail to the Jewel in the Lotus.'

We walked into the jumble of narrow, uneven streets. The dry-stone walling of the houses had been reinforced with pats of yak dung and was heaped with branches for the fuelling of winter fires. Pierre and Jacques had been ahead of us: many villagers were adorned with safety pins and clutched photographs from Pierre's Polaroid camera. They were obviously delighted, but again I felt annoyed by this doling out of gifts. A stocky man appeared wearing a faded T-shirt which bore the logo of the American expedition of the previous year. In a smattering of English he told us that he was a porter and wished to work for us. Touring us around the village he presented us to his friends and neighbours, and soon we had an entourage of dusty, ebullient children. The girls' hair was plaited up on top of their heads and the boys wore pigtails or had shaved scalps. The women of the village were dressed in layers and layers of blouses and long skirts, and high colourful boots of a felt-like fabric. Many of them suffered from goitres – one girl, quite young, had two huge growths on her neck – and Denny told me that this was due to a lack of iodine in the diet.

On the edge of a smoky courtyard, under the shade of a veranda, nine Nepalese people were busy trading. The wares spread out on blankets on the ground made up a strange assortment of goods: plastic bangles, kettles, conch shells, silver bracelets, boxes of snuff, an old box of matches, a straw hat, a broken watch, old coins. The men spoke with Denny in Nepali and told him that they had portered on several expeditions, as was obvious from their well-worn fibre-pile jackets. With them were two girls, a seventeen-year-old whose dark hair was plaited to below her waist, and her younger sister who wore a colourful hat with a matching belt that wound around her hips. This group trekked to and fro across the pass to Nepal, which was still closed to foreigners in 1982, each of them carrying packs of at least fifty pounds.

Denny returned to camp with the T-shirt man and I crossed the river by the rickety wooden bridge and nervously approached the neighbouring village of Shika. I wondered how its inhabitants would react to a lone woman, especially one dressed as I was, in trainers, shorts and a rainjacket, with my hair in two short plaits and round, metal-rimmed spectacles on my face. I thought I probably presented a bizarre sight, and my suspicions were confirmed when the first group of children I met ran away, screaming with fright. I stood in the dirt street, unsure of what to do. The children re-appeared, peeking out from behind the skirts of three women, two of them young and holding babies and the other very old. They huddled nervously in the gateway to the courtyard of a house, staring at me fearfully as I smiled, nodded and walked uncertainly on. Around a corner I came across two more small children who promptly burst into tears. I was about to quit the village and leave its occupants in peace when a young man arrived, probably sum-moned by the women in the gateway, and took charge of the situation. Without a common language we managed to introduce ourselves, he ascertained that I was on my way to Chomolungma and invited me to see round his village. He ushered me into a courtyard where the two women I had first encountered rocked their tiny babies in baskets and ate from a bowl of boiled, unpeeled potatoes. They chuckled as I bent over their offspring and pressed me to share the meal, but I declined, aware of their extreme poverty and the comparative wealth of food back at the camp. A cry came from one of the rooms off the courtyard – the small, windowless space was empty save for some straw on the dirt floor and a young child playing with a scrawny puppy which had just nipped her.

The re-erected *mani* wall was a source of obvious pride to the villagers, and a small crowd gathered around me as my guide pointed to the stones. Children squatted by my bare legs, amazed at the down of hair growing on them. The adults, meanwhile, had discovered the Velcro strips on my jacket and were ripping them open and patting them shut repeatedly. Our curiosity and delight was mutual. I regarded these people in open wonder, marvelling over their hair, their skin, their clothes, the turquoise jewellery that even the seemingly poorest wore and, above all, their smiles. These smiles seemed to indicate a strength of spirit which, in the face of their harsh and impoverished living conditions, made me ashamed of the ease with which I allowed myself to slip into depression.

I left Shika reluctantly, wanting to stay on but knowing I would cause concern if I wandered alone for too long. Sure enough, Zhiang was waiting anxiously at the bridge, with a bottle of beer ready for me. He had not ventured into the village for fear of upsetting its inhabitants, and I was sorry for putting him in a difficult position. It was becoming increasingly obvious that Zhiang had great empathy with the Tibetans but, despite the fact that he spoke their language, his Chinese uniform forbade any communication, bar that concerned with his official duties.

Dinner was ready, my stomach was settled and my appetite restored. Our meal was interrupted by two women who came to the tent and asked for Hilary and me. News of our visit had spread and they were anxious to see the Western females. We stood outside in the evening light while they gazed at us, patting our faces and chuckling together. Like the people in Shika they pointed up the valley. 'Chomolungma?' they asked repeatedly, and shook their heads in disapproval when we nodded.

The women returned in the morning with a basket of newly-laid hens' eggs. Zhiang traded these for sugar and fried up a delicious second breakfast while we waited for the arrival of the yaks. All the gear for our trek up the Kharta and Karma Valleys was packed into rucksacks and sturdy red boxes from the Everest expedition, festooned with the now-familiar Jardine logo stickers, red, white and blue thistles. While we were in Hong Kong Adrian Gordon had taken us to what he called the 'Everest Surplus Store', a walk-in cupboard at the Jockey Club where he worked which was stuffed with equipment left over from the Kongur and Everest expeditions. His employers had obviously been tolerant of his involvement in the two trips. The red boxes stood floor to ceiling and we sorted through them to find things that we needed for Tibet.

In Joe's front room there had been a permanent pile of those same red boxes in the months before he left, with gear spilling out of them. He was squirrel-like, hoarding things in case times ever got hard. After each expedition the quantity of these 'freebies' bestowed by sponsoring companies increased.

'I suppose I should give it away or sell it,' he would say from time to time, surveying the mound, scratching his beard and frowning. 'But you never know. Anyway,' as if by way of an excuse, 'if you think this is a lot, you should see what Chris Bonington's got.'

Adrian had been kind and sensitive in giving us help and advice over what to take, but it was as hard for him as for us. The gear was so familiar to him, and it must have brought back memories. I had a strange envy of Adrian, and of Chris and Charlie and Dick. They had been so close to Joe over the final months of his life; a bond had grown between them all, the intimacy of shared concerns and goals. Joe's letters to me from the mountain had had their usual detachment, and I looked to the surviving members of the expedition to link me to him in some way, to tell me what they knew of his thoughts and worries and joys, to fill in the spaces between what he had written. They tried, but they were in mourning for lost friends and needed time to let their own feelings settle.

The boxes on the grass were battered from use on the last two trips. It was strange to think of them going back towards the mountain. There was merriment as we waited; Denny sneaked away and made some very convincing yak mooing noises, and to his delight we began to look for the approaching beasts. Dong suggested that we trekkers set off, leaving him and Zhiang to catch us up with the loaded yaks, their herder and the two porters, as with Jacques' poor health and Denny's injury progress was going to be slow. Tele was staying at the camp site to guard the truck and we bade him farewell. He was a tiny figure next to his huge vehicle.

The path was a narrow goat-track that clung to the hillside, gradually gaining height. Groups of children followed us as we passed Yupa, plucking at our sleeves and asking for gifts. From time to time I turned and gazed at the winding valley behind me, its terraces leading down to the slash of green along the riverbanks.

134

Wind swirled through a field of yellow corn and beyond it were the brown hues of a village. After the now familiar reaction of alarm, the villagers welcomed us warmly and crowded round. An old lady walked along with us, bent double under a basket of wood but laughing loudly and merrily, displaying a toothless mouth and discoloured gums. She left us abruptly, turning into her courtyard through a gate decorated with a hanging pot of yellow geraniums. Beyond the village we waited in a herders' shelter for the arrival of the yaks. They were not far behind us, and we munched on fruit cake and enjoyed the break. Our yak driver was small and wiry, and was accompanied by his young grandson. Both wore ragged clothes with no hats or socks. The yaks were domestic and shorn, not shaggy-haired like the ones I had seen two days before; their herder treated them gently, urging them with a light touch of the switch as they lumbered along, laden with boxes and scrabbling at the stony terrain with cloven hooves. The path was steepening; we stopped to catch our breaths. Zhiang opened tins of lychees and passed them around. Sitting near the sad-eyed yaks as they nuzzled among stones, it finally struck me how remote I was, how far, far away from the everyday life back in England that was continuing without me. I wondered what my family and friends were doing at that moment, what was happening at work. And I felt a contentment, for it was impossible to imagine being anywhere else but on that barren, windy slope in Tibet.

Four rock 'steps' over passes were ahead, each leading to a higher valley. The first was the most strenuous – I was affected by the altitude and poor Jacques looked grey. The second led into a valley green with trees and alpine plants; Hilary pointed to gentian and edelweiss, and the scent of a stunted juniper transported me back to the Tashilumpo and the chanting of the monks. We crossed a river by a makeshift bridge of rocks and branches, and skirted the opposite side of the valley. A heavenward-pointing finger, the high spire of rock spied from our tent that morning, came into sight until the clouds closed in and the rain came down. We could have dreamed we were in Scotland, trudging through wet grass and mist beside a stream of white water rushing over rocks, but for the yaks and their driver and the scent of juniper bringing us back to the reality of Tibet. At the pass into the next valley one of the porters stopped to add a prayer-flag to the others fluttering from the cairn, and he seemed unsurprised as I joined him and tied my piece of green silk to one of the canes.

There were two more hours of trekking through driving rain before we huddled inside the hastily-erected wigwam, warming ourselves with whisky and trying out our supply of Chinese chocolate which tasted surprisingly like chewing gum. Denny presented the yak driver's grandson with a white peaked hat and I gave him my share of the chocolate, so he beamed with delight for the rest of the evening. Pierre and Denny volunteered to cook dinner and I withdrew to the little tent to think and write. Rain beat down on the fabric walls of my shelter as I contemplated how close we were coming to Chomolungma. We were headed for the east side of the mountain, towards the Kangshung Face. It dropped, almost vertically, for thousands of feet from the East-North-East Ridge down to a jumble of crevasses. Joe and Pete were last seen moving behind a rock pinnacle on the Ridge, towards the edge of the Face. What happened next remains a mystery but Chris Bonington believed they fell to their deaths down the Face, and the rest of the team agreed. My mind could not accept the reality of Joe plummeting through so much space and terror, although mountaineers who had survived long and near-fatal falls assured me that it would not be the horrifying end I imagined. Nor could I bear to dwell upon the picture of broken bodies lost in crevasses, a grave so bleak and far away from home and love. Yet still I wished to see the Kangshung Face, and to be as close to it as possible, even though Chris and Charlie had expressed concern that the sight might bring us nightmares rather than some semblance of peace. After the disappearance they had come from Base Camp to Kharta by truck and then trekked up the valley, clinging to the faint hope that by a miracle Joe and Pete might have survived the fall, or that there would be at least some sign of them or their remains on the Face. The weather had been clear then, giving them the chance of viewing the Face for a full day. There had been no sign. We were on the same path three months later, and they had warned us that conditions in September were often unstable, that we should expect cloud and rain, that we might not even see the mountain at all. But we would, I was sure of that.

My thoughts were interrupted by Zhiang bringing me a cup of coffee. 'Dinner!' he announced with a wide grin, pleased with his newly-acquired word, and I followed him out into the rain.

It was shameful, and it arose from guilt, but I felt uneasy about sharing the food tent with the porters from Yupa and the yak driver. They eyed our gear, our food, our protective clothing;

later that night they would sleep in a nearby cave under woollen blankets. The three Swiss men seemed to have none of my qualms and excluded the Tibetans when handing round steaming bowls of pea soup. An escaped yak drew them out into the rain as we ate, and they returned during our second course of spaghetti, ham and cheese. They asked for the water that had been drained from the pasta and drank it from the small wooden bowls they each carried. My food was sticking in my throat. I spoke up.

'Can we share this with them? There's plenty.'

Denny frowned at me.

'They have *tsampa* which they will eat later,' but he handed them the fat from the ham which they eagerly divided up.

I could neither enjoy my food nor bear to meet the gaze of the men who had carried our loads all day. The justifications for what was happening were familiar to me: with Joe I had discussed the role of the porters on his Nepalese expeditions. They would carry heavy loads on the walk-ins, make 'bed tea' which they served to the climbers in their tents and generally take on a subservient role for very little money.

'But you have to remember what the average wage is in Nepal. To give them more causes trouble. You can't sit here in Britain and make judgements about it: it's not that simple.'

Of course it was easy to be altruistic for a few weeks and then walk away, but still I felt that in one tent the first and third worlds were sitting together yet were as sharply and unfairly divided as ever. At the end of the meal Denny gathered up the remaining pasta and sauce and handed it to the Tibetans. I was still poking half-heartedly at my dinner and gave them my share of ham, but it did nothing to alleviate my unease. Denny left the tent, annoyed with me, and Zhiang handed beers around to everyone and encouraged one of the porters to sing. While his tune rolled out the others prepared their staple food of *tsampa*. They mixed ground roasted barley with black tea and shaped it into balls which they ate with hard, unleavened bread. I said goodnight and withdrew again, full of confused thoughts.

THIRTEEN

The rain fell relentlessly through the night and into the morning, turning to snow as we crested the valley and moved into a landscape of rock and sparse vegetation. I walked alone, locked into private thoughts and listening to the sounds of my own body moving through the silent surroundings.

Hilary's footprints were ahead of me in the snow, and I found her waiting in a small cave on the edge of a lake of the clearest blue which reflected the rocky slopes above it. A thermos flask and food stood ready: since our little expedition in the Alps her sense of when my energy was about to flag was uncannily accurate, and she would always be there with supplies. Our trekking team was spread out as we moved along at individual paces, each reacting differently to the altitude. Hilary and I had been the first away that morning, carrying packs in case we reached the next camp site long before everyone else and wanted to put up our tents. The track was easy to follow, and Dong had given Hilary careful instructions. It was good to feel so independent, and to realize that we had gained the trust of our Chinese guides.

We set off again after our snack and I hung back until Hilary was out of sight, reassured by her tracks but wanting to feel the solitude and remoteness of the place keenly around me once more. My pace settled into a regular plod and I moved slowly and easily, feeling warm and comfortable despite the low temperature. Wet snow fell around me, flakes landed on my face and immediately dissolved. The protective clothing was a cocoon, my breathing was amplified inside the jacket hood. A sense of peace settled over me. Suddenly, and totally unexpectedly, I felt Joe's presence. I have no explanation for this; my rejection of Catholicism in teenage years left me suspicious of the spiritual side of life. What happened on those high slopes in Tibet may have been generated by my own mind or may have been a manifestation of some form of energy from Joe. I really do not know, but I had experienced this awareness of him before. Shortly after hearing of his disappearance, I had asked Sarah to drive me to Derbyshire. I wanted badly to be in the house and among all his things, yet it was a dreadful journey, knowing that I would not find him at home, not then or ever again. I sat in the car, distraught, unable to speak to Sarah, feeling sucked towards a horrible finality. And then, as we left the outskirts of the city and headed towards open country, I felt him there, all around me, comforting and reassuring. Sarah got out at her cabin and I slid over into the driver's seat. I wanted to go to the house alone.

'Are you sure you're all right?'

She bent down to look through the open window. Her face was concerned.

'Yes, I'm fine now. It's not far. I'll see you in a while.'

I drove along a back lane, and experienced the same heightened awareness as when Dick had first told me about Joe's disappearance. The afternoon was vibrant, trees reached out their branches towards the car and the leaves on them shimmered. Joe's presence was still there when I arrived and unlocked the house. I had been too preoccupied with work on my own place to visit it while he was away. It felt like minutes since the day we had left. I wandered around inside, soaking in the familiarity. On the bed I wrapped myself in the duvet, my nostrils filled with his smell, and I felt him about me then most powerfully. I cried, talked aloud like a child, and finally slept. A deep, dreamless, peaceful sleep. When I awoke the sun was still streaming through the window. Leaving the house was difficult. My impulse was to stay there, and wait. Only when I parked the car at the bottom of the track leading up to Sarah's cabin did the feeling of Joe gradually fade.

She was standing in the garden among long grasses, shading her eyes against the sun to watch my approach. The scene was uncannily still, as if she were a figure in a painting. I began to tell her.

'I know,' she said. 'He was in the car when I was driving. I felt him. It was really strong. I wasn't going to say anything in case it upset you.'

It has happened several times, only infrequently, but always intensely and without warning. And so, in Tibet, heading towards the Langma La Pass from where I hoped to glimpse the Kangshung Face, I did not try to block the feeling but allowed it to flow. Without knowing how or why, I felt infused by Joe as I plodded along. I listened to him talking to me, encouraging me. He was all around. I felt the gentle pressure of his hand on the back of my neck. This was utter contentment, a sense of rightness as I headed up the wintry slopes.

Joe, or whatever the sensation had been, ebbed away, leaving me relaxed and smiling and still walking at a measured pace. A dog bounded into sight, ahead of a herd of yak driven by a preoccupied man. Fifty beasts lumbered by, their shaggy coats brushing the snow. They were rounded up by a wide-eyed child who had already, I later discovered, been scared witless by an initial encounter with Hilary. Straggling along at the end was a baby yak which stopped in its tracks, refusing to pass me. The little boy, frightened anew by the sight of another strange woman, could not pluck up courage to urge the animal on. My attempts to walk past them only caused the yak to scamper about in terror, and for a few minutes we executed an impromptu matador scene until the boy suddenly made a break for it and drove the yak past me with a switch.

The track became very narrow, cutting through a steep scree slope along a valley side. Far below me lay a long, densely grey lake with no reflection. Snow fell lightly, the air was damp and the cloud cover so low that mist swirled around me from time to time. My boots crunching on the loose rock broke the silence. In the distance, where the track curved and was swallowed by mist, some shapes took form. Several scrawny cattle swayed along the track until I had to scramble up the slope and make way for them. Behind the animals, carrying staffs and walking slowly and steadily, were an old man and a young boy. The man was slight, his face narrow, wrinkled and serene, and from his chin a long white beard fell in two strands. Their grey woollen blankets and felt boots seemed insubstantial against the snow and rocks. They stopped and regarded me seriously. 'Chomolungma?'

The old man pointed to where he had come from, towards the Langma La Pass. I nodded, and waited. All morning I had felt a stillness within me, a tenuous but undeniable link to a dimension outside the well-known and understood parameters of my world. Being high in the Himalayas, sensing the solidity, force and sheer permanence of the environment, as against human transience and fragility, was opening up my mind and allowing in a chink of awareness of the full scope and mystery of existence. This man and boy seemed creatures wholly connected to the mountain they stood upon. The child gazed up at me, unsmiling, with an air of wisdom and experience far beyond his years. His companion shook his head gravely. 'Chomolungma, Chomolungma,' he repeated, and taking my hands in his he intoned a prayer, perhaps a blessing. I welcomed this: I wanted to draw from the knowledge of ages that he surely possessed. He raised his hand in farewell and moved past me with the boy, towards their cattle. I watched until they went out of sight and imagined how we must have looked from high above, three tiny figures passing through a vast and unmoving landscape.

Beyond the prayer-flags of the Langma La Pass a bank of thick cloud lay over the Kangshung Face. Hilary sat very still, gazing towards it. I put my hand on her shoulder.

'The man and boy – did you meet them? Did he bless you?'

She nodded. We waited together, silently willing the mountain to reveal itself, until the rest of our team arrived.

Jacques was in bad shape. We were now at 17,400 feet, he had pains in his chest and his pallor was a worrying grey. We divided up the contents of his small day-pack and Denny, still limping, stayed close and kept a watchful eye on him. Coming down the steep path from the pass, into the Kharma Valley, the yak driver and one of the porters prayed loudly at a high, sheer rock face and left offerings, small piles of food, on a ledge. At the head of this valley was Chomolungma, a sacred mountain, and they were showing respect.

On the valley floor the waters of a lake, startlingly blue from the copper salt, reflected our progress as we filed along its shores – heavily-laden yaks and porters, tired trekkers. A crowd of beaming girls appeared seemingly from nowhere and crowded round as the tents were erected. When they left I discovered that one of my gaiters and two stuff-sacks had gone with them, articles that had belonged to Joe. My fury was unreasonable, but I couldn't help feeling that they had taken away a tiny part of him. I drifted into a disgruntled sleep, woken near dawn by Hilary shaking snow from the tent roof and lighting candles to dry out the interior.

Chomolungma kept her Eastern Face shrouded for the next two days as we moved closer to the mountain across dramatically changing terrain. Moonlike landscapes on the high plains transmuted to muddy trails through lush vegetation in the valleys. We pressed on, crossing and recrossing rivers by rickety bridges or by precariously hopping from stone to stone, trudging through mud, willing the clouds to lift. I remembered Charlie's and Chris's prediction that there would be little chance of good weather on the east side of the mountain, but I was still convinced we would be lucky. The feeling of drawing so close was intense. Hilary was voluble in her grief: she talked and cried openly. I became increasingly withdrawn, conscious of tension building inside me. If Chris was right, if Joe and Pete had fallen down the Kangshung Face, then they were not far away, they were somewhere in the crevasses at the foot of Chomolungma. I immersed myself in an awareness of Joe's proximity, allowing it to override my loneliness and the reality of the loss. Asleep and awake I dreamed of somehow getting to his body, wrapping myself around his frozen form and breathing warmth and life back into him. It was an illusion, born out of hopeless desperation.

Drying out round the stove at the end of the fourth day of trekking, we made a group decision to turn back. Going further towards the Face meant crossing a glacial moraine that could be unstable after so much rain, and there was no indication of the weather clearing. Early the next morning Hilary and I walked up to a rocky knoll to make our private goodbyes. The Kangshung Face was ahead of us, hidden by the heavy mist that clung to it so resolutely, but I could feel its presence. Joe could be nearby, held somewhere within its folds. Perhaps this was as close to him as I would ever be again. With that thought the illusion snapped. There were no miracles to be had, the relationship was over, except for what I could cling to in memory. Chomolungma could not give him back to life. I sat down and began to weep, heaving sobs which bent me double as in the early days of grief. Hilary held me until I quietened and then I leaned on her and tried, brokenly, to express my thoughts. She looked over my head.

'Zhiang is coming.'

He walked slowly by, placed something on the cairn at the very top of the knoll, and then stood and looked towards the cloud-covered mountain. When he returned his face was set tight as if holding in feelings, and he did not glance in our direction. We went up to the cairn. Two cans of beer were set there, and a small posy of flowers lay between them. An offering to the mountain and a sign of respect to Joe and Pete.

'That was more apt than any church service,' said Hilary.

It was a gesture which helped me to walk away from the knoll towards the waiting yaks.

Halfway down, much to my surprise and bewilderment, there was a familiar tugging at my bowels.

'Hilary. I've got to stop for a shit.'

'OK, I'll wait for you.'

'Christ, I feel embarrassed.'

'Why?'

'I don't know. It doesn't seem like a very suitable thing to do. I mean, here. Now.'

'I'm sure Joe will think it's funny. And Pete won't look: he's very considerate that way.'

I couldn't wait any longer, and, despite my tear-soaked face and the outpouring of grief which had left me weak and wobbly, I imagined I could hear amused laughter.

We retraced our steps, back through the dense vegetation, up the muddy slopes and onto the windy plain. As night fell the mist rolled in around the camp site. In the big wigwam I chopped vegetables, drank whisky and tried to socialize, but I couldn't concentrate on conversation. My mind was outside, out in the mist and heading towards the mountain. After dinner I walked through the fog until I was out of earshot of the camp and away from its light. Squatting on my haunches, I felt the cloud close in and I imagined Joe walking towards me with his relaxed, loping stride, dressed in his usual garb of jeans, boots and sweater which varied little with the seasons. Had his ghost emerged from the mist I would hardly have been surprised, but nothing moved, there was no sound. I remembered an American girl I had met years before, in Patagonia. I had just arrived at Fitzroy National Park and she and her team of Italian climbers were preparing to leave. Her boyfriend had died on a nearby mountain the previous year, and she had travelled to South America to find his body and bury it. One of the climbers was a priest. They had reached the point on the glacier where her boyfriend and his companion had landed after the fall, said Mass and lowered the bodies into crevasses. She was young, in her twenties. As we talked she was using an ice axe to hammer nails into the wall of the wooden hut that was at the 'road head' of the park.

'This was his,' she said, waving the axe.

'You mean . . .'

'We found it beside him. I may as well use it. These nails will be good for hanging stuff on. And who knows, I might come back some time.'

'Are you glad you came?'

'Sure I am. Now I can believe he's really dead. Now I have a picture of him. Now . . .' she stopped for a second, her voice caught. 'It was good to at least be able to say goodbye.'

That girl . . . I couldn't remember her name, or what part of America she was from, or why she was with Italian climbers. But the feeling I had had on that day came back clearly, my admiration of her composure and my wonder at her strength. I could never have foreseen it back then, but now I was envious of her, for her chance to say goodbye.

My legs had begun to cramp, and I was cold and damp. I stirred, stretched and returned to our tent, which was aglow with the light of several candles.

Crawling in I discovered Hilary in the middle of a full-scale nose bleed. Her red thermal underwear was matched by the mounds of bloody tissues scattered around the sleeping-bags, and she was distraught with a mixture of grief and frustration at not being able to stop the flow of blood. I calmed her and the bleeding ceased, but her confusion carried through to her sleep. During the night her anguished cries woke me.

'No! No! Pete! *Pete!*'

She sat bolt upright, suddenly awake. In the dream she had relived her avalanche experience, but I and her two nieces were with her and Pete was trying to dig us all out. For a while, then, we lay awake and she talked about the real avalanche which happened when Pete and Joe were on Everest, six weeks before they disappeared. She wrote to Pete about it and he replied, 'What is important is that you are alive and so am I.'

The sharp frost of the morning gave us hope the mountain would appear. The clouds were playing a teasing game, allowing a glimpse of a peak and then covering it up again. Makalu appeared for a time and there was confusion over whether or not it was Chomolungma. We ran up a slope for a better view, our lungs heaving and burning in the thin, cold air. The face we saw was massive, spectacular and terrifying, but it was not the Kangshung.

Jacques was weak and despondent, so we took turns at walking with him and giving him encouragement. As I plodded up snow-covered slopes behind a yak, past tiny blue lakes, with the sun breaking through and snow peaks appearing, the loveliness would send a shiver through me and I would be glad to be alive and to be there. Hilary and I hung back at the Langma La Pass, watching the clouds around Chomolungma, willing the curtain to open and show us the awesome vista behind. Three times the mists rolled back to reveal the summit, but the Face stayed shrouded. Zhiang was hovering anxiously, wanting us to leave and follow the others, but we needed the steadying of those minutes, letting our thoughts settle before heading down from the mountain. It occurred to me that perhaps it was no coincidence that the Kangshung Face was not being revealed to us. Perhaps it was, after all, easier for us this way. I blew a kiss towards the east side of Everest and turned away.

Verdant hillsides pungent with juniper, and the gentle colours of irrigated fields and villages; after the landscapes of the high passes I felt I was seeing the lower Kharta Valley with new eyes. And as we began the drive to the northern side of Chomolungma I was calm, almost happy. Two eagles hovered high above us on the air currents. Joe and Pete, I thought, watching us leave. It was a fine place to spend eternity.

FOURTEEN

Leaning precariously out of the truck, I craned my neck to look up at the steep, fluted, colourful walls and down to the tumbling river rushing through waterfalls and rapids. The gorge opened out onto a wide plain, so flat it must once have been a lake. Villages rolled by, cornfields splattered colour across the aridity and cows tethered to stakes grazed hopefully among the windswept, stunted grasses. Denny became agitated in the back of the truck, his photographic desires frustrated by the relentless movement of the bumpy vehicle. Despite his periodic banging on the cab roof, Tele, encouraged no doubt by Dong who was anxious that we reach Rongbuk before dark, drove purposefully on. I sympathized with Denny, who needed photographs for a travel brochure, but for myself I didn't mind. The images forming and transforming before us, day after day, were being imprinted on my memory. And it felt right to be pressing onwards, skirting the mountain in a long loop to reach the northern side before the light faded.

We stopped briefly at a dusty village where Zhiang tried to bargain for a sheep. I was dumbstruck to realize that he planned to put the live animal in the back of the truck and slaughter it at Base Camp. My relief was great when the deal fell through, but Zhiang had been delighted by my dismay and from then on would bleat at me regularly.

Pieces of a bridge recently washed away lay scattered along the banks of a wide, meandering river. Zhiang leaned forward for a rapid discussion with Dong and Tele in the cab, and the truck plunged in. I watched water rise almost to the top of the tyres and recede again as we began to climb the far bank, before the unmistakable sound of wheels spinning in mud signalled a sudden halt. We clambered over the cab roof, across the bonnet and stone-hopped to land. Tele, his feet bare and trousers rolled up, lowered his skinny

146

legs into the icy water. He threw ropes to us and we heaved on them as he revved the engine until the truck came free and mounted the bank, dripping from its undersides. Tele climbed down again, still shoeless, folded his arms and smilingly surveyed the river, obviously delighted by the manoeuvre and its success.

'Like a rock-climber looking at a route he's just done,' laughed Hilary.

Late in the afternoon, as light was fading, we reached the Rongbuk Valley. It is windswept, stark and cold, and totally dominated by the vast bulk of the mountain at its head. Chomolungma, silent and majestic, seems to emanate an ancient power. I imagined what Joe must have felt on this approach, seeing the scale of the challenge he had taken on. I remembered how the yak drivers and porters in the Kharma Valley stopped to pray and leave offerings to the mountain.

'Can you see?' said Hilary, as we balanced against the cab in the back of the truck and scanned the East-North-East Ridge through binoculars. 'They were almost at the part where it levels out. They'd done the hardest stuff. It would have been a long snow plod to the summit.'

There were no clouds on that side of the mountain: it stood hard and clear against the sky. Seeds of understanding were slowly, slowly germinating in me. I had been tortured by unanswered questions – why were they so drawn to this mountain, why did they push the limits instead of turning back and coming home? But, little by little, the puzzle was beginning to fit. Le Grand Combin had begun it and now, the closer I drew to Chomolungma, the more I began to feel that perhaps their deaths were not as senseless as they had seemed.

> 'He is a portion of that loveliness
> That once he made more lovely.'

Familiar words slightly adapted and carved on a granite bench atop the windy hill behind Chris Bonington's house in Cumbria. They are there in memorial to a local boy, Mick Lewis, who died at sixteen in 1944. The first time I walked up High Pike with Hilary, Chris, Wendy and the dogs, and we rested on the bench and read the words, I had been moved; now, in the Rongbuk Valley, the sentiment seemed right for Joe and Pete. As the sun was dipping out of sight and an orange glow spread over the mountain, we arrived at Base Camp.

Joe had described the site to me in letters and once enclosed a photograph: he posed against a backdrop of grey, moraine hillocks with Changtse and Everest beyond, and held onto his hat to prevent the wind whipping it away. 'This is a desperate place,' he wrote. We pulled up outside a large tent where a small group of Dutch climbers and Chinese officials stood waiting to greet us. There was a pile of trunks and cardboard boxes full of tinned food. A generator hummed and two trucks, identical to ours, stood next to it. One-man tents were dotted about the flat, dusty site. It was an orderly scene, set in a wilderness. Mr Wang, the Chinese liaison officer, made the introductions and insisted that we eat with them in their food tent. Hilary and I quickly withdrew to erect our tent before the light was gone, choosing a spot next to the wide and shallow glacier river that formed a boundary on one side of the Base Camp. Close by was a hillock, another boundary.

'Ladies on left, gentlemen on right!' Mr Wang had said, referring to the large boulders, on either side of the rocky outcrop, which afforded a little privacy. And on the top of the hillock stood memorial cairns for climbers who had lost their lives on the mountain. I smiled at the intimacy of the connection.

There was barely any soil to catch the tent pegs, and we paused from hammering to watch the last rays of the sun on the ridge. I hugged Hilary; it seemed a long time since the morning she had suggested the journey to Everest Base Camp, and our friendship had grown deep and enduring along the way, through all the highs and lows.

Our names were being called, a meal was ready. Inside the spacious tent a circle of picnic chairs was illuminated by a single lightbulb, and several propane stoves formed the kitchen area. Porters lounged in the darker recesses, resting and eating. We were ushered in, seated and served with delicious food. Mr Wang talked kindly to us of Pete and Joe, whom he had met earlier in the year. But it was not an easy evening for us to socialize and we soon thanked him and left. Night had fallen and the outline of Chomolungma was just visible against the brightly starred sky.

'It's strange to think of them here, Hilary.'

'Pete described it so well. It's exactly as I imagined.'

'How do you feel?'

'Close to Peter.'

'I wish . . . . I wish Joe had got my last letters. And my birthday cards.' I had sent him two, one funny, the other romantic. They, and the three letters, had been returned unopened.

'You must stop worrying about that, Maria. It doesn't matter now.'

'It's horrible to regret so much. You're lucky in that way.'

'No, I'm not. I regret that Peter's baby isn't growing inside me.'

We were nearly at the tent. I knew she had begun to cry.

'In one letter he joked about sending frozen sperm. I was sure I was pregnant before he left. I had to write and tell him I wasn't. I wish I was pregnant, I wish I had been left with a part of Peter.'

'Hilary, Hilary.' I soothed her. 'It's cold. Let's get inside.'

We crawled into the small nylon shell that had become a familiar home. Two insulation mats were laid out to give some protection against the cold, stony ground and at night we made an extra layer with our clothes. On top were the voluminous feather-filled sleeping-bags. At the end of the tent stood two rucksacks and along the sides, in the limited space next to the sleeping-bags, were diaries, water bottles, tissues, washbags, towels. Hilary's belongings were organized, but I still tended towards a frenzied scramble of unpacking whenever I needed something. With the onset of darkness the temperature, at 17,500 feet, was dropping rapidly and we wriggled into the sleeping-bags still wearing thermals and socks and drew the hoods tightly around our faces.

'Let's go up to the cairn in the morning.'

'Yes. At first light.'

My sleep was disturbed by dreams and I tossed and turned until the alarm finally startled me fully awake. We dressed quickly and gathered together the things we had brought to leave at the cairn. Hilary had a piece of gritstone, the Derbyshire rock Pete had loved to climb on, and some poppy seeds to scatter in the hope that they might germinate and bloom. Joe's family had given me a religious medal and a prayer card to leave there, and I had brought pressed flowers and the translation of a Chinese poem. Suddenly I was reluctant to leave the tent and my stomach knotted with tension. As two mourners we were about to take offerings to a grave, to perform one of the rituals of death, and this had an air of finality which I still resisted. Angry, frustrated tears fell on what I held, the papers, the flowers and a round of metal. This was all that was left, memories and flimsy representations.

'Come on, Maria,' urged Hilary. 'We must go before everyone gets up.'

The morning air was sharp and frosty and rocks crackled under our boots as we climbed the hillock. They had not been the only ones to perish on the mountain – there were several mounds of stones holding memorial plaques. We found the granite slab on which Charlie Clarke had chiselled their names:

'In Memory of Peter Boardman and Joe Tasker May 1982.'

I traced the letters and numbers with my finger, wiping away ice crystals, and thought back to May 17th, four months before. I had been taking my course then; I walked to the college and called in for a friend on the way. We sat outside in the morning sun of that unusually warm spring, waiting for classes to begin. My thoughts must have drifted during a lecture because in my diary page for that day there is a complicated doodle of snow-capped mountains with the sun setting behind them.

Three days later, while spending a weekend in the Lake District with Sarah, I had had a vivid nightmare. I was running down the windswept streets of Ambleside, rain was washing over my up-turned face and I was screaming. She remembers me sitting up in bed, rubbing my eyes and saying, 'I dreamt that Joe is dead.'

There had been no way that I could allow myself to dwell on the possible implications of that dream. It had to be a manifestation of the fears and worry I had been tamping down into my subconscious for weeks. Or so I had assured myself, and Sarah. And maybe it was. Or perhaps I did pick something up, some disturbance through the realms of time and space that are not yet understood. Because, as far as we know, the dream had been accurate. By then he was already dead.

Hunkered before the cairn, looking beyond it to Chomolungma, I felt no more anger and frustration but simply a great sadness. On May 17th I had been so excited about Joe coming home. The house was almost finished, he would be delighted by the transformation, he could retreat there while his building work went on. We had a whole summer ahead of us . . . But it was over, everything was over. I missed him so much. Hilary was planting poppy seeds; it was time for my private ceremony. I stood up and quietly read the prayer, and then the poem:

> '. . . Oh that I had a bird's wings
> And high flying could follow you . . .'

Papers, flowers, metal; I slipped them into a plastic envelope and dropped it inside the cairn. A breeze blew up, lifting my hair and raising a little dust. No other movement, no sound, no bird cries.

'Are you finished?'

The question pulled my gaze away from the memorial cairn. Hilary was standing very close, and speaking in a low voice. Our ritual was over.

'I can see Denny coming.'

We sat against a nearby boulder. Denny reached the top of the hillock, nodded to us and took off his cap before standing in front of each of the cairns. One was for a girl, Marty Hoey, a climber with the American expedition which had been trying a different route on the mountain at the same time as the British team. Within days of Joe and Pete's disappearance she slipped from a harness and fell 6,000 feet to her death. There were other plaques for Japanese climbers. And somewhere on the East-North-East Ridge were the bodies of Mallory and Irvine, names I was familiar with as a child, never dreaming that some day I would be a tiny part of the weft and warp of the history of Everest. Denny put his cap on, saluted us and left. The camp was stirring below us, it was time to go down.

'Sometimes,' I said, 'when you do things that you were really dreading, they turn out to be much easier than expected.'

Hilary smiled.

'Joe's making sure you learn that lesson, isn't he?'

Over breakfast we discussed plans. Hilary and I wanted to get to Camp Three on Joe and Pete's route; we should really have stayed at Base Camp for a few days to acclimatize, but time was short and our driving force strong. I had no idea of how I would fare, trekking at that height, but I was ready to push myself. To the perturbation of Dong and Zhiang, who were not allowed to accompany us beyond Base Camp, we decided to set off that afternoon.

We were blessed with fine weather and Chomolungma looked benevolently down on us as we laid out sleeping-bags, clothes and the tent to air, in preparation for the trek. Concealed behind a boulder on the riverbank we stripped off and bathed in icy waters that ran straight off the glacier. My head ached from the cold as I washed and rinsed my hair, but within minutes the pain was replaced by an invigorating glow. As we packed our rucksacks a Dutch climber hesitantly approached. We had decided to avoid contact with the team as much as possible, fearing that our presence and the reasons for our journey might unsettle them.

'I just want to wish you well,' he said, 'on behalf of all of us.'

Lin, the Chinese cook, was already spoiling us, and for lunch he had prepared his speciality of *momos*, spiced meat wrapped in pastry. It was 2 p.m. before we set off across the plain towards the jumble of moraine at the end of the glacier. Clambering over and around the big boulders was exhausting, but before long the path began to cut through the loose rocks of the valley sides and become easy. Below us the rock- and mud-strewn glacier was zig-zagged by wide, shallow crevasses, and above us stood sandstone pillars, high and wind-eroded. Shadows fell across the slope – our guide and interpreter were coming up behind me.

'But, I thought . . .' I began.

'We will take your packs. Follow us to Camp One,' said Dong.

They were bending the rules to give us moral and physical support. Before we could begin to thank them they had hurried on ahead.

Camp One was next to a tiny blue lake; the tents were already erected and Dong and Zhiang had a brew of tea ready for us, but as soon as we arrived they left quickly, making their goodbyes for the second time that day. The Dutch were using the same site and some of them were spending the night there before going back up to their Camp Five on the North Col of the mountain the following morning. On most expeditions a camp system is set up, as the altitude, the terrain and the weather make it impossible for the mountain to be scaled in one straight push. Tents, with supplies, are erected at various stages up the mountain and are sometimes replaced, very high, by caves dug into the snow. This allows the climbers to work a relay as they gradually establish their route, going increasingly higher up the mountain and often leaving fixed ropes. A team goes a certain distance, sets the ropes and perhaps a camp, and then retreats to a lower altitude, sometimes as far down as Base Camp, to recuperate.

One of the Dutch came over to our tent as we finished a meagre dinner of tinned ham and bread. Johan's head was swathed in folds of white cloth, Arab-like, and his gingery beard framed a face prematurely lined by wind and sun exposure. He knew who we were and talked sensitively of his plans to climb Changabang, following the route Joe and Pete had taken and described in Pete's book, *The Shining Mountain*.

'They were remarkable men,' said Johan. 'It must be strange for you to be here.'

We accepted his invitation of tea and biscuits and joined a cheerful group of climbers all squashed inside a four-man tent. The nylon was picking up the rays of the setting sun and made us all appear to be suffering from advanced sunburn. They told us that the site of the British expedition's Camp Three was easily identifiable.

'Just look for the empty whisky crate!'

Their camaraderie and the ease with which they accepted us on the mountain was reassuring. They offered us the use of their large food tent at Camp Two, a thousand feet below the point we hoped to reach. This meant we could reduce the weight of our packs by leaving the tent and cooking equipment behind, and we accepted gratefully.

Outside the tent the spectacle of the night was spine-tingling. The sun had slipped behind the western, snow-peaked horizon and an ethereal light of deepest orange spread over the surrounding mountains. Stars were beginning to twinkle in the darkening blue sky and the air was sharp, impossibly clear and totally still. I caught my breath at the beauty of it and had a strong sense that something was about to happen. Just before he left for Tibet, Joe and I had watched *Close Encounters*, and the appearance of strange ships in the sky on that night would not have surprised me: we were in the perfect setting. Hilary laughed when I shared my thoughts.

'This *is* close encounters!' she said.

I lay with my head poking out of the tent door for a while, watching as the sun's rays faded, the night stole across the sky and the purity of the atmosphere allowed the heavens to display their full celestial beauty. We were finally on the mountain that Joe and Pete were part of, and I wondered if they were somehow aware of us. It was hard to believe that all their vitality, talent and joy in life had been blotted out. Surely it had been absorbed into the energy of Chomolungma, an energy I imagined I could feel as I lay on my back, star-gazing. My eyelids grew heavy and my face numbed with cold. I slid into the tent, zipped it shut and snuggled down into the sleeping-bag, happier than I had been for a long time.

FIFTEEN

The reflection of snow peaks rippled and broke when Hilary dipped a can into the still lake. I watched her light a stove and boil water, but the tea she handed over did little to rouse me from the tired and sluggish state in which I had woken up. She waited impatiently as I floundered about, misplacing things and packing up slowly. It was a clear and warming morning and we wore britches and sweaters, and put scarves on our heads for protection from the strong sunlight. The track to Camp Two was along the glacier. It was easy ground and the crevasses were obvious, but Charlie had warned us to watch out for stonefall from the rock towers and steep scree slopes high above. He and Adrian had nearly come to grief on this first section when high-speed missiles narrowly missed them. I walked along with sharp eyes and ears, and the eerie sensation that the slope above me had a mind and an evil intention of its own. Despite our steady pace across this dangerous section we were overtaken by Johan and then a succession of Dutch climbers who, far fitter and more acclimatized to the altitude than we were, trotted by with chirpy greetings. Beyond the menacing section of the track was a forest of ice pinnacles, remnants of the slowly dying glacier. These teeth-like formations of white and blue ice towered to thirty feet, bright against the greyness of the surrounding rock and sparkling with prisms of light.

The sun was high and intense; we peeled off sweaters, pushed down socks and rubbed sunblock onto the exposed parts of our limbs. Hiking at 19,000 feet was a strain to the lungs, but we pushed on up the slope, following the small cairns that marked the route. The valley narrowed, below us a stream ran along one side of the glacier, coursing through tunnels and bridges of ice.

'Is it the altitude getting to me, Hilary, or is that a telephone wire?' I couldn't believe what my eyes were seeing: something which snaked along the ground among rocks and gravel.

'I thought I'd told you about those,' she said. 'Pete wrote about them in his diary. They were put down for one of the big expeditions, Chinese or Japanese. At least we're going the right way!'

But by mid-afternoon we were no longer sure of that. Hilary went ahead to check our position, leaving me to rest. She moved behind a hillock and out of sight.

It was a welcome stop. Several hours of walking in hot sun at such an altitude had left me weary and I had begun to watch my feet, fearful of stumbling and spraining an ankle. I sat down on the loose grey scree. Boulders lay scattered all around. Nothing was growing, not even lichen. A total wasteland. With Hilary gone and my own body unmoving at last, the air became utterly still. Such intense silence was unnerving. I glanced anxiously to either side, drew my knees up and hugged them against my chest. I was afraid. It was like my childhood fear of the dark which I had never really overcome. There were nights when I still lay awake in bed, wanting to go to the bathroom but paralysed by an abstract terror that only the flicking on of a light could dispel. I reassured myself – there's nothing to be afraid of, stand up, stretch, do something to blot out the anxiety. Some crevasses nearby hovered on the edge of my vision; I moved over to them and peered down at the solid blueness below their lips. They yawned into black space and I felt that strange urge one gets on the top of cliffs, wondering what it would be like to jump. A sudden rustling swung me round in alarm – who's there? No one, of course not, pull yourself together, Maria. It was ice slithering from a slowly melting pinnacle. *Creak!* The glacier shifted imperceptibly far below me, but the noise travelled up through hundreds of feet to where I crouched. Blood began to throb loudly in the veins of my ears. The demons of loneliness and isolation crept nearer. Hilary was not far away, logically I knew that, yet it could have been a million miles as far as my oxygen-starved brain was concerned.

'Maria! This way! Round the back of the crevasses!'

I moved cautiously towards the voice. Her scarfed head appeared; she turned her face up and grinned widely.

'Nearly there!'

We had miscalculated after all: we were too high. But three tents were in sight, and a Dutch flag fluttered from one. We bent our stiffening knees and set off down the steep slope.

The camp made a desolate picture. It sat on one side of the narrow valley, and was diminutive amidst a stark and massive landscape. A wind blew down the glacier, flapping the partly unzipped door of the bungalow tent as we approached. I was suddenly overwhelmed with tiredness.

'Hello?' called Hilary.

'There's no one there,' I snapped. 'Johan said they were all going up the hill this afternoon.'

As if responding to his name, he appeared in the doorway and welcomed us in.

'The others have already gone up to Camp Five. I will leave at first light in the morning. I'll get there in time for breakfast.'

He had stayed behind to ensure that Hilary and I arrived safely, although he obviously did not wish it to be alluded to. I felt reassured by his presence.

'Relax,' he said. 'I will make tea and some soup.'

Relaxing at 20,000 feet did not prove to be easy. My head was heavy and aching, I felt listless and irritable and could not find a comfortable position in which to sit or lie.

'I feel like an old woman,' I grumbled.

Johan laughed. 'Yes, you look like one, too!'

He paused from stirring the soup, delved into a bag and passed me a mirror.

'See?'

The face reflecting back at me had deep lines that ran from nose to mouth and were etched between and around the eyes, and the skin underneath the sunburn was a pallid grey. I knew this to be only a temporary change caused by altitude, but it did nothing to improve my feeling of ill health. Unable to face anything solid, I drank as much tea as a I could and lay in a stupor listening to Johan making his 8 p.m. radio call to Base Camp. Something was wrong: although he could hear the incoming calls they were not receiving him.

'Are your group expecting you to call?' he asked.

'Not unless there's a problem,' I heard Hilary answer.

My headache was worsening and we realized that we had left the aspirin at Camp One. It was impossible for me to join the conversation. I lay in a stupor and listened to them discussing Joe and Pete's books, and to Johan describing the avalanche which had injured Eelco Dyke. Restless, uncomfortable, and helped only a little by a sedative, I dropped into a fitful sleep. With the silence of the night

156

came the sounds of the glacier – loud cracks, bangs and creakings from beneath us would start me awake and I would feel freezing air on the exposed part of my face; I would move my tongue around my mouth to try to relieve the dryness, and wriggle about on the insulation mat to seek a comfortable position. Once it was a pressure on my bladder that drew me out of sleep. I lay for a while trying to will it away. Frosted plumes of breath rose from the mounds of the other two sleeping-bags. Hilary was closest to me: she sounded hoarse. It was no good, I had to get up. I wriggled out of the bag, pulled on inner boots and a jacket, unzipped the tent and squatted right outside it, my teeth chattering. Relief. Another sound began as I settled down again and tried to sleep. *Rustle.* Silence. *Rattle.* Silence. *Crunch, crunch.* Of course. It was the mouse. Johan had talked about it earlier. No one knew where it had come from, but it was presumed to have followed the team up to the camp and moved into the bungalow tent, lured by the feast of dried foods left there. By morning it had munched and nibbled its way through several sesame-seed bars and a packet of dried soup. The idea of the soft little animal busily feeding close by was comforting, it took my mind off the cold and the effects of altitude, and I drifted off into a dream. I was in Derbyshire, dozing in bed at Joe's house. He was pottering about downstairs. I could hear him opening and shutting doors. He had often got up very early, leaving me to sleep while he worked on his slides or his writing, bringing tea and joining me some hours later. He let one door bang shut so loudly that I jolted awake. Where was I? Another door creaked open; where *was* I? I groaned aloud, recognizing the sounds of the glacier below me, and distressed to leave the comfort and familiarity of the dream.

At 5 a.m., in the dark, Johan got up and made tea. We slurped down the hot liquid and mumbled our thanks and goodbyes as he left, then snuggled back into the sleeping-bags for three more hours. The sun was creeping up in the sky by the time we roused ourselves, but my contact lenses were still frozen into their solution. I was grateful for the inners of my plastic boots, warm from being inside the sleeping-bag with me all night, as I watched Hilary trying to defrost her solid, leather ones. Breakfast was just a cup of hot chocolate, as neither of us could stomach solid food. As I sipped it I thought about the thousand more feet to the site of Camp Three. I wanted badly to get there but my body was not functioning well, every movement was an effort and my head still hurt.

It was an easy walk up the glacier, a gentle gradient across loose stones. But each step was painful. I inched along like an old, old lady and my head pounded dangerously. Hilary was getting smaller and smaller. She came back to where I had sat down, clutching my forehead.

'I don't want a case of cerebral oedema on my hands, Maria. You have to decide if you can go on.'

The words were firm, but kindly spoken.

'I'll be all right. I will. I'll just take my time.'

'OK, I'll wait for you. But if your headache gets worse, you must tell me.'

Very slowly, with many rests, I continued up that slope. The whole of the East-North-East Ridge came into view and then, over a final knoll, we reached the site of Camp Three.

Circular areas cleared of sharp stones showed where the individual tents had been. The team spent a lot of time here: it had been their Advance Base and they had tried to make it as comfortable as possible. Pete had been proud of his temporary home, and in one letter to Hilary he described his search for flat stones to use as the foundation for his tent. She picked these out immediately and sat down on them, looking up to the Ridge. I didn't know where Joe's tent had been, although perhaps it was where I found the label from a movie-film canister. Scattered about the site were the singed remains of the bonfire Adrian must have made hurriedly when packing up camp. A tin opener, a few paperbacks, a film box, the whisky crate, odds and ends that proved they had been there not long before, eating, laughing, working and sleeping before setting off together towards the Ridge. Hilary was crouched immobile in Pete's tent area. I felt disorientated, physically uncomfortable and not knowing if I should sit or stand or walk. I leaned against a boulder and surveyed the site and the Ridge above. It seemed so close now. We could go no further along the route; from that point on we would be on snow, we would need equipment, I lacked experience and neither of us was acclimatized to the altitude. I remembered the slide projected onto a wall in Chris's house, the picture he had taken of Joe and Pete setting off for the summit attempt. Their backs were to the camera and they carried big rucksacks. I could see where their path must have been. That was May 15th.

'There is a big job for Pete and me to do,' Joe wrote in his last letter, 'but hopefully it could go well . . . and if fortune, weather and spirit favour us we could be up the mountain in a few days from when we start.'

Before they left there was a celebration for Joe's birthday at Advance Base. They had a party and champagne. He was thirty-four. I thought ruefully again of my cards sent from England that did not arrive in time.

'You and I will age,' Hilary had said to me when we looked at the slide of them laughing and catching the fizzing wine in a jug, 'but they won't. They will always stay as young as this.'

And the last photograph, the very last one, taken with a powerful telephoto lens. Two tiny dots in the col between the First and Second Pinnacles, mere pinpricks on a vast and forbidding landscape of snow and upward-thrusting rock. 27,000 feet high, with no oxygen, climbing difficult ground for hours, since dawn. The Pinnacles – we had talked about those so much since June. 'They were last seen moving behind the Second Pinnacle.' Time and time again I had said that without understanding the full import of the words. Over the past days I had looked at those rocky towers standing up from the Ridge, looked and looked, from the truck, from Base Camp, from our trek up here and now, finally, from this place. And still it was impossible really to understand what it had been like for Joe and Pete up there, so totally and ultimately alone, to glean anything of what might have befallen them or to grasp the fact that it could be a long, long time before anyone else gets that far along the route, and that even then they may find no trace.

I slid my back down the boulder and sat on the stony ground. My feet looked big in the plastic boots. Hilary had still not moved, and yet I was so restless. I thought of the others, Charlie, Chris, Dick, Adrian. How it must have been for them when Joe and Pete set out. Dick was on his way back to England by then, with Charlie accompanying him as far as Chengdu. Chris and Adrian went up towards the North Col to leave supplies for Pete and Joe on their way down. They had the last radio contact with them on the evening of May 16th. The following day, back at Advance Base, Chris and Adrian watched their progress along the Ridge, through a telescope. At three o'clock they opened up the radio but Joe and Pete did not come through. They were still visible at 9 p.m., two tiny dots moving very slowly at the foot of the Second Pinnacle. But when the night closed in there was no sign of any light from a tent up there, and Chris presumed they had moved behind the Pinnacle to camp on the eastern side of the Ridge. The morning of

May 17th dawned clear. A perfect day for climbing. Good conditions for Joe and Pete. But there was no sign of them. Chris and Adrian went back up towards where they had left supplies. And all day they watched the Ridge. No sign. On May 19th they reached the North Col. The hope they had been clinging to, that Pete and Joe were delayed on the east side of the Ridge and would reappear at any moment, began to fade. Charlie had returned from Chengdu and was at Advance Base. They talked to him by radio, told him what had happened. He wrote in his diary, 'I think we must prepare for a disaster. But there is still hope. If the situation is the same tomorrow I shall have almost given up.'

It was the same the next day, and the next. Weeks later, Adrian wrote to me, 'My thoughts have been with you since that awful moment on the mountain, when we finally realized that our hopes and prayers were in vain.'

I remembered Chris's tears in my house, when he first came to see me after the accident. He cried because he had not followed them up the Ridge. Because he had not gone to help, to rescue or at least to discover what had happened. But he was already stretched beyond his resources by the mountain, and Charlie and Adrian were not experienced enough to go with him. He could not have followed Joe and Pete alone, even if he had been stronger. Poor Chris. He had never really forgiven himself, and yet it would have been suicide. Sometimes he gave me the impression that he felt guilty to be alive. But I was glad he had survived. For Wendy and their boys. And for me and Hilary. We needed him, just as we needed Charlie and Adrian and Dick: they were our links to the final part of Joe and Pete's lives.

Adrian had stayed in wait at Advance Base while Chris and Charlie hurried round to the east side of the mountain, to scan the Ridge and the Kangshung Face through binoculars and telescopes. They must have known Joe and Pete were dead; I think they did it for all of us left at home. Closing my eyes I could see the photograph of the Face they took, blown up to show detail and projected against the wall in Chris's cottage. Even though the clouds did not lift for us on the other side of the mountain, I still knew of its scale and of its great slabs of fluted snow. If the snow had given way beneath Pete and Joe, as Chris thought it had done, they would have fallen a great distance, down to the steep glacier below. He and Charlie scanned the Ridge and the Kangshung Face for a day. No sign. While they were gone Adrian packed up the camps. A ghastly task, I thought, to collect up Joe and Pete's belongings and to know that bringing home the news of the tragedy was their responsibility alone. I found the singed remains of a book I had given Joe, the story of a train journey through Patagonia. I fingered its blackened pages. It was comforting to think of him reading it in his tent. I imagined Adrian making a bonfire to burn debris and surplus gear that could not be carried down the mountain, watching the flames and looking beyond them to the Pinnacles . . .

Back in Britain we had endured three weeks of silence from Everest. As day after day passed, I screwed down my fears and worked feverishly on the finishing touches to the house. And then opaque messages began to arrive on Jardine Matheson's telex machine.

'Expedition about to leave Base Camp.'

'Arriving in Hong Kong, June 9th.'

I talked to Ruth, Charlie's wife, in London.

'Maria, they are all dead,' she said.

Ruth was always dramatic, she was overreacting, it was impossible that anything had gone wrong. Wendy Bonington expressed disquiet. I listened to her quiet voice on the telephone and told myself not to worry. And Dick, back in Cardiff with Jan and their little boy, was hesitant in reply to my questions, but then he usually sounded like that.

Sarah and I had then gone to London to see a production of *The Oresteia* at the National Theatre. For over four hours masked actors had conveyed to us the timeless realities of death and grief.

> 'Suffering comes first then after awareness
> The future's the future you'll know when its here
> Foreseeing the future's to weep in advance . . .'

Coincidence or not, it was a portent. Within a week I had received news of Joe's disappearance and, a few months later, Sarah heard that Alex had died on his descent from Annapurna.

Now, high on Chomolungma, gazing at the Ridge, my head began to swim with the memories of the day in June when Dick had appeared on my doorstep. My fears for Joe had been so tightly coiled up by then that I had asked Dick what he was doing in Manchester, almost 200 miles from his home. His first words, 'I've got some tragic news,' ran through my mind again and again, as if he were sitting next to me on the rock, speaking into my ear. The suddenly-frozen faces were all around me again as I backed away, into the yard, to be alone.

Hilary stood up and began to walk slowly around the site. We hadn't spoken since arriving. She seemed very calm and concentrated. But I was besieged by memories and thoughts, my head hurt, I wanted to cry yet did not have the energy. I felt as if all emotion had been sucked out of me. It's time to leave, my body was saying, it's time to go lower. I called to her that I was moving. She turned and nodded. At the hillock I attached a piece of Joe's scarf to a pen I had found at the site, and stuck it into a little marker cairn. My tiny prayer-flag fluttered towards the summit of Chomolungma. I took a long, hard look at the Ridge and the Pinnacles, before turning away.

A tingling sensation spread from the left side of my face and down my arm as I moved weakly along the glacier. This warning sign of altitudinal damage to the body registered only faintly in my brain amid the overwhelming desires to stop, lie down and drink. The tents appeared and grew larger as I stumbled along. I unzipped the door of the bungalow, reached for the water bottle and fell onto my sleeping-bag. The thudding in my head and my heart gradually quietened. I must have dozed off because Hilary was suddenly sitting next to me, cross-legged.

'Here,' she said, handing me an unopened packet of Panadol. 'This was left up there for you.'

I stared from her to the packet, astonished.

'See!' she laughed. 'They knew we were coming!'

We were expected back at Base Camp that day, but it was too late and we were too tired for more exertion. Repeated efforts to call Dong and Zhiang failed; we could hear voices over the transmitter but they were obviously not receiving us. It was Hilary's turn to be flattened by altitude and I, from some inexplicable source, found a short burst of energy which I used to collect water from the stream and make soup. By seven o'clock we were deep in our sleeping bags; I was more relaxed than the previous night and the paracetamol had eased my headache. We chatted and began to drift into sleep. Suddenly, from above us on the glacier, came footsteps. A tension stretched between us as we strained our ears to listen to the feet crunching across freezing stones. There were two people moving towards the tent. My mind snapped into a fantasy I could hardly bear to recognize and I held my breath as the tent door was unzipped. A dazzling flashlight beamed around.

'You are the English girls? Has our mail arrived?'

An accented voice.

The fantasy, mercifully short-lived, crumbled around me as two Dutch climbers, arriving from Camp Five, came into the tent. They got tea going and made another, unsuccessful attempt at a radio call.

'They are asking what has happened to you,' one translated for us. 'They want to know if you are here.'

Curled in a ball inside my sleeping-bag, my face almost covered by the down hood, I slipped again into fantasy about Joe and Pete emerging from the darkness. Since their disappearance I had imagined them returning, after some miraculous survival. I would open my door in England and find him there, or they would be alive in Hong Kong, in Lhasa, at Kharta or Base Camp. As time progressed, the dream would adapt to the circumstances I was in. Allowing myself to indulge in these fantasies gave comfort and a respite from the ache of grief. And each time I returned to the reality of my situation, each time I pulled myself out of the daydream and faced the fact that I would not find Joe at an airport, in a hospital or hotel room or remote village, I gained a fraction more of acceptance and was a little further down the road towards emotional healing.

My sleep was calmer that night, but was still disturbed by the sounds of the glacier and the rustling of the mouse, and by a dry racking cough which was echoed by the others in the tent. All that Joe had told me about the harshness of life at altitude became a reality over those two nights: the unrelenting environment, the effort of the simplest of tasks, the awareness of physical deterioration. And for him this had been a resting place, a relief from the higher camps.

It was a long, long trek back to Base Camp the following morning, trying to hurry, aware of the concern that would be growing for us. We lingered by the ice pinnacles to rest before moving as quickly as possible across the unstable moraines. Hilary made me run across a steep gully – I scrambled up the far side, lungs heaving, and through the sound of my panting heard the tumbling, crackling and bouncing of a rock fall behind me. Before long she turned to me.

'I can see Camp One. There's someone there, we can stop for a brew.' It was Denny and Jacques, waiting with coffee and biscuits. There had been anxiety the night before when we failed to turn up, they told us, and we should get back to Base Camp as soon as possible. The awareness that shelter, food and rest were close by seemed to allow my mind to accept the exhaustion of my body and I staggered along the track, high above the jumble of crevasses, stopping repeatedly to drink orange juice and trying to stomach a sesame-seed bar. I thought about Joe descending from Dunagiri, going for days without food or water. He had persevered in far more weakened states than this. I wondered what he would think, if he could see me, straggling along behind Hilary beneath the peaks of Pumo Ri and Nuptse. Zhiang was waiting at the strenuous, boulder-strewn section.

'Hello! Hello!' he said, and he took both our rucksacks.

Back on the dusty plain, walking slowly towards the tents, a despondent feeling grew in my chest and made my throat ache. This should have been Joe and Pete returning from the summit instead of Hilary and me from the remains of their Advance Base Camp. Dong and Mr Wang came to greet us. There were no admonishments for the concern we had caused them but, instead, congratulations that we had coped with the altitude and reached our goal.

The shade of the big food tent was a great relief. Hilary answered questions while I drank green tea and tried out a few of Lin's *momos* on my shrunken stomach. In a corner two large bowls were piled high with lumps of marinading meat and Lin was busy skewering them for a barbecue. Zhiang caught my eye.

'Baaaa! Baaaa!' He was gleeful.

In our absence he had returned to the village and had finally been successful in his quest for a sheep.

'Well, I'm glad I didn't have to get to know it,' I said.

We were dusty, sweaty and in need of a wash, but we couldn't face the icy river. Taking some water from a cauldron that was always on the boil in the food tent, we retired to a large empty wigwam to strip off and bathe. A wind suddenly blew up, threatening to lift the loosely-secured tent.

'I bet Peter and Joe are doing that,' said Hilary.

While she went back to our tent to read Pete's diary, I walked up to the memorial cairn. Someone, probably Zhiang, had left two cans of lychees there. The gesture moved me, more deeply than I could explain. I returned to the tent and wrote a long letter to leave behind in the cairn, disconnected thoughts of love and grief and hope to Joe, or in his memory, I didn't really know which. The act of expression settled me, and when Zhiang called us for dinner I was ready to face everyone. The meal was delicious: tasty, tender lamb kebabs and potatoes boiled in their skins. My appetite was restored, I was suddenly ravenous and the Chinese cook laughed heartily.

'He says – one shish kebab eating many shish kebabs!' translated Dong, setting off much good–natured bantering about my skinny frame. A group of Dutch climbers sat to one side of the tent, sharing the meal but involved in their own discussion. Near them, out of the light, was a group of high–altitude porters, wild-looking men, dark and striking, whose eyes flashed across the tent at us. As the sun was setting we stood outside in our down jackets drinking coffee with Dong and Zhiang and watching the changing colours of Chomolungma. Our guides were relaxed and began to talk a little about their personal lives. Dong's wife was studying in Australia for a year and Zhiang was married with a small baby. Chinese etiquette demands great social reserve, and these disclosures displayed a sense of trust by which we were very flattered.

We had one more day and night at Base Camp. Our Swiss companions left early in the morning for a trek, and we arranged to pick them up on our way out of the valley. It was good to relax around the tent and to soak in the atmosphere of the place. The wind had dropped, and we sat outside in warm sunshine listening to the river, which had swollen in our three-day absence. The truck that had taken the Swiss men down the valley reappeared, raising clouds of dust all around it, and rolled into camp. Zhiang jumped down from the cab, strode purposefully over to where we sat, handed us each a posy of tiny yellow flowers tied with red shoe-lace and left, smiling shyly at our thanks. We taped the posies one either side of the memorial stone, and between the cans of lychees placed a foil-wrapped cake that Lin had baked and asked us to leave there. I slipped a piece of the silk scarf underneath one of the cans so that a corner fluttered out in the wind. Hilary began to dig up plants with her hands and a stone.

'Help me to make a garden.'

After an hour's work we sat back to look at the result. Ringed by rocks were two types of mosses, a miniature edelweiss, a strong-smelling green herb and a delicate plant with tiny purple flowers. These were age-old and instinctive rituals, beautifying a grave and leaving offerings to the spirits of the dead. I sometimes wonder what has happened to the cairn, its garden and the things we left. Friends have gone on expedition to Chomolungma since then and used that Base Camp, but I have never asked them about it. The cairn and the stone will eventually fall and be weathered down, the articles will rot or rust or blow away, the plants have surely died, but above them all the mountain stands as steadfast as ever, and it is the true grave.

In one of the emotional swings that I had come to accept as a natural part of grieving, over lunch we laughed and sang and played music with our Chinese hosts. Dong and Zhiang had been curious about the tapes we listened to on our Walkmans, so we brought them to the food tent and watched their bemused expressions as rock music blared from the portable stereo. Mr Wang put on some Chinese popular music. 'Sing along! Sing along!' he urged us, and our efforts reduced them all to helpless laughter.

At the start of their expedition, Joe and Pete's team had picnicked at the site of Mallory and Irvine's 1921 Base Camp. We tried to cross the river by foot to reach the picnic spot, but the water level had risen too much. I trekked up the cairn from the far side of the hillock, suddenly hit by the realization that in the morning we would be gone.

'How will you ever leave the mountain?' several people in Britain had asked, and I had replied that when the time came it would be a simple, inevitable and timely step. Sitting by the cairn, I realized that I would indeed have to turn calmly away the next morning. Joe was gone, he was no longer moving about the earth, he was frozen somewhere on that beautiful mountain looming above me, never to be called back. I had come to be close, to make my peace with Everest and with him, and now I had to leave accepting all. My questions about our relationship remained unresolved, but I had reached one simple conclusion. We had not had the time together that we needed to work things out, and regretting that was of no use. The important thing now was to continue to face the fact of Joe's death. It was not possible to 'get over' it, instead I had to accept all that had happened without anger or bitterness or remorse, and reconstruct my life around this acceptance.

Hilary was reading Pete's diary in the tent when I crawled in. She looked up and smiled.

'Shall we build a house here?' she said, and we laughed to think of the horror it would cause if we were to sell our properties in England and set up home in the Rongbuk Valley. She had become so dear to me. Her strength, wisdom and complete generosity were only part of what made her a special person. It was easy to see why Pete had loved her so. She began to read to me from his diary, the symbol of the closeness and resolution of their union, and as I

166

listened it struck me that for the first time I was not experiencing pangs of envy and sadness over this. Those were early days; I did not know as I sat in the tent, arms around my knees and watching my friend read, just how long it would be before I felt happy and whole and able to see the past as a part of life's pattern, but I could tell I was on my way.

'Come in! Tea? Tea?'

Mr Wang ushered us into his 'house' tent. It was warm and friendly in there; foam mattresses on the floor were covered with heavy, fur-lined coats, a tape machine played Chinese music and a card game was in progress. We had come with thanks for his kindness and generosity but he waved these aside and pressed us to sit down and talk for a while. He told us stories of other expeditions he had worked on. In 1975 four hundred people were camped at Rongbuk during the Chinese attempt on the mountain, there were seventy 'house' tents, a makeshift volleyball court was set up and a Tibetan dance troupe performed. As we left he gave us each a dried lotus flowerhead.

'Come back to Tibet, you come back soon?'

We smiled but did not say that no, we would probably never return.

We lingered outside for a while in the cold air. Electricity from the generator illuminated the large food tent, and laughter and people spilled in and out of its flapped door. Smaller tents glowed with torch or candlelight as climbers settled down for the night. Beyond these spots of brightness the night was dark, still and silent. The sky was full of stars and one fell and burned out.

'Make a wish, Hilary.'

'I've made it. It won't come true, though.'

Within hours we would leave, but all this would still go on. Expeditions would arrive and set up, some lives would be lost and others, like ours, would be enriched by being on the mountain. I was glad we had made the journey. I slept deeply and peacefully and imagined Joe there with me, — we were curled up like two spoons throughout the night.

During breakfast in the food tent, heads popped around the door in farewell. We packed up and threw our rucksacks onto the truck. Then quickly to the cairn for a final goodbye to the pile of rock that had become somehow significant and symbolic to us. I reached in for the plastic envelope, slipped my letter inside and pushed it back deep among the frosty stones. One fell and hit my finger, and the blood-blister it caused was a reminder of that morning for days to come. I looked at the little garden, the cans of lychees, the silk peeping out, the names carved onto granite and the mountain beyond. Words from the poem among the stones ran through my head, 'In my dreams I see the light of your face.'

Swallowing hard and blinking back tears, I walked steadily down and climbed onto the truck.

A little group formed to wave us off. Mr Wang and Lin reached up to grasp our hands and I was glad we had said our goodbyes the previous night, because neither of us could manage any words at the moment of departure. The truck pulled away, then stopped abruptly as Wilhelm, a handsome Dutch climber, ran out of his tent calling to us and stuffing a letter into a hastily-addressed envelope.

'Please, could you post this for me in Hong Kong or London?'

Probably to his girlfriend, I thought sadly. And we were off, bumping and jerking out of Base Camp, the two of us alone in the back. Dong and Zhiang, sensitively, had climbed into the cab with Tele, allowing us private space to watch the mountain recede. I stared hard at Chomolungma. I was leaving calmly, as I had wished. The image of the mountain at the head of the valley filled my eyes and my heart, and I knew I would carry it with me for a long time to come.

SIXTEEN

'Hilary, Maria.'
The truck had stopped outside the ruins of the Rongbuk
Monastery. Dong called to us gently.

'Tele wants to show you around.'

He stood waiting for us, gap-toothed smile and woolly hat,
shrunk even smaller by the landscape around him. Chomolungma
lay cradled in the V of the valley, at its most magnificent, for me,
from this vantage point. A flag of snow streamed proudly from its
summit. The highest place on earth. We are at peace now, I silently
told the mountain, and I will never forget you.

Tele had set off into the remains of the monastery, and he
beckoned us to follow. Its destruction, the work of the Red Guards,
was horrifying. Every roof torn down, shrines ripped apart, walls
crumbling into rubble. I shook my head in dismay and Tele nodded
his agreement. He pointed into what was left of a monk's cell, a
stone square with a bench along one wall. I tried to visualize
the daily life in that place: praying and meditating, overcoming
cold and deprivation, and watching the dawns and sunsets of
Chomolungma and the passage of seasons across it. Joe had
written to me about the monastery: 'It is hard to imagine anyone
choosing to live in this remote, bleak place. Just an hour's walk
away from it is another ruin – that used to be a convent! The
mind boggles!'

I remembered his letter and smiled to think of the ribald comments he must have made to the others about the proximity of nuns
and monks within this isolated valley.

Dong was calling. It was time to go. We settled ourselves among
rucksacks as the truck rumbled and rattled away. The mountain
gradually grew smaller. Joe, I thought, our relationship has been
full of farewells. With no attempt to hold back the flow of tears, I

looked up to the ridge near the summit of Chomolungma and made myself say goodbye.

The Swiss men were waiting for us at the first village, and when we drew up the headman came out, a striking sight in the orange down jacket which had been a gift from the American expedition. His hair was plaited close to his head and framed a sculpted face lit by a wide smile. A very old woman hovered behind him, peeping up at us, her pancake-flat breasts visible through the folds of her dress. Filthy, barefoot children, dressed in rags and with long and matted hair, climbed onto the sides of the truck, poking their tongues out in greeting. '*Namaste. Namaste.*' I wondered at the harshness of their existence: it seemed inconceivable that life could go on in this high, remote place, that people could survive and raise families, that they could even withstand the winters.

The truck rumbled away; children chased alongside us until we picked up speed and the older people stood and waved. We turned out of the valley and back onto the high plains. Lhasa was a three-day drive away. Tele relished being behind the wheel again and careered along at speed. He took an exhilarating but precarious zig–zag route across a river, recrossing it later by a rickety low bridge which collapsed as soon as we were over it. From time to time I looked behind, to catch a glimpse of the mountain.

A steep pass finally slowed Tele's driving. The truck ground its way up, and sometimes on hairpin corners it seemed that the engine was about to fail and send us hurtling back down the road and into the gorges below. When we stopped for lunch I walked along a stream-bed picking some purple flowers, remembering my surprise when I had come back into the Swiss Alpine valleys after mountaineering with Hilary, at how lush the grass and flowers had seemed after the barrenness of higher places. I presented Tele with my little posy; he accepted it with grace and solemnly placed it on the dashboard above his steering-wheel.

At the top of the pass, 17,000 feet, Dong leaned over to us.

'Zhiang says,' he shouted, 'to say goodbye to Chomolungma.'

This was to be our last view of the mountain. Hilary plugged us in to Pete's favourite tape on the trip, 'Bare Trees', and she smiled at me over the words 'lovers have to say goodbye'.

And it was gone. Tele took the downhill side of the pass with a vengeance, whistling along the track with such speed that I was sure the brakes had failed. We clung to the sides of the wildly bouncing

170

truck as colours, rock formations and snow peaks streamed by in a blur.

'I'm scared!' I yelled.

'I'm not,' Hilary shouted back. 'I think I'm becoming a Buddhist!'

We did arrive, in one piece, at our camp site on the grassy flood plain of a deep and narrow valley. Tele started to prepare a meal and fought with the propane stove which was by now resembling a flame-thrower. I washed the socks that I wanted to give him as a gift and rolled them in a towel. They would dry against my body that night, an emergency drying trick taught to me by Hilary during the rainy trek through the Kharta Valley. The night was clear and starlit again and she pointed out the direction of the north side of Chomolungma, under the brightest star of the Plough. Telephone wires ran along the side of the road and another truck passed by; we were back into 'civilization'.

Zhiang picked a dwarf bush on the way into Xigaze. It had tiny blue flowers and its trunk and roots were knarled and convoluted like a bonsai. I held it as we rolled past the monastery and into the streets of the town. Protected by buildings from the wind of the plains, it was suddenly unbearably hot in the back of the truck, and we began to pull off layers of clothing. The Dutch expedition doctor, Charlie, was standing in the courtyard of the military compound next to a jeep when we pulled up. Hilary ran over to talk to him.

'I am going now to visit Eelco,' he told her. 'Come with me, it will be good for his spirits.'

He had accompanied Eelco on the slow, tortuous journey from Base Camp and was tending to him daily in the hospital.

'Me, too?' I asked.

'Oh, yes, of course.'

We hurried to our room, filled bowls with cold water from the urn on the porch and carried them inside. On the wall was a mottled, stained mirror, and once again I was startled by my own reflection. My jeans hung loosely, and when I took them off hip-bones and ribs protruded. I had not realized the extent of my weight-loss. There was no time for concern. I brushed dust out of my hair, rebraided it and found some clean clothes. Carrying the 'bonsai' plant and two tins of lychees, presents from the ever-thoughtful Zhiang, we climbed into the jeep. It had been customized: it was lined with fabric and had comfortable upholstered seats. Stickers from the British expedition were on all its windows, and I wondered if Joe had been ferried around in that vehicle. We drove along busy, bicycle-filled streets, through a wrought-iron gateway and up to the hospital.

It was a long, low building of grey stone set in dusty grounds. In contrast to the warm afternoon sunshine the corridors were cold and dark, flies buzzed about our heads and there was dirt on the walls and floor. Open doors revealed rooms where patients with hands, feet or eyes wrapped in bloodstained bandages sat on iron bedsteads. Most of them were soldiers.

'The doctor tells me they shoot each other,' said Charlie enigmatically.

A child's cry drew me to look through a doorway; a young Tibetan woman sat holding a wailing baby while a bewildered toddler clutched at her ankles.

The glassless window in Eelco's door had pieces of yellowing newspaper taped over it.

'I'll wait outside,' I said. 'Call me in when you feel ready.'

A group of Chinese nurses came by clad in green trousers, stained white coats and caps with red stars above the peaks. They looked at me curiously as I stood against the wall clutching our gifts. The door opened and Hilary took my arm. Eelco was lying on the bed, propped up by pillows, wearing blue salopettes.

'Let me introduce a thin Maria to a thinner Eelco,' said Hilary, and I shook his hand, struck by the blue eyes that shone with such spirit from his wasted body. His extreme thinness made him seem childlike, a shadow on the bed. 'Like a cancer patient,' Hilary said later. She sat on his mattress, Charlie and I on the bed opposite them, with ancient bedsprings squeaking under our weight. The room was appalling: dirt-smeared walls, an unswept floor, blood-stained sheets, flies. Eelco was happy to have our company, he talked and talked, sometimes missing a word as he caught his breath in pain. He had been on his way to the North Col when the avalanche hit him, breaking nine of his ribs. His companions, including Johan, bivouacked on the mountain to keep vigil over his unconscious body, fearing that he would not survive the night. Four high-altitude porters, the group we had seen in the food tent, carried him to Base Camp on a stretcher, one of them insisting on taking the load the whole way without a break. To reduce his pain on the journey to Xigaze the team rigged up a hanging bed in the back of the truck with ropes, inner-tubes and foam. On arrival at

172

the hospital he was found to have internal bleeding, and an operation was immediately performed to remove blood and fluid from his lungs. I winced at the thought of an operation in such conditions.

'But the doctor here, he is excellent,' Charlie reassured me.

Eelco had worked on preparations for the expedition for three years and was bitterly disappointed at being halted by the avalanche.

'But I am lucky . . .'

Earlier that day he had been taken out of traction, and he asked us to help him with his second attempt at walking.

'Charlie and I managed one hundred metres this morning!'

We eased him off the bed and, with the aid of ski sticks, he took slow, painful steps to the door. Out into the hallway – 'Watch out, here comes an Everest climber!' he called to some startled nurses – and along to a courtyard where the sun made us squint. A trench had been dug near the doorway, with a single plank the only way across. Charlie was watchful, but did not impose help, as Eelco tentatively negotiated it. Exhausted, he sat down on some rocks. The hospital had no running water and I came back from a visit to the nearby filthy and fly-ridden outhouses in sheer horror. Eelco laughed at my disgust.

'Use my pee bottle next time!'

Pieces of wood were flung from the top of a half-erected water tower that was being constructed nearby, and we were suddenly showered with debris.

'Time to go,' said Eelco.

He moved slowly and unsteadily ahead of us like a very old man, his limbs almost as thin as the ski sticks, and I recognized the breaking of another half-suppressed fantasy: that by some miracle I would find Joe in a Tibetan hospital, almost wasted away but alive and recovering.

Back in his room Eelco lay recovering for a few minutes, then began to tell hospital stories.

'It is very organized here today. Yesterday was haymaking and everyone left for the fields. Except for the patients. It was crazy. And every day, if I want some help, I have to shout. There are no bells. Have you ever tried shouting with nine broken ribs?'

Charlie had made up a list of words and phrases that Eelco would need in the hospital. 'Please give me water,' 'I need to go to the bathroom,' and so on. The interpreter had translated everything into Chinese except 'Please hold my hand.'

'But you do that for me,' said Eelco to Charlie, and the trust and affection that passed between them at that moment was almost tangible.

The door opened and two young nurses appeared, clad in dirty white coats, shuffling and giggling at the foot of the bed.

'They come in here all the time to stare at me,' said Eelco. 'What do you want? Go *away*!'

His sharp reprimand made me jump, but had no obvious effect on the girls. Reaching into the drawer of a little cupboard next to him, he pulled out a plateful of dried biscuits, offered them to us, ate a couple and then handed the plate to the girls. This had obviously been their mission, because they immediately left.

'There is only one plate in the whole hospital. We share it around,' remarked Eelco casually, and we roared with laughter. I marvelled at his spirit and humour in such a dire place. He was leaving the hospital the next day to spend a week of recuperation in the Guest House, and then, he told us, he wanted to return to Base Camp. Charlie made doubtful noises. The hospital doctor, a tiny Chinese man, joined us as we wandered back down the maze of dark corridors.

'Eelco, a brave man,' he said.

I stepped out into the evening sunshine and gulped in the fresh air, appreciative yet again to be alive and healthy.

SEVENTEEN

Dong and Zhiang encouraged us to sightsee during those last two days of our journey back to Lhasa, but I was having problems with being a tourist. I made the motions, trying to prod myself into absorbing all before me, knowing how unlikely it was that I would ever return to Tibet. But my head was full of the mountain, of the East-North–East Ridge.

'In my dreams I see the light of your face.'

Asleep and awake I thought of Joe; all I saw, everything we did was tinged with the knowledge that this was a homeward journey that he had planned but had never made.

'We have had to make provisional bookings for flights from Lhasa,' he wrote at the end of March, 'and our best projection is that we should be ready to fly from there on June 1st. If we don't book we don't get seats. If all goes well we should make that and that would mean we would be back by mid-June, but if storms or setbacks occur we will have to postpone our flights.'

Storms or setbacks, postpone. Words of confident optimism. And yet. . . always, before his expeditions, he would talk of 'when I come back', and there would be a tiny, barely discernible silence between us, an unspoken knowledge that 'if I come back' was, of course, a more realistic statement. His final six months in Britain had been taken up with writing a book, the days before his flight to Hong Kong were a headlong rush of finishing the manuscript and preparing for his role as cameraman on Everest. It had always been like that: there were never enough hours in each day for Joe, as if he accepted the fact that his life might be cut short and he was thus impelled to accomplish as much as possible.

He would have disapproved of the way I was allowing the past to hold me back and prevent my enjoyment of the present moment.

But the monasteries and temples we saw only reinforced my feelings, for they echoed with a lost life and vitality. Being with people was easier.

In Xigaze, when Hilary and I returned from our hospital visit, we went with the three Swiss men to a performance by the Lhasa Operatic Society. The street outside the wooden hall was jammed with young Chinese soldiers on bicycles. Inside, the crowd was mostly Tibetan, and heads craned to stare at the sight of five foreigners. There seemed to be no seats left but, after a great deal of shuffling and discussion, room was made for us on a long wooden bench. I sat next to a group of giggling young women, whose long plaits were wrapped around their heads and colourfully ribboned. They leaned across me to marvel at Jacques' large nose and Denny's hairy arms. It seemed to be an important social occasion – whole family groups were there, and the noise level rose to a deafening pitch as friends shouted to greet each other across the hall. A sudden clash of cymbals caused a hush to fall, and was the sign that the performance was about to begin. Music started up from a hidden orchestra pit and the curtains opened. I had not really known what to expect, and I was taken aback by the three-act performance of Chinese propaganda that unfolded. But the audience was enraptured. The actors sang in high-pitched voices, executed fast costume changes and danced with excellent timing. After two hours the Opera Company assembled on the stage and signalled to the orchestra to stand. As I began to clap, the woman next to me poked my ribs and shook her head, stifling her laughter. Everyone around me was silent, staring intently at the stage while the actors applauded their audience.

Outside Gyantse, Hilary and I wandered through the crooked streets of a village and into a market place. Horses and cows were tethered to the stalls, and the people were friendly and obviously used to seeing Westerners. They were extremely clean and all smelled, mysteriously, of the same brand of soap. I came upon a small, well-groomed sheep sporting an ear-ring and eating the remains of someone's dinner on a plate set on the ground. As I started to photograph it a large and smiling lady rushed out, eager to pose with her pet. The sheep seemed to want its own limelight and butted her furiously until she beat a laughing retreat. A little girl took my hand and we walked along together looking at the wares for sale until we found Hilary crouched down, her headscarf only just visible amongst the crowd of smaller heads intent on the workings of her camera. Two horn blasts made everyone jump and sent us hurrying back to the waiting truck.

The final pass before the descent to Lhasa was at 14,700 feet. Speeding round the bends on the way down I was moved by the beauty of the now familiar contrast of colourful rock and irrigated green, and the intense and brilliant light of Tibet. We hurried from the Guest House on that final afternoon to visit the Jokhang Temple and the Potala. The feeling of a missing presence was overwhelming in the exiled Dalai Lama's palace. Room after room, flight after flight of steps echoed with the loss of the God King in the once revered home that was now a museum. The calendar and clock were set in his bedroom, and the blankets folded back, as if time had stood still and he had just left. Part of a Chinese poem ran through my head:

> The things are there just as before
> But the man they belong to is not there.
> His spirit has suddenly taken flight
> And left me behind far away.

It was how I had felt when I went into Joe's house for the first time after his disappearance, and saw all the familiar objects in their usual places. I could not believe that he would never again walk through the door and be among them. It was unbearable for me that anything should be moved. I wanted everything to stay just as it had been when he was at home so that I could soak up the feeling of his presence and cling to it. I had a vision of dust settling, of cobwebs stretching between chairs, while I and the house waited for his return. His dressing gown hanging in the bathroom, the smell of his soap, the piles of papers on his desk, his jeans thrown over a chair: they gave me comfort and a sense of his existence. His family quickly packed his belongings and took them away, and the house was put up for sale. I had some of Joe's clothes, and for months I slept each night curled around a sad bundle of sweaters and shirts, on which his scent seemed to linger. The Potala was a stunning and impressive building, but it stirred up too much pain and I was almost glad to leave.

The sun rose during the two–hour drive to the airport. I sat on my rucksack in the cool morning air, listening for the drone of the approaching plane. It was an immense wrench to leave Tibet, and Joe.

'There is nothing else we can do for them here,' said Hilary as we boarded. The plane took off again quickly, into the brilliantly blue sky, carrying us over snowy peaks and glaciated valleys, back to China and away from Everest, Chomolungma, Goddess Mother of the World.

Chengdu was a cloudy, drab and hectic contrast to the mountains and high plateaux of Tibet. We plunged into a crowded market to shop and I was tempted to buy a wolf-skin. To reach the restaurant for lunch we crossed a bicycle-jammed street where nothing could be heard above the ringing of the bells attached to each set of handle bars. Curious eyes followed our winding progress to the pavement. All three storeys of the restaurant were packed with customers and we were eventually ushered to a table in a far corner of the third floor.

'Specialities of Chengdu,' Dong proudly told us, as plate after plate of unrecognizable food was set down. Remembering Al Rouse's story of asking what he was eating during a banquet in China and being told that it was sea slug, I decided to keep my questions to myself.

Zhiang visited us in our room that afternoon. We had come to be able to communicate with him through a few words of Chinese and English, gesture, and much shared feeling. He showed us photos of his wife and baby and asked if we had any of Joe and Pete. He looked intently at the pictures we took out, and he began to cry. Culture, language and politics kept us apart from Zhiang, but somehow he had transcended all that to understand and share our experience on the mountain. He put his arms around Hilary and me, and for a few moments in that Chinese hotel room the three of us were linked completely by the puzzling but universal nature of life and death. Later that night we wrote a letter, for Dong to translate, trying to convey our gratitude to both of them. We gave it to them at the airport the next day. They made their public farewells formally and stiffly, with no show of emotion.

On September 30th, a month after we had left Britain, our plane from Hong Kong approached Heathrow Airport. Just as I had felt reluctant to begin the trip to Tibet, now I did not want to end it. I wanted the plane to land briefly and then take off again with me still aboard, back towards Chomolungma. I could not conceive of returning to my job, my house, my daily life and the approaching winter. But there was a reality I had to face: Joe would never come back from the Rongbuk Valley. There were no more of his foot-steps to follow in; I had to make my own. Another, much longer journey was ahead of me, I had a life to reconstruct and fill with meaning. And so, aware that the journey was already beginning, and with the image of the mountain of which Joe was now a part firmly in my mind, I took a deep breath, stepped off the plane and set out.

EPILOGUE

Six years on and the story is not yet over. When my phone rings here in Canada, early in the morning or late at night, I sometimes hope that it will be Hilary or Chris, with news of an expedition finding some trace of Joe and Pete. A British team recently made the first successful ascent of the East-North-East Ridge, to a point beyond the Pinnacles. But they found nothing – it was the monsoon season, and the deep snow on the route would have covered any traces. I long to know what happened, high on Chomolungma, for only when I know will I finally put them completely to rest in my mind.

Meanwhile, my life has reconstructed itself. The healing took a long time, and writing this story has perhaps been the final part of that process. At last I can accept my past, quite calmly and without regrets. Yet hearing of friends and acquaintances dying in the mountains always brings back some of that old pain. When I am in England I occasionally go to parties and see the gaps left by missing faces. It is hard to imagine a world without them: Joe and Pete, Nick, Alex, Pete Thexton, Al, Simon, J.P., the list goes on for too long. Perhaps they are all together somewhere, carrying on a party of their own. It would certainly be a good one.

A few days after the news of Joe's disappearance became public, Carolyn Estcourt called round to see me.

'What a waste,' she said bitterly. 'What a stupid waste.'

'No, don't say that, Carolyn.' My tone was urgent. 'It wasn't a waste. It wasn't.'

Seeing it that way was far too brutal for me, back then. Their deaths had to have some meaning, otherwise it was unbearable. But now, I sometimes wonder. Many of the mountaineering books and articles seem almost to be written to a formula. The preparations, the walk-in, the climb, the tragedy. And then, always, the self-questioning. A year after the Everest expedition, Charlie Clarke wrote: '. . . I question the nature of our journey – to venture with a small team on unknown ground on the highest mountain in the world. The outcome answers the question, "Was it worth it?" It would not have been had we been able to peer even dimly into what was to happen.'*

They had embarked on that expedition in full knowledge of the odds they were setting themselves against. It was a calculated risk, a decision which had far-reaching consequences for the families, lovers and friends who had no part in its making. Yet, despite the outcome, Charlie, Chris and Dick continue to return to the mountains which hold them, as so many others, in thrall.

Joe, Pete and all the lost friends – climbing was their dream, and an important part of what made them so vibrant; we survivors have to try to accept that, while coming to terms with the fact that it also took them away too soon. I am fascinated still by mountaineers, and full of admiration for their courage and drive, but I am glad to be distanced from that world now. It taught me enough.

On the fifth anniversary of Joe and Pete's disappearance, Hilary sent me a card, a photograph of Skiddaw in the Lake District illuminated by winter light. She wrote: '. . . we are the lucky ones, who have the ability to stand back and look at what happened like witnesses now, without remaining in a chasm of regret. Thank you for five good years, Maria. I sincerely feel now that they have been good, to plumb the depths of our being and evacuate all that was in there.'

When I first met Joe he was telling a story about a near-fatal descent from a Himalayan mountain, and it held the essence of all I have learned since then. The climbers put themselves at risk, and survival sharpens their perceptions and increases their love of life. But it is the same for all of us really. Everything can change in an instant, even though we try to lead the safest of lives. These days I feel blessed by a surfeit of love and good health. Yet such happiness, however soundly I imagine it to be based, still trembles on an edge as fragile as that on which Joe and Pete stood, and from which it

*Chris Bonnington and Charles Clarke, *Everest: The Unclimbed Ridge* (London, 1983)

could just as easily slip and fall away into oblivion. And so I try to appreciate it all, day by day, and to remind myself that there is no time to be lost and nothing to be taken for granted.

TERMINATOR

TERMINATOR

POEMS, 2008—2018

Richard Kenney

ALFRED A. KNOPF

NEW YORK

2019

THIS IS A BORZOI BOOK
PUBLISHED BY ALFRED A. KNOPF

www.aaknopf.com

LIBRARY OF CONGRESS CATALOGING-IN-PUBLICATION DATA
Names: Kenney, Richard, author.
Title: Terminator : poems, 2008–2018 / Richard Kenney.
Description: First edition. | New York : Knopf, 2019.
Identifiers: LCCN 2019002031 (print) | LCCN 2019003045 (ebook) |
    ISBN 9780525656647 (ebook) | ISBN 9780525656630 (hardback)
Subjects: | BISAC: POETRY / American / General.
Classification: LCC PS3561.E443 (ebook) | LCC PS3561.E443 A6 2019
    (print) | DDC 811/.54—dc23
LC record available at https://lccn.loc.gov/2019002031

Jacket art and design by Tyler Comrie

Manufactured in the United States of America
First Edition

For Carol and Maeve, Hollis and Will

CONTENTS

III. *World Enough*

IV. *Personae*

v. *Self-Portrait in Lemon Juice*

vi. *The Terminator*

TERMINATOR

Definitions

Word: an interval,
a needle biopsy
of a waterfall,

making digital
the rinse of experience
by jot and tittle.

Poetry, I think,
is the distant-thunder sound
in the drying ink.

Annunciation

Imagine a loved face reflecting on the side-
edge of a scimitar-shaped shard

of a breaking mirror—just thus
it was: sun-whet suddened at the oculus

of the Pantheon one day,
just barely, along its under

eyelid—
Look! Eyeliner, I said,

unimaginatively,
and you looked. That genitive

moment was too long, by an age.
You saw the sickle, not its just-touched edge,

that thinnest paring of light released,
lasting

less long
than a whetstone's ring.

Because then the image began to oxidize
and thicken, smear, fade, as bronze does,

as everything eyestruck does, once
announced

into a noun.

Terminator

The Terminator
is the line separating—
not the hemispheres,

that's the Equator—
but the one separating
certain metaphors.

One terminator:
that knapped core, the inner curve
of the crescent moon.

Another, later
in our romance, that scythe-swerve
down the face of soon.

One is the future
severing, leaving the past
to its own story.

One a new suture
down the calvarium of
memento mori.

I.

ANYWHERE

NOT PARIS

Our shimmer of days
sucked through the howling wall-clock's
macerating blades—

Signs

Slung
like an ancient
baseball

across
long
space

past Ursa
Major
enter

invisible
the Cybele
Meteor

unwelcome
in the Milky
Way

or so
we'll
wager

*

Look up, Alley Oop!—
pressure-flaking a flint core
in your unflown coop,

Deep Time, that egg-blown
old dark under the Dordogne—
there's blood on your door:

Somethings in the sky—
something's scratched your cornea—
blink. Don't rub your eye.

*

Tell, Sibyl, huffing sulfur,
intuiting tomorrow,
your mind's reticulum in shreds,
your vital signs a horror:

They've seized the Cybele Meteor.
They're bringing it to Rome.
Is that a good idea?
Gaia grim in a black stone?

Anywhere Not Paris

1. Edges

About the time one starts to grow suspicious
of the world, to lose one's faith in edges,
verges, borders, boundaries, that cusp
comes at which one's own biology
begins to cross them with abandon. Bulge
and salient balancing retreat: here hairline and shrunk shank, there the more general her-
niations supervene: belly occludes belt;
dewlaps brim the buttoned collar.

*

Deeper pattern shatters. Ventricular
percussions stutteringly muff the rhythm
of a lifetime: *lub-dub-dub*: the world's withering
fire. Grotesque foreign proteins trickle
though the blood-brain barrier. *Not-You*
enters the city in triumph, to clarions and cheers,
while *You* hammer the portcullis, howling. Does Nature
have edges? Tell me that, you smudge, you faint Venn
diagram whose membrane-lines have proven solvent
in the stream of things?

*

                    As words as vessels
fail to hold their little maelstroms, all selves
lose outline, so. Nouns leak; verbs leak worse,
and that's the news. Our poor suppressor cells

don't recognize us any more than What's-Her-
Name, from whenever-it-was, fumbling words
with me on the street the other day. She, too,
shape-shifted like a blink of myth: Ishtar
Resartus in a paisley shawl; Apollo reappareled
in papyrus and bone—what a pair!
Say, Siri—Pythia—what's flesh anyway but shadow-
garb a gone god's doffed? If ours seemed a touch
déclassé, it's only by unfair comparison
with what divinity was wearing in—I want to say *Paris,
1972?*—Good grief, she was a pretty
Muse!—

          And who's not shapelier today than soon,
a thousand years or so from now, redistributed
according to surfactant properties
of Time? Her name?— I want to say Beauty,
though it might have been Betty. The point is, even proper
nouns bleed out like all the rest of us.

*

Not the street, the bus. It was on the bus.

2. *Taxa*

To my friend the physicist, who still resembles
his yearbook picture, things seem simple.

Acknowledging her name, conceding her avian
properties, her moods, her modes, her raving

beauty, he'll insist she is a *mammal*, and feel
the firmer settlement of saying something real.

I ask: are avian dinosaurs, *qua* birds,
reptiles? And then my friend and I have words.

3. *Under the Oculus*

Turn the mirror edgewise, time sideways,
so to speak. Here's the waist
of the hourglass, our porthole oculus,
cervix of the future
which, like everything accelerated,
swells
and thins:
thus
memory shreds in the solar wind,
the quartz porthole, bleb on a blowpipe, spills,
the skull rises through the face
behind its mica visor, slung in the centrifuge—
no refuge:
lick the mirror like a glacier,
like aluminum in winter—
lick Antarctica, that'll slow your bosons,
won't it?

4. *Unlikely,*

we say, involuntarily invoking a Land of Unlikeness
where no echo augurs a far shore,
nothing accrues to a human cry.
The mirror like Loch Ness

coughs up its plesiosaur.
A decade ricochets by.
Hear the Doppler foghorn through the shaving glacier?
Check its edges, calving.

Having
read somewhere that certain sorts of humor
depend upon surprise, a sly
low-slung irruption of the unexpected, I—
oh, my!
That's why the mirror gets so *funny*.

5. *Don't make me laugh,*

we say, meaning something like, *No*.
About the time we stop stropping like barbers these blades
of nouns and verbs against the spinal cord,
the hard thought having once for all occurred
they'll never prove keen enough to resect the clade
from the light-waves washing all this flotsam in—

About our lot: loss.
About the courage one might wish to summon,
about that sang-
froid, the saying-goodbye sans tears—

About the time (as I was saying)
one starts to grow suspicious of the lexicon,
to lose faith in defensible frontiers,
to sicken
somewhat before the calving berg
of the funhouse mirror (horribly

a liquid, as the pedant puts it), the glass bags
in and out, flimmering like a windy bubble:

Now here's belt uncinched, subtending belly
now debouching
into neighboring space—

Feel that elevator-lurch-and-pause?—

And now Biology
like punched dough no more plump and jowly
bugles its retreat: cheeks scoop; thews
thin. The world's fire withering.
And still a good deal left to lose.

6. So, for the moment

never mind the Time Machine, that ever-cracking mirror,
syntax, cervix of the sandglass, oculus, our kind's quartz
porthole blown like a soapy bubble flimmering through the
Kuiper Belt and Oort Cloud, occluded at the terminator,
minatory as it is in mind, always, us tongue-stuck, indistinct
in a moon-calf wince windmilling backward—what an
image!—into origins or epitaphs, it's life, still, though
thought stall,

and not the worst laugh ever laughed.

The Time Machine

1. The Pantheon

Watch, at the stoneless cope
of the open oculus, its keen kerf
slice Time. Acetylene sun—

ice moon—the strobe
accelerates. Earth's verdure
winking in the onset:

instants!—seasons!—eons!—the snow-globe
spinning like a pitched ball back the coffered curvature,
all its flakes a flurry of unsettling—

*

Now wing-whirr of the four-foot dragonfly—
Pock-ploops the early asteroidal rain-drum din—
A blood-red placental moon drapes a third of the sky—
Whoops!—now lithosphere slips like pudding-skin—
Syntax enters the ape—the world splinters—
Enter invisible: the Cybele Meteor spins past Pluto—

*

Pilot-
less, queasy, we lisp *Abort!*
The time machine creaks to a halt.
Through its quartz porthole
the page stretches, endless, white as salt.

2. When Are We?

After tree ferns, their whispery soughing;
after predator-drone-sized darning-needle's whizz.
After armored fish
dragged up clanking from the benthos.
After Amazon and Congo run confluent.
Certainly after our one moon tore off, dripping,
but well before aurochs
(great big aurochs bumping our cavewall,
oilcanning our cavewall,
denting it to get in!—
a flock of handprints pushing back—)
After also smilodon, dawn horse.
Well after that dead stegosaur
with its plates unstacked,
its veined tongue lolling,
dirt-stuck, breaded like schnitzel—
(note iridescence on the oily onyx shell
of the stag beetle staggering
up the medial valley
of the dead stegosaur's lolling tongue—

*

Zoom out:
Iridescence streaks the lens
against a thick galactic talc.
As though as hoar
from a pane
the great corrugated thumbnail of God
scrapes a starless line
across the screeching empyrean—

*

3. The Meteor

Well, that was how it was. Maybe we dreamt it.
That was a ride. Time torn open like a hydrant.
That was sure hair unbound and lips apart,
lapels aflutter in the flume of the photon-torrent.
We stood looking up, and a bit of iron scratched the oculus,
and that was just our luck,
start to finish, we fishtailed, and treed,
and fell, and it didn't kill us,
though the hands horrored up
and we hit the quartz screen,
and it starred.

Madsong

Origins suggest edges;
middles, too, as also ends;
the horsehide baseball just so sketches
an arc from hickory to fence

(whose little horse, just poodle-high,
once fled the sabertooth's embrace)
but here the ball is said "to fly"
above the runner and the base,

the flaxen laces spinning, spun
like inks in the Book of Kells;
thus Africa was somewhere once,
the Arctic somewhere else—

as also, too, magnetic north
and also, too, Polaris,
and this and that and so and forth,
recalling me to Paris:

I meant *appearances,* I think,
like a scholar in a study—
The Keats Equation!—sing, sing,
since her name must have been Beauty.

II.

SCIENCE

TUESDAY

Fragment

There's nothing any-

where but guessing. [Frag. thirty-

four, Xenophanes.]

Conceptual Thinking

A polyp would be a conceptual thinker if a feeling of
"Hollo! thingumbob again!" ever flitted through its mind.
—WILLIAM JAMES

Re Names:

Finical,
perception
its pen-knife,

nerve-long
language
feels for an edge,

teasing out the rim
of a perimeter,
muttering

Hollo?— Polyp
to Apollo:
Bob's your uncle,

Mr. James

Agnostic Gospels

Do I believe in Fahrenheit degrees?
Of course I do, they're real enough, as, please
the little gods, also the little gods,
and big ones, too, but grudgingly, the odds
against them feeling somewhat longer. Muse,
too, who hardly ever calls. Also the news
from what used to be called Frontiers of Science. *Science!*
that mortgaged curator of psychic sins,
in this case Curiosity: what killed his
cat may serve his proudest faculties
the same, since Reason scums its petri dish,
endangered now, with every wilting wish.

But weren't we speaking of *belief*? Schrödinger's cat?
What's reason got to do with that?

Reason May Not Mean to Be the Sophist

Slip the Problem from its sleeve. The vinyl's
scratched. And that's the problem, finally:

the nature of emotion's analog,
while languages are digital. Too few long-

playing feelings, inkily remastered,
long survive by heart. This mystery

runs deep, requiring deeper magics. *Look,* we
say, by darksome sleight ventriloquy,

referring to a nerve potential triggered
by a pressure in the world, recurring

now in a lung, in a laugh, in a poem of Sappho's.

Schrödinger's Elephant

Once upon a time in Copenhagen
the blind men met to scratch the quantum noggin.

They hashed things out, agreeing to decree
that the wave function of the pachyderm
collapses into rope, or spear, or tree,
or fan, or wall, as senses will confirm,

but only when the moment's brought to measure.
Till then, it's all-and-none. It's worse than Escher.

The key, you'll note, is human observation.

Human?— How in heaven's name?—

                             The answer's
mathematical as all Creation,
involving Probability and Chance. . . .

Laypeople simply can't—look, no offense,
but try now not to think of elephants.

Science Tuesday

The first human-chimpanzee chimera,
christened *Pan sapiens,* was born today
at Brigham and Women's Hospital, in Boston.

The Hubble's Very Wide Spool camera
regained partial function of its data
module, and is now on track for the Sirius starburst.

Dr. 32B, chief of research at Merck,
again replied, "No comment." "Ever," he added,
to op-ed columns suggesting he's hostile to the Press.

The Sentient Rover, assembled in America
from Chinese parts, parked since Saturday
in a no-load zone on Mars, appears depressed.

Spokesmen for the Generation Meerkat
Energy Corp. assured critics that the shudder is soldered,
stressing again that "containment vessel" is at best

a metaphor. The starburst—a miracle!
The drug had side effects. The Rover broke. The "baby satyr,"
Pan sapiens, died at his surrogate mother's breast.

He was hard to look at, she is reported to have said.

Pan sapiens 2

The first human-chimpanzee chimera
looked searchingly into the shaving mirror.
His hairline—was it?—yes, it was advancing.
Another blow, albeit only glancing.
For, having clever fingers (who'd forced fire?)
he'd simply boost the amps in his blow dryer.

Later, glaciers shrank from their moraines.
Seas rose above the knees of fishing cranes.

Venice, once resembling Tycho's Mars
now swamped like Venus, where the brontosaurs
rent heaven with hoarse hoots in praise of gods
who lent such swanny necks to sauropods.
And if you can't believe a noon so strange,
consult your own defunct nouns, for a change.

The Blank Slate

Concerning Common Ancestors, in verse:

Might chimpanzees once raised by bonobos
reach deep into your trousers and propose
engagements polymorphous and perverse?
Who knows.

Or would (here note initial terms reversed)
a bonobo by chimpanzees once nursed
and raised to adolescence come to blows,
or worse?

The question is an old one, cast in fable—
the oldest one, maybe, rephrased by Abel,
marking Cain, the line forever cursed—
though what an ape'll

say to that (in ASL, of course,
if non-recursive, and a touch terse)
may not refer to the matter of the Apple,
or Ancestors

at all. Or Babel.

And never mind what it means to say "refers."

Pan sapiens *3*

I am *Pan sapiens.* I don't speak well,
and so I write. Some say I look like hell.
I think that's hard. I think I look like you.
Pan in, however—never mind the view:

You've seen it all your life, the diorama
stinking with the crowd of us, from *Rama-*
pithecus to poor Neanderthal,
who's lost his lisp at last, and, standing tall
peers like any fool into my eyes
where once upon a time, a wild surmise—

Now, dip your quill into the pupils' ink:
it isn't how we look. What is it? *Think.*

The Arcturan Vivisectionist Explains

This specimen's common name is *Mirroreye.*
Observe (retractor, please) just *here*—a rare
non-adaptive anomaly in the so-called third
lid—common enough, of course, in lizards, birds,
sharks, et al., all perfectly unremarkable, save
that the nictitating membrane is *silvered*
inside, enabling these creatures to see themselves
reflected *everywhere:* in wood-grain, in moon, in clouds,
in others of their kind, even; also imparting an odd,
not uncrabwise aspect to their gait, backing hell-bent,
headlong, as it were, into what's already happened.

Horcrux: A Romantic Landscape

—AS SCORED FOR CRUMHORN BY EDWARD LEAR

You need some genes for jumping,
but none for not jumping too high,
since that information is stored on location,
between the earth and sky.

Our ancestors hadn't to worry
about too many sweets before lunch.
What protected their livers? The veldt could deliver
just so many berries per bunch.

Memory is a secretion
externally fertilized, so,
that a landscape revisited still may elicit
a shiver from ancient snow.

Some writers have interesting minds;
most don't. Yet by poem or novel
they somehow find thoughts the way tubers in plots
may surface, when stirred with a shovel.

The brain thinks it does all the thinking,
but likely it doesn't, at that:
too much information is stored on location.
It couldn't be done from a vat.

As birds need genes for flying
but none for returning to ground,
and the human mind is not born blind
to the conditions of its surround,

if the world's a bouquet of answers
to the questions the senses pose,
its lies of omission would be the conditions
that Heaven only knows.

Forget what you can't imagine,
the edge of the measure of man:
since what's unfurled as the sum of the world
must be what you can.

And that's not terrible news.
It means we *are* some place.
That's some reassurance. Where it leaves the Arcturans?—
But Lunch is served. Say grace.

Brains in a Vat

Step inside, please, spake the elevator,
hissing, reminiscent of Lord Vader
also in its little shudder. Later,
lobbed, too, through the black hole labeled Vela
X-1, judging by an indicator
blinking upward through the blank abyss
between the tenth and millionth floors, the Muse
of Relativity would disabuse
me of my geocentrism, for this
was Einstein's gravitational caboose,
and I was in a thought experiment.
Or was one, which is what I might have meant.
Still, the simplest things seem paramount:

That elevator *talked,* and I can count.

Numbers

Seethe on silicon
like bacterial plaques.
Somehow they liken

to appearances.
They have a seemliness from
which all earth rinses.

Elegance! Log on:
the algorithm resets
as *LaOcOOn.*

Unlikeness yaws thought.
Timor mortis is the thought.
That land Time forgot.

This—no mere mirror.
Nor is an error message
like no tomorrow.

Ecological Meditation,

or Space Is Closer Than Chicago

Even from Peoria.
Much closer, on the flat.
The wide yonder's wide indeed;
foil-thin, for all that.

The mountains puncture most of it,
their human climbers, too,
who wriggle dressed in oxygen
to a sky scarcely blue,

where helicopter blades won't bite
and sound itself thins.
A fifty-minute walk at most
on legs which once were fins.

The sea is similar, whose deeps
a dipstick shows as shallows:
wet an apple—that's the earth,
a scarcely moistened chalice.

What to make of thoughts like these
when the mind wants a yonder
wide enough to hold itself?—
I don't know. I wonder.

Horcrux Redux,

or Good Luck

I recall the earlier lecture, now
(or the fact in verse inflected)
that the human genome turned out somehow
to be "smaller than expected."

You need genes to rise off earth,
to crawl or jump or fly—
for all baroqueries of birth,
if none to fall or die.

The operator's manual
for returning to dirt, they say,
is locked in the physics of fare-thee-well,
not in the DNA.

It's so for so much else in life,
like appetite for sugar.
There's only *Go*. To add a *Stop*
the box would have had to be bigger.

Now, thinking of the Pleistocene
while reading above the fold,
reflecting on rapacity
and limits in a world

which vomits hordes of murderous apes,
eyes afire, amok
(to summarize what history
forecasts for human luck)

I could wish a few more base pairs
had been salted down the helix
to stitch us more securely to
the future: *Homo felix.*

The Drake Equation

1. They Were a Kind of Solution

Say one Spaceman, when she lands, will touch
down in a human sentence, speaking Dutch,
a dialect of Mentalese. Her torch-

song (loosely rendered from the Arcturan): "Baby
Let's Get Square with π," or "You're the Apple
of My Eye," or "Boola Theta Babel

Bye-Bye." It might make sense. This is a heady
thought. The traditional verse, *viz.* "Who's Your Daddy,"
as sung in *The War of the Worlds,* and signaled *Mayday,*

mayday—a little like Beethoven's 4th in digital
redaction—may underpin what limbic Dutch
must once upon a time have bloomed beneath the sagittal
crest of *Homo*—

        Who? What? This news just in!—the starry
sky is empty. Spacemen are out. Sorry.

2. Exo-Statisticians Change Minds, Cite Insufficiency
of Planetary Bodies of Right Type

What, no aliens? Or, with greater dignity,
life elsewhere in the universe? That window's
shut, we learn. Astronomers, indignant

desert birds, eyes screwed to the long cinder-
scuttles of their telescopes, will voice some doubt,
one hopes! This is too *lonely*. Heliocentric

humility's a habit hard to shake. Endowed
with what we've called "intelligence," or "powerful
intelligence," like-minded creatures, each an end-

point in a home-world's evolutionary raffle,
well, just *must* across the vasty deeps of space
and time yearn forth to find each other with awful

big radios. That's how the Book of Revelations
we knew used to read, rephrased so, π be praised.

3. Binary

My friend the Geometer, when asked if π
were in the sky or in the skull, replied

π's the pontification of a ratio.
Bisected, so, the circle: π. To show

that in a well-formed sentence, well, that's human, sure.
All language is. So ever since that fateful shore

of Lake Turkana where tongue forked, where first
flaking syntax split the atom into force

and mass, thing and verb, the copula
has groped to reanneal it: *this* opulence

is equal to the sum of *those* simplicities. . . .
So here's the mystery: across the placid

surface of the water a salt of stars
once scattered, hissing. Caliban stammered *Are*

stars. Then, *Look, look up at the stars!*

4. Prose Obtrusion Concerning the Keats Equation

Hold it there.

Would you say, whereas Beauty is a recognition of *the world*, that Truth's an attribute of *sentences*?

So that mysterious predictive gift of mathematics is precisely that of sentences like *I predict the sun will rise tomorrow*?—isn't *that* the leap that left the chimpanzees behind?—and adding time of sunrise just adds increment to the precision?

So that Platonic realm where mathematics *must* exist to be discovered by Ramanujan or Hardy or Arcturans tucked in anywhere in Time or Space is *just* that space where earlier equations live, like *love's a rose* or *tears are rain,* which Hardy's *and* Ramanujan's respective ancestors discovered independently?

That if in England *two men feed a horse, the horse stays thin,* the axiom would hold as well for two Tibetan yaks or fat Jurassic stegosaurs (assuming less that that's what the Arcturans use to carry mail than that, like us, they pinch their pence)—

That *that's* the realm where poems and equations likewise lie unspoken, quietly awaiting their *discovery?*

And so those famous instances where mathematics efflorescing on some blackboard purely for the play of it turn out to have a shocking congruence with patterns in the world is just *exactly* like the case where poetry is news before the news it stays?

That hadn't the acclaimed predictive potency of mathematics best be cast as *a reminder of forgotten shock*—the shock our shaggy kind must once have felt, framing for the first time well-formed sentences about the world that was, and then about the world about to be, and so extended human sensibility and thrust it forth as backward through the night of Time?

Yes, if diffidently.

5. Postscriptum

The aliens are back, incidentally. Astral
systems dropping planets like nuts in May. Exo-
biology leaps again into likelihood. A straw
poll proves the numbers may be multiplex.

No small relief for this slow versifier,
who, peering through this poem's decades-long zoom-
lens has seen what changes?—sapphire
heaven bleached of all biology?—*shazam!*—

and then revivified, less abruptly,
with a thought. In the same blink of the clock
the pupil of a black hole was seen to matter,
some dinosaurs grew feathers, and (this one for Ripley's)
Pluto got demoted from a planet to a rock.
Also my family died. Also I had a daughter.

III.

WORLD

ENOUGH

That parabola?

Galileo. See also:

bola, *and* hula.

The Problem

Feeling can't defend itself
in the court of reason
where every jot's accounted **for,**
minus frisson.

But logic has its own failures
in the bed of love,
(of which there's sometimes **t**hese days too much
speaking of).

The court of reason?—what **is** that
but a closed fist uncurled?
The bed of love?—what is th**at,**
but the world?

How?

As hours back up in the clogged drain
of the glassy water clock,

as the assignation of the wind and spun vane—
I'll love you as the foghorn vague in rain—

Magnetic swipe to the blinking lock
is me to you.

As cat's-paw cowlicks eddies in the spring grain—
that's my eye on you.

How camels catch the scent of far water clear
through obfuscating myrrh,

that's me for you. True:

I love you as the summer hammer
stuns the wold

(the *what*??)—
I tell you what:

I love you as our mer-
child loves the strong signal of the world,

as the whorled fingerpad loves Morse,
but more so. Worse.

Primavera

Sky a shook poncho.
Roof wrung. Mind a luna moth
caught in a banjo.

This weather's witty
peekaboo: a study in
insincerity.

Blues! Blooms! The yodel
of the chimney in night wind.
That flat daffodil.

Small birds exit skies
whoop, the way smoke, or Kleenex
up a Shop-Vac flies.

With absurd hauteur
new tulips dab their shadows
in water-mutter.

Boys are such oxen.
Girls!—sepal-shudder, shadow-
waver. Equinox.

Plums on the Quad—did
they?—blossom all at once, taking
down the power grid?

Foreboding

As one may infer, I've been laboring lately
under a looming recrudescence
of optimism.

The data support it, more than a little.
It has some of the marks of *mens
sana.* An abysm

of butter into which I've evidently fallen
resists dismissal, whether analytic
or summary.

The lessons are counterintuitive. Call in
no air strikes. Requite the ludic.
Swim. Marry.

Spring Wedding

IN FURTHER DEFENSE OF MARRIAGE, AFTER
C. LIGHT'S "RAYNAUD'S WEATHER"

1

Spring equinox today. Its augury:
two starlings, chill March harbingers, now exit
sky ceremoniously as—what was it?—Kleenex
up a Shop-Vac?— *Fuck this,* they hack. I scurry

into the bakery, wanting no biscotti.
Spring's—you've got it—*just around the corner,*
murmurs a plastic groom, grim as a coroner,
ankle-deep in icing. Judas Iscariot,

I elaborate stalely, hating myself only a little
less than everyone else, including the cashier
who wrings me up. *How's you?* He grins. We share
a glance. His mouth snaps shut. I'm volatile,

I know. I'm a trifle low. Outside, higher,
the traffic light is bucking on its wire.

2

Memory adjusts its monocle, correcting
for parallax. Now *two* grooms wade that cake,
Woozles, as it were, on a spinney. OK,
more luck. And have you lost your wedding ring?

Recall that ground-hole leaking yellowjackets
like sticky smoke between your sandals?—the wild
batting at the face, wrists outflinging like violent
blown kisses, and the filigreed ring's trajectory

into the blackberry patch, and dusk? All's well
that ends well: we slaughtered hornets in their hole,
borrowed a metal detector, dredged the thicket

against all odds—and undeserving, under owl-
light, got it back. Detecting love is holy
work, or so—salud, grooms!—we've come to think it.

Cave, Reversed

Sleepy stagger into the kitchen this morning, wherefore wife
blindingly backlit by the conflagration of the sunrise—
stunning!—and looking only a little less like Athena
than one might expect, on account of the peculiar little finger-motions
she's making with her outstretched hand. "You look like Athena, but thinner,"
I say, but she barely notices, so intent is she on these twitchy digitations
I don't understand. "I don't understand," I say. *"Rabbit,"* she replies.
"Duck." I turn into the shadows, where, unmistakably, *"Wolf."*

Wolf, Not Yet

Wolf, not yet undone,
lies abed with Riding Hood,
reading Jack London.

Canis

lupus:

There is no man in our moon above.
Our howl is the extruded second syllable of *eleutheria,*
the longing middle of *moon.* What else is there?
Weak Dog, despicable Dog!—who'd trade this for a chain.

familiaris:

Listen to old Shit-for-Brains
howl his hoary old dinner-for-freedom theory!
Ow-woooo! Really, it's too much. Now attend carefully, Wolf: not food; *God.* Not chain; *Love.*

Love Arrived

(Jalaluddin Rumi, from transliteration to imitation)

1

Mordeh bodam zendeh shodam

Gerych bodam khandeh shodam

Doulateh esgh Amad-o man

Doulateh pawyandeh shodam

2

Dead I was alive I became

(Crying; Tears) I was laughter I became

(Wealth; Fortune) love arrived—and I

(Wealth; Fortune) everlasting I became

3

Once dead I was. I woke alive—

Once tears I was To laughter turned—

The wealth of love   Arrived, and I—

Eternal wealth!—   That wealth became.

4

Dead I was. I woke to Life.

Tears I was. I turned to laugh.

Love came!— Flame's coin:

Wealth I was, whom Love reclaimed.

5

Once I was a corpse
capsized in a tear.
Love's lens righted me
in its larger sphere.

Coins lay heavy
on my lidded eyes.
Love came! The sun's doubloons
glinted a gold sky—

Once I was unalive.
Eternity was tears.
Love in laughter lifted high
the glass globe of years—

6

Once a thumbed quarter
under rain, or stream, or tears,
or other water.

Coin on the eyelid;
shadow-pressure on the wrist:
those darks Love undid.

Love came! Laughter joined,
and now the wrist is pure pulse,
now the sky, all coin.

Three Prayers for My Daughter

1. Annus Mirabilis

Tumbling octopus
traces little braille cursives
under a hand's press—

2. Cackle & Snort

Listen!—child, my lamb,
laughing in your sleep . . . I wish
I was there.
                  I am.

3. Little Crime

She mumble-spoke, her
voice a tremor (so it seemed).
Thinking then to spare

what was not nightmare,
but in fact a flying dream—
her first!—I woke her.

Gone World

Mixing pancakes this Saturday morning with my five-year-old,
I'm thinking how strange, how strange, the gone world.

Which gone world, then, since there are so many?
Well, not those famous ones
in which we didn't act
and ruined everything, or the ones
wherein we did, to identical effect.

Nor that Hall of Antiquities to come
where our placarded combs and costumes
all seem quaint,
our trash and grocery notes curated,

nor that lopped bract
of future possibility
where *nothing* is,

but rather the one I'm sensing so sharply now
its proximity fills me with such a mix of joy and rue
at the brain-beggaring quotidian squander of luck
dissolving in the howl of time,
right now, here,
the one gone world we're square in the middle of,
the one Maeve, too, may rue one day
as the gone world.

IV.

PERSONAE

Cubicle

Your neighbor?—that's Fred.

Subdued, but wild inside. Well-

dressed, in infrared.

Biography

Darling! I think our toddler **just** said AMOUR!
How his mother smiled, eyes **abrim**
with omen.

In fact, what the little sport **had** said was LAWNMOWER.
And that's how the years **ahead** would go, with him
and women.

For the Unitarian Martyrs,

or *She Vacuums in Fury*

Weather—
oh, it's bad. It's
like London during the Blitz
without the all-pulling-together.
Earth: scorched.
He: gone to the garage
on important business.
Dog: under the porch,
practicing is-ness.
Their thoughts rise like barrage
balloons.
Imagine
marriage:
once couched pasha and harem houri,
now Jack Palance
and the later Madame Curie.
Radiant are the moon's phases.
Inscrutable are forces and graces.

Breathe.

Muted

Barking through a tennis ball,
she's somehow not so menacing.

I wish her luck in all her quarrels
with postmen, passersby, and squirrels.

I think (like other not-quite-dumb pets'
plugged intentions) muted trumpets

everywhere should be applauded:
like the tycoon under audit;

Herakles, caught in a leg-lock;
city-mouse, trapped in an eclogue—

any plan gang half-agley,
especially when a sphere of play

obtrudes to soften duty's slog
or worse, ferocities enfogged

with folly, instinct, ignorance,
or any irritant that rends

the better angels of our nature,
even when it isn't major.

Ars

We like our poems (even verse!) if
they're transgressive and subversive.

We love their sexual unsober
maunderings, as of a toper.

We ever valorize an Other,
(whatever fashion deems our druther).

We love *de trop,* like Oprah, yet—
abjure the *inappropriate.*

Tattered Coat

Here arrayed in Kevlar tweed,
hectoring students concerning a screed
about which none of them cares a fig,
he mildly envies the thingamajig
they've hidden to diddle and swipe in their laps,
wishing his lecture were one of their apps.

Poetry Exam

Whinging toward its wan catastrophe,
our class redoubles on its syllabus
like Ouroboros gumming his own rattles.

What what what, we ask Professor Stuffy.
Who's your Sibyl? he Beelzebubs us.
Sibyl? We suppose his problem's marital.

He needs a steeper dose of lovey-dovey.
We all do. Poetry and school. All bells,
bells, bells. The words aren't what the song retells,

or so he says, adrift on his second coffee.
Pretty soon we all start crying. Labile,
that's us, lost, lapped in an end-term riddle.

Literary

Poet

He's not commercial.
He's a seeker after pearls,
clamshell by clamshell.

*

Critic

Abandon all hope,
he mutters, peering darkly
through the stethoscope.

Personae

Poet

Who goes on hands and knees
under sun, through sweet corn snow,
portaging his skis.

*

Mathematician

Excitedly leaves
just the equals-sign. The rest
erased by his sleeve.

*

At the Gym

Such ferocity
of face! Of fungicide! Of
men from the city!

*

On the D Train

Crumpled in his seat,
palms steepled between his thighs,
the cassocked priest sleeps.

*

Co-Boss-Boss-Boss

The farmer's matin,
hand cupped to mouth, calling cows
in fossil Latin.

Dispatches from the First War

1. Plans

December's

Hair: *cut.* Lexus: *wax.*
Shoes: *shine. Shave.* Insofar as
possible, *preen up.*

*

May's

Curl hair. Do nails. Wax
pantyline. Who's the fairest?
Go for no Pre-Nup.

Some Gods & Goddesses

Circe

No "feminine arts."
Just glass-and-cat-fur prickle
at a thousand yards.

*

Zeus; Hera

Re supper and rue:
She: *Zucchini soup tonight.*
He: *What did I do?*

*

Artemis

This is not occult.
If men do it, it can't be
all that difficult.

Mirror, Mirror

Is This a Dagger? or
The Tragic Prince Notices Himself
Reflected in a Steak Knife

The knife, thus flattered,
is made foolish. Sheathe the knife.
Tripe, the knife mutters.

*

In the Reflecting Pool

The Princess catches
her own eye. The Queen watches,
too, lips like matches.

Over Coffee

Kay is often getting cancer.
Conjured tumors swell and ebb,
like rumors do, when worry answers
night's alarming aches abed.

Cells dividing everywhere
below the microtome of Time
know DNA must needs beware
of anything but perfect rhyme.

So, Kay describes her symptoms. Patience.
Ghost sarcomas, waning, wax.
The morning's mortal intimations—
Kay's—again conturbat Jack's.

So breakfast conversation darkens.
Years go by. They've little time.
The pillbox rattles. Lines of Larkin's
flit uncomfortably to mind.

All patterns in a life may shatter.
Rarely is it really cancer.
Never mind the doctor's data.
Dread is dread, and love should answer.

Arithmetics

The first fall, into the world, winks on the sun.
This is the fall from nothing into one.

The second, into irony—O rue!
The child's chapel cloven into two.

The third fall, into sin, is more than fun.
It tries and fails to rhyme two back to one.

The fourth fall is apart: by toll and knell,
hale Integer becomes a decimal.

The last fall, into earth, is that which *I for
once* subtracts *for all* into the cipher.

Arithmetic is tragic. Which is why
the gods first taught us how to multiply.

V.

SELF-PORTRAIT

IN LEMON JUICE

Portrait of the Artist Post-op

Post-op, I'm pure style.
Mona Lisa dishabille,
Oxycodone smile.

Self-Portrait in Shorts and Furs

Summertime

I am the Vicar
of the Hammock! Lemonade!
Cloud-scud my ichor.

Hammock Redux

Mind leaks through the mesh,
leaving me behind. Filtered,
so to speak: pure flesh.

*

First Frost

The hose crackles, coiled.
Arteries too, maybe. I'm
thinking of the cold.

First Freeze

A kind of vigor:
pumpkins melting on the porch
evince new rigor.

Not Gone

A snowcloud just sheared
the mountain at its base. *What*
mountain? *I'm* still here.

Can-Do

I used to be damned effective, I actually
hear myself mutter to a young person in patchouli
patiently waiting while I kick my legs apart
and pat myself down for the fourth time, upward
from the pants pockets to the top of the scalp. Sheerer
fury, farther back in the line.

                              The cashier
alone, bored, fated, remains tranquil.
She knows I will prevail. My bank will
honor my debit card, once I stop
swiping it upside down. I will. I strop
it three or four more times. Time passes.

Where, I ask, O God of the Israelites, are my glasses?

Siri! Why Do I
Wear a Necktie?

1. A necktie is upward-tending, like a noose
   or a steeple.

2. A necktie is the ancient ceremonial dress
   of my people.

3. A necktie honors Our Lady the Muse,
   who is our occasion.

4. A necktie whispers low to me the news
   I'm not on vacation.

5. A necktie, for cleaning reading glasses,
   is handy.

6. A necktie irritates certain University dudes who're
   ostentatiously unaffected, and abhor
   a Doodle Dandy.

Le Soleil

L'état—c'est pas toi,
opines the shaving mirror,
in its grim patois.

So: if not the Sun,
what then? A cadaver? *Oui.*
But quite a good one.

In the Chamber of Periodontia

Although such diagnoses ought, perhaps,
to be left to mental health professionals
or their respective iPhones and their apps,
my dental hygienist, Miss Chanel's

convinced our interactions fall outside
the range of the abnormal. In this I trust
Miss Chanel. She gives me nitrous oxide.
(Trust me: next time, you too—try the nitrous.)

Our relationship is based on trust. I know
that this allows for feelings somewhat muted
when the steel probe dips below the gumline, *whoa,*
and the torso leaps as though electrocuted.

Did I say *feelings*? Muffled, I meant *screams.*
Just thinking of it makes me cringe. Of all
the things to write about! Find other themes,
I tell myself. Eschew the gingival.

I shall! And so vouchsafe my signature
and word and bond. Beyond, I only ask
that should I fail, may Miss Chanel be sure
to be at hand with canister and mask.

Return to the Organic Co-op,

or The Nuns of Gaia Wag Again

Their fingers. They are wise women, wise
to my ways.
They can see these in my eyes:

my nine-miles-per-gallon extended-cab Chevy pickup, cherry;
my respect for flirtatious witchery,
and what they call dairy.

I ask if they happen to have burdock root
and chaga fungal mushroom tea. The mood
changes. They give me high-fives, and call me Dude.

Thus, O Best Beloved, is the guise
of gender abandoned in the true church, which is Gaia's,
where everyone is sometimes still just guys.

11.99

The grocery store sommelier smiles.
I figured that's about where your palate's at,
he adds, as he rings me up. His decimals
amuse me: Eleven *ninety-nine* (?!) I call that
a twelve-dollar bottle. I always pick in the middle.
It's a trick I have. Keep the wallet in quality! Lordy,
who on earth—for *wine*?—I mean, it'll
be a chilly day in Mudville when I pay *forty
ninety nine*. Take my advice: Comparison
shop. Be smart. Don't just buy by the label.
People! It's appalling how manipulable
people are. Versace? Prada? Paris in
the springtime? Shop Gap. And for a sensible *frisson,*
try Montreal (I'd spring for the shoulder season).

Professor Stuffy Wonders

How can one tell insolent from stupid,
in a kid

whose range may be broad enough
to encompass both? It can be tough.

Lecturing into the uvula
of a yawn, you'll've

appreciated the wish
to distinguish.

Some questions are ineffable.
This one, eminently effable.

I meant that grade-
wise. But also in the alphabetically cognate

bilexical expression typically ending in *you* (passim),
and I don't mean you, I mean him.

Voir Dire *in Superior Court*

The best-dressed lady in the waiting room wants to know
what's going to happen to the ones who didn't show

up, because it isn't fair. The bailiff says he guesses some
are sick, probably. He says it's time. He says no hats, no gum,

follow him. We echo through to the far side of the frosted glass;
TЯUOƆ ЯOIЯƎꟼUꙄ sighs chilly shut behind. We gawk. They seat us.

There—that must be the guy! He's knife-edge creased and staid, in
a tie. Did his attorney tie it? He looks guilty as Satan,

as we all do, now. Now the judge tells us how it is.
We do swear. Now the lawyers give us a little quiz

which some of us fail. I fail it. I'm a Full Professor, for
God's sake. Glum, I slink clacking from the courtroom, Luciferian,

whorl down the long oaken staircase, echoing, out the brass hiss
of the revolving door, dour as the guiltless grass is.

Where is there justice in a world so full of suffering
elsewhere? And from which we've been so summarily dismissed?

It's Always Yourself That You Find in the Sea,

or In Dreams Begin Responsibilities

Yes, but what a shame.
What a wasted opportunity. Who'd
have predicted we'd wind up so blasted *constrained*

—in our *dream-life*? Why not flame
the guttering charcuterie,
when there's so little hell to pay? Steam

the mussels! What kind of lame
god designs a dietary dessert-cart? Screw Duty.
Think of what a man could *do,* in dream!

Why prosecute those self-same
thrill-killing scruples and pruderies
shackling waking life so deaconly in dream? Why deem

doom on harm-
less illicitudes
here, in the consequenceless Eden of dream?

Poor spanceled animal! REM-
revels wrecked, the supple pole-dancer suited,
zipped, chaperoned, a never, an ever nothing but a dream.

I'm Going to Have to Fire the Dream Master

Who fabricates our dreams? Well, we must, or
anyway some *part* of us. The mystery's
the utter
ambush of it: how, in night's apparent theater,
our fingers clutch the velvet armrests, our eyes
widen with surprise. . . . But how could we surprise
ourselves? And so,
we posit the cloaked figure of the Dream Master. Mine's got to go.

To be clear, the problem's not
in the theater itself, albeit shabby, old, ornate,
a nighthawk's haunt, a lonely man's demesne.
Nor in the mothy, slow unrolling screen.
Nor in the projection equipment—a little flickery, as to
that; still, the problem's with the Dream Master.
Ask Carl Jung, spooning *schlag* in the Schnitzel Platz.
The problem? The problem? The problem's with the *plots*.

Not naked, late. Not naked, late, at the lectern, hearing
one's name announced: Quantum Engineering
Colloquium—again!—the keynote speaker!
Not naked anywhere obliquer
than doing taxes after a day of doing taxes;
likewise dishes, any dully punishing repetitive praxis
requiring finer motor skills and better
eyesight than one possesses, like disassembling a carburetor
by dying flashlight, or like—oh, never mind.
These lines
are beginning to seem

a little too much like one of those damned, idiotic dreams
from which, dear audience, you may take
the Master's word, you are now requested to awake.

Self-Portrait in Lemon Juice

I considered calling this Swan Song of My Self,
but it seemed derivative, and I'm resolved
to be original in this, my Art,
if not in this, my Life, wherein, from start
to finish, top to bottom, late and soon,
I may be a bit of a William Steig cartoon.
And that's not bad! Of the many things I'm not—
Hero—Rogue—Roshi—Astronaut—
there aren't too many that I really rue.
I'm mostly glad I get to be with you.
But back to what to call this manuscript:
my title's strange, I know. All inks encrypt,
including blood. My*self*? *My* Song? Whose?
Lie: ***here writ*** *one no name in lemon juice.*

The Man in the Iron Magnet

Here follows, in boilerplate armor,
the story of my
MRI.

Confessions first: no history of _____,
nor _____, nor_____,
nor _____.

Privacy laws
require that I leave these fields blank. No claus-
trophobia. No metal in the body. Don the green gown. Clasp

proffered headphones. *You want for music Rock?*
Classical? Easy Listening?—a close look—
Classical for him, concludes the tech

so decisively I'm dispirited from the outset.
He explains the equipment, the magnet, the whatsit,
and its wattage.

I stop nodding.
Now I am dough on a tray sliding
into the—no, now I am wadding

in an immense siege mortar,
only a little shorter.
I shudder

into what I imagine will be a cool, sepulchral,
enveloping silence, an expectation cruelly
abbreviated by a sort of percussive lead-sap pulse

against the temples—a swaddled jackhammerish DUH-DUH
DUH-DUH-DUH-DUH-DUH, eliding
into more of a little-

boy noise, tongue-to-tooth,
machine-pistol style—T-T-T-T-T-T— though, in truth,
you can't make a sound like this with your mouth.

Just now the headphones begin to make sense: *Classical*
kicks in like a sickle
through the eardrum, resecting the so-called

ossicles. But never mind Stravinsky
skinning the auditory nerve: the raving
inscape

of my circumstance has magnetized
my attention at last. Slowly I imagine
somewhere in me something old, unnoticed,

forgotten, unconfessed,
some slight sliver of ferrous
metal stirring now in the ferocity

of the magnetic field, nudging north now.
I imagine iron-rich neuronal
cell-bodies arrayed like North Korean

infantry. I imagine—what?—*Muse,*
line please—a lone adverb scrabbling for its mousehole,
sucked back into a vacuum hose, held,

perhaps, by a cat. Jack-
hammered, Dvořak-
thrashed, I banish Disney and Marine-crawl toward the verge

of meaning: What might so large a magnet
not,
I think, attract? I make

an effort to reason out my own story's end,
the wherefore of it all—the why am I here?—but find,
in truth, to be serious for one undesigned,

naked moment—
you can't make a thought like this with your mind.

Leadership

The chimney is hoarse.
Under doors

the weather-stripping's loose.
Another lightning-flash. Grumblesome Zeus.

Twice I've woken with a wet nose in my eye.
Poor dog. He quakes with the sky.

It's just thunder, old pup,
I mutter irritably. His fallible pope.

I call him a cowardly cur.
I counsel courage.

I advise him to master his fear.
To hear

is to obey: he obeys.
Aye, aye, Boss,

he seems to say with his crazed eyes,
rigid, shaking uncontrollably on the floor

beside my bed. *I'll try.*
But you don't hear what I hear.

VI.

THE TERMINATOR

Memento

Rattle, rattle and dirt, Sky-
Eye,
Tongue milk,
Blank
Slate, blank—
Mind,
The baby!
Sweet baby,
That's the day you're born!
The bone in the old joke
Seemed barely apparent,
The chuckle that cackle whose point
Time sharpens—So? So what?
There's time.
Years!—See—
And now you're shaving:
Note that razor hands of the stopwatch strop too,
Sermonizing Tyrant Time. Whyever?
Just so (bored, half-
Dying) we must endure
No dotard nor crone but croak their quaint,
Endless, querulous, jealous, dyspeptic displeasures,
No doubt. No
Matter for us, though!—we're *young*: let
Crooked teeth grin! Wink the world's eyes!
Whistle past the headstones
Forever
And kiss a girl whose lips
Whisper love—

Mori

Whisper love
And kiss a girl whose lips
Forever
Whistle past. The headstones'
Crooked teeth grin. Wink: the world's eyes
Matter for us, though we're young. Let
No doubt, no
Endless, querulous, jealous, dyspeptic displeasures,
No dotard nor crone but croak. Their quaint
Dying we must endure,
Just so. Bored, half-
Sermonizing Tyrant Time—why? Ever
Note that razor hands of the stopwatch strop, too—
And now you're shaving
Years: see—
There's Time.
Time sharpens, so. So: what
The chuckle, that cackle whose point
Seemed barely apparent?
The bone in the old joke?—
That's the day you're born:
Sweet baby,
The baby-
Mind,
Slate-blank,
Blank
Tongue, milk-
Eye:
Rattle, rattle and dirt sky.

VII.

PORTRAIT OF

A GENTLEMAN

What Am I?

Cut forest?—a moor.

Drained swamp?—a field. Extinct sea?—

that's a prairie. Love?

Sword Upstairs

This tower is an excavated well
where robed scholiasts
crank a windlass.

*

A bucket ascends
from the abandoned benthos
bearing the heavy reflection of their peering.

*

Is this tower the chanter
of the sky's pipes, or the dry syrinx
of the dead bird of the sky?

*

Flutelike,
this tower is a tipped-up lava tube
exposed by erosion.

*

The tone windblown
over the hole
is a mouse on the snow of the spine.

A Winter's Tale

Once upon a time, un-icily
in Sicily (so, the old story nestles
hearthwise), earth stirred, birds stilled,
wind hearkened in the sterile wild, until
at last it caught a new sound. The sonnet
melted from a string. It was a bonnet
full of phlox and meadowsweet, of posies
gathered to a spring, a poppy-woozy
sweetheart-song, a lovely, lissome, lutely
thing. It was that—melodic and a little
ludic, before it was anything.
                       Then Pluto
up-plunging, chariot root-ripped from deep time plowed
the planet's skull, recalling a time when the crust was moony
with the craters of his coursers' hooves—how many
ages his dark banishment?—well,
he was back again, and he was hell.

Mantle-rock like pink jelly parting around him,
spattering stone like spume, he pierced the rim
of vision, seized sunlight by the hair,
and vanished with it forever. Blink. And there
you have it: the winter's tale, the tale of dawn.
Yours. Mine. All love's. Gone.

Sans Everything

As marketers might put it, Romantic passion
is a sort of package dislocation:

along with lip and kiss and dragging curve
of the gaze in its involuntary swerve

unto the lidded eye and pursed nipple
comes gratis Paris, and the Bay of Naples,

and the moon, all mildly discouraging
without it. Travel! What but perishing

in nature?—cheerless, parched, occluded, clouded,
unnourishing as sunshine is, without it?

Diptych

Quick, flame-slim, she'd lanced
flickery his egg-blown skull,
kohl wick to lit sconce—

*

That's how it works, lens
to quickening. That happened
upon a time, once.

Eros

She

White wristmarks. Cut wire.
Freed at last from the fleering
succubus, Desire?

*

He

Clearly not so saved.
Across endocrine chasms
widening they wave.

Diptych

Meeting on the Street, After Years

So. Much the same face.
And that ridged scar? Memory
fingering its trace.

*

Wrong

Gray heads shake. Hands wring.
The young presume it's *judgment*,
not *remembering*.

Triptych

What can he recall?
Sclera. Moon-swab on smooth skin,
cool as alcohol.

*

A curl of butter,
a little schnitzspahn of sun
sent in a letter.

*

Turn the pillowslip.
Dark side of the moon, cool breeze
against the cheek. Sleep.

Dream

The moons of his youth thudded underhead—
how?—
like coconuts in the hold
of—
of a rolling dhow?—

No: cannonballs, unmuzzled after a false alarm
beat the crew to quarters
in the midst of a storm
of something
other than water.

Apotropaic

He spins on the spit of sleeplessness, that the moon
may chill him equally on all sides.

Mummywise, he drags his sheets
as earth drags her tangled mess of tides.

He paints iambs on the ceiling. Blink
eyelash is the brush he'll use.

Think. Think. Think. Until he'll think
the sleep is not the least he'll lose.

Night Gallery

Night thoughts nose gar-like
across the ceiling, schooling
through moon and carlight.

*

Thud, thud: they drum dire
like shadows tied together
in a distant dryer.

*

Black pluck-and-rasp. Crow-
like. Crow crowbarred off offal.
The hell of Velcro.

Very Well, Thank You

Some people, asked how do they do, say, *Great!*
Others—*glad you asked!*—enumerate

aches. Assume the aches are general:
though lumpily distributed in neural

space, by genes or biographical
contingency, and subject too to the fickle

dumb vicissitudes of Time and the scything
clock—still, *general.* And so he thinks

the next time someone's kind enough to ask
how do he do, he'll readjust the mask

of courtesy, nod, and repeat the question
like a talk-show host, ensuring that the djinn

and poltergeists and pookas lurking
on the far side of the cell-wall hearken

well: he'll wish for them to mark his sang-froid.
He'll wish them shivering in his cold blood.

Luck

Though the eyelid's vein-blue
is a fool's refuge, since
in this world are needles and pins
sharp enough to puncture through,

still he'll close his eyes.
Still the blades of the world sling by,

whose little wind he takes for ill.
How from the throne of dudgeon he'll
imagine ought but luck's a real
measure of his stature. Still,

he dabs his brow with a little soot.
That's the way, in Lilliput.

Another Sunset

Time passed. He gained elegance
and lost force. Fears surfaced: scorched
linen underneath the chafing wish.

The world went shiny, ironed. Gone the gay glance.
Meanwhile, the whole day proved discouraging,
like cherries—were they cherries?—in an orange dish.

Oracular

A natural sentimentalist mugged into satire
by jovial gods and circumstance, he tired
of love as subject, if not as praxis, exactly.
His job?—Did he deserve to be sacked?
He might yet linger decades longer, unless
illicit cells should whistle up the sunless
lands a little sooner. Who's the fairest?
Prithee, Pythia, in thy swirl of sulfur,
tell us, was this man a force for good?

Forgot, forgot,
the Priestess gibbered
through the membrane,
For lo!—
then, whispering his name,
lapsed into Old Egyptian,
where he couldn't follow.

Portrait of a Gentleman

True?

A picture assembled from the wreckage
of memory. You shouldn't trust the rakish

angle of the hat, for instance—a fedora,
certainly, a Borsalino, or a

baseball cap with the peak cocked off
like they do, like a slung Kalashnikov

or a rogue erection dialing Venus:
that's *a man*. It'll evanesce;

they all do.

VIII.

PERSONAE

From sound sleep, Isaac

cries out! Again, Father's eyes

hung with icicles—

Blessing

Bless rage, lest it pass,
leaving them to the mercy
of the looking glass.

Sympathetic

The grand piano
in the resonant Great Room
rings, strings still astir

with the yelling. *Pain*
echoes also. *Child* its rhyme:
eye-white long upstairs.

Night Lights

This Apparition of Faces

In the coffee-shops,
cars, homes, beds, by the laptops'
fungal shine, life stops.

*

Still Life with iPhone

Eyes unquiet, set.
Think how shimmering rainbows
fade in a gill net.

Rigor Google,

or The New Universal Tableau Vivant

Neck: hunched, something like a defecating dog's.
Palm: supplicatory, crimped to the horizontal.
Gaze: blank. Note, though, the rigor isn't al-
together unrelieved, since thumb or index
crawls a continual little clitoral tickle-
wipe across the touchpad, *slip-slip*, like this.
One hypothesis:
this is a *genuine addiction*. Another: to call
it so (derogatory epithets
aside) would seem to presuppose a cure.
What cure? Ergo: together on the skewer
of that data stream which begs to pith us,
sympathetic, stunned, our brains aligned,
we shrimp into the future of the human mind.

Redirect:

But, really, *addiction*? Industry lawyers object.
They file a restraining order. They suggest *tech-
savvy*? *Necessary skill-set*? *Salutary multitask*?
No answer goes unquestioned now, so why ask
me? Why don't we *just check*?
I'm checking now. Consider my neck.

Ask Me Anything

Half a dozen boys surround **her**,
laughing uproariously. They **egg** each other on.
They make improper **suggestions**, which she counters
with impertinent repartee **from** Cupertino.
We're not afraid for her. She's **Oberon**,
she's Circe, she's Siri, who **knows** we know
no misery. The whole thing **gets** repetitive. The voice
changes. Now we're afraid **for the** boys.

Electable

One surprise they rarely failed to mention
was ordinary people's genuine
pleasure at finding him
so—well, *ordinary!*— in person, that is, affect-

wise, so *approachable,* so *easy to talk to.* Tension
vanished in the odd sudden of his boyish grin,
the metonym
for what came next, so predictably catastrophic.

Tell It to the Marines

What doesn't kill us
makes us stronger. So they say.
No Fear!—that's a plus.

How could it be wrong?
Ask the fireman with two kids
and much of one lung.

The Young See Age as Old-Fashioned

Somewhere, say, between a moral failure
and an avoidable foible. If the old fools
just took the trouble to go to the gym!
When you're hale, who's hearty enough
to fear, far-off, the little *puff,* the black silencer
screwed to the barrel of the future,
short or long as that may prove? Furtive
earwig of the unconventional cell,
slick of lymph leaking out, in answer . . .
no nicer, surely, the shy embolism
ambling through those precincts of familiarity,
the old elm-lined neighborhoods of the cerebrum.
Far better: battering the chest, sudden
as the D train taking its tunnel, *whump.*
But all this is just imagining the actuarial worst,
not *age,* which often comes first.

Books

3 a.m., he'll rummage his shelf
for a mirror he can stand.
Some book where he won't find himself
in mind unmanned.

His legs?—they've stalked off into the sunset
accompanied by what looks
he ever had. Love goes unsaid,
except in books.

And even books aren't what they'd been
when read with his kids at night.
It's been a little while since then.
Switch off the light:

Life is short? Time's a River?
Only Art is long?
We, knowing our loves will last forever,
know we're wrong—

That's Auden, of course, speaking of *death,*
the End to all our ends.
This isn't that. But that that comes
in increments.

Sentimentality

Age coughs and says, *Life drives you to your knees;*
Some call it prayer, some call it being clubbed.

The youth consults his heart: *lub-dub! Lub-dub!*
Strong! He says the sky is his to seize.

Which? *Each,* opines Chiron, wrinkling
his nose, whinnying. Tell what's between

Truth platitudinous and Truth stropped keen?
Not the words. Time trickles out that inkling.

Musketeers' 50th

They didn't need the name tags. They'd been like brothers.

The one with the Scotch and the spatchcock back, in overalls,
rejecting a white-collar future for which his folks prepaid,
once wagered all, in order to be *real*.

And this one, who, out of a cognate zeal
"went into teaching"—? What does he do, all weekend? He grades.
Roommates, in college. (Both on Demerol—

lumbar nerve roots, the one; carpal tunnel,
the other.) That one over there, with the mineral water?—well, AIDS,
we understand. Controlled, though he looks autumnal.

D'Artagnan didn't come. Intel
held its own retreat, in Santa Fe. So sodality fades
into the eternal.

Sunday departure. There won't be another.

Three Songs for Ithaca

Whose nose a rutabaga?
Whose chops show what he chews?
Who hirples down the ways where once
he sprang on mighty thews?

Did someone say *Ulysses*?
What happened to him? God,
see what the angels do for sport
before they stamp the sod?

The sword outwears the sheath, sure;
that doesn't keep it keen.
What's a *self*, and who says *I*?
and what could such words mean?

What do ash and clinker coal
have left in them of flame?
How ever can he have the gall
to answer to his name?

And yet he does. So did his crew,
when he mentioned the horizon.
So call him Ishmael, and wish
him one more wild surmising:

In selves again they'd sail the seas
(as Dante's pen predicts)
they'll thread the pillars of Herakles
in Canto 26—

2

Tennyson sniffs *it's sentimental*;
Argus barks *it's old*.
Penelope mutters *try a cento,*
since your pencil's cold:

3

Ah solving that one brings the doctors
in their long coats: run—run—
In the valley of the foxes
gleams the barrel of a gun—

Long coats trailing, doctors, priests
running over winter fields;
sky a clay-white in the east,
cornstalks like a creel—

Laughter is Satanic: thus
profoundly human (Baudelaire).
From the crow, a dust, a dust
of snow sifting through the air?

Trolls run scolding through the wood?
What's (dear heart, a change of mood)
different whined at than withstood?
Some part of a day I'd rued?

Tell me, is it something human?
Profoundly human: gills gaffed
blinking little to illumine:
Laugh the worst laugh ever laughed—

The Bad Joke That Depends on What?

That Everest of concepts (James Merrill)—
that's the rub, the subject, the dubless lub
of the heartbeat held at the hyphen. Here's the feral

snarl, the animal trapped in time, that lupine
look, that cornered look, the occluding corpse-coin
sliding like a manhole cover over the lapis

sky. This is the line that won't scan.
All those metaphors involving roads and rivers,
and spinning and spools and threads and scissors—the can't-

can't dance in the lap of luxury, lazuli, verso-
recto respecting Heaven and its blank unintentions,
the rectal thermometer of this cold, howsoever-

unavoidable thought: change, that wind chime, the far chime.
That's what I'm thinking, O Best Beloved, and it's about Time.

Memory Care

Long life

    loved

left poorer,

    ores of the word-hoard

played out, struck sparks

    arcless, anode-less

in an absence of oxygen,

    search conditions

becoming unfavorable

    over a rubble

of organic molecules,

    cooling ecologies

where the cursive script,

    clipped in its upswoop,

denatures, simplifies,

    snags an ankle,

dragging bottomward,

    wyrd-ward, equipped

with fire-axes and sledges,

    lecturing ourselves in rhyme

about the notional

    nature of the good life

loved

    afterlife long.

Afterlife

On time to the strike of a silent bell
inside the chapel of the cell

the heretic is whispering.
Spittle flickers on his lips.
The lizard into shadow slips,

the winter wasp staggering.
Soon the lymph begins to leak.
Telephones commence to speak

the stars back to their westering.
Earth laps up above the shins.
Another afterlife begins,

which sometimes feels like lingering.

Pax

So, Love, when that celebrated clarifier,
chemotherapy, calls back—*for us,*

this time, with his white, apologetic smile,
his porcelain saucers of carbolic acid and lye,

his banker's insistence on reality-based accounting,
well, we'll want these chances back. The canting

hours, the fund of unkisses, the mind, unMidas-
like, immodest ever in miniature amidst

the molten metals of the morning, his brazing-iron
of petty anger held against the pure ore

of the already-gold world.

IX.

WORLD

TOO MUCH

Hobbes obtrudes. Rousseau

recedes. Father the mirror

mouths I told you so—

The Pythia Goes Too Far

Goddess, give it to us straight —

Right:

The males are dominance engines. They trade in pain.
They will do anything. They think with their pricks,
which tell them: assemble a terminal moraine.

Females are complicit. They hunger leanly.
They trade sex for security. They are pure praxis.
They smell Time; it's what they fear most keenly.

Review: copulation is human being. Culture
is talk and handshake. Half: wet handshakes.
Half: dry handshakes, equally worthless. Killjoy

Hobbes had it right. The Great Apes cannot speak,
and yet they lie. The mirror shows shrike,
ichneumon wasp, The Doctor's perfumed beak —

Enough! It's wrong — maybe not even right —

When I Lose

When I lose the heart's long rhythm—

When I have fears that we may cease,
another genus losing its single species,
then I lose speech.

Not that it's likely, wholly,
or tomorrow, necessarily, but we know the road,
revolting with its bones.

And now that the pert, postapocalyptic
entertainment trades have trod the pocked
planet raw, wreaked every dystopian havoc, lopped

each greening branch imagination might yet
proffer to its dove. . . . We watch our midget
politicians wave their tiny arms. Jets

pepper forth. The wind is thick with them.

Money; Worse

Money is killing the world, you worry?
Re: murdering democracy, oiling the shore,
shearing the rain forest,
fracking the aquifer,
quaffing the rainbow from the bloom of the future?

Phht, the Arrow of Dream.
Drum hope, we're thinking. Draw straws at which to clutch.
Cash rules, they say—but wait: fresh news
now seeps up from the interior, the shattered hypocaust
of History, I mean, an omen:

Money hath a master. Money to unreason stands:
hands down, *Ideas trump Money!*
(Moony hope stabs the gloaming. . . . Long nursed,
nascent optimism stirs. . . .) But is this good news, really?
Rifles crackle in the nearing distance.

Family Men

Listen—radar domes
ululate. A dry wadi's
silent muezzin.

Remote robot drones
drum mayfly-like on windows
in Arizona,

whose pilots have dreams
they don't share with their widows
in the dinner zones.

Jeopardy

Clay terrarium.
Trees like smoking runes. The roar
of artillery—

—And all that barbed wire,
right. *What is the Western Front,*
in the First World War?

Searchlights scissor sky
plated black with bombers. Low
engine-drone. Sirens—

—This one's easy. *What's*
(we know this from the movies)
London, in the Blitz?

Concussed, the Humvee
bucks, shakes itself like a dog.
Screams in the convoy.

Hmmm. Afghanistan's
possible. No: *What's Iraq?—*
the clearer instance.

Vestments viols side-
ways-storming plate glass cats car-
doors dads deicides

burqas burghers chipped
bits bullets spalled concrete skeet
clot keens cloves giblets—

This is no poem.
This is a little too close
to what we call home.

Time Change

Here: POTUS holds codes.
They tingle in his pocket
under Dakotas.

Here: geeky cyber-
warriors crunch cheese Cheetos
over bruised keyboards.

Here: plastic sabers
across snoozing nominees' knees.
There: Siberia.

There: vodka defends
the spider-holes. Damp silos.
Rust streaking tail fins.

There: buzzard-throats bend
over their wilted map. Teeth
long. Breasts beribboned.

Where, the bezoar,
Plutonium? Click *Gotcha-
stan*: click *Grand Bazaar*.

There: no god but God.
Click there. Click here. Click the speak-
easies of Riyadh.

Here: POTUS holds codes.
They tingle in his pocket
under Dakotas.

Homo faber

Trinity

A disk of fused sand.
Contact lens floating on the
future? See *Glass, stained.*

*

Lament for the Makars

O whittled world. Cold
cadmium wands. Dark metals,
our unpaid wergeld.

Diptych Unspoken

A scrap of rainbow
caught in a cobweb? That's soul
in nerve aquiver.

A sky akimbo
in transmuting isotopes?
That's never-never.

Easter Wings

Where else but Airport
Security, coffee-deprived, bored?

We're under Apollo's lyre,
here (Auden, again): dire

order is the line we hold.
We're told

no liquids.
Now I am randomly selected.

*

Preferring Hermes,
my students assure me

poetry, too, is characterized—
terrorized,

one might say—by what they menacingly
call semantic indeterminacy,

or instability, or contingency,
or chance.

Usually they call it *disjuncture.*
Unsure

of what they mean, exactly, I prove it,
removing

my shoes.
What shows

on the full-body scan—
no wish to imagine.

*

The whole security line's a campus
akimbo

with collegiality. It's mid-semester;
most are

flying off to copulate
in Mexico. Good plan! Our pilots

arrive carrying briefcases. They skirt
Security,

flashing badges.
Unsuspicious,

I am deemed no Saracen.
On a blaring TV, Risen

Christ is advertised:
I infer

Easter. Agnostic,
I believe in no hand on the joystick.

*

Instability characterizes the situation.
Wishing

it away, I infer
fear,

and wonder about its half-life.
Lufthansa lifts off

under me. The set sun disinters,
a fanned cinder.

The Pacific Plate aches north another inch.
Ancient Japan leaks cesium into her grandchildren.

The saltwater
is contaminated with tears.

Embolism

Zero—little clot
astray in the data stream,
lights in the wrong slot.

Now try the lights. Now
try your bank. Look up: contrails
scar sky. Why? What now?

X.

ROME

Sales spike with the "toll."

Again guns flood the system

like black cortisol.

Civics

As kids we're taught it's safe as Pyramids,
unshakable and permanent amidst
a sordid history amok with ids

frocked in all those lesser-*ocracies*
the mind of man has proffered up, all crazy,
and all doomed to end up like the auk.

(Plus, it's *Athenian*, we think. Pax Plato;
smart man, but no one bats a thousand.) Later,
though, we see it's really safe as plates

awhirl on broomsticks. Trump! And now we're all
ears, waiting for the fools with whom we've quarreled
to aggregate a mob for all the world

like all the mobs in storybooks: the slaking
rage that spatters from the joke when Loki
rules the moot: *we thought it was OK.*

Thought nothing could go really wrong. We thought
the fire we played with wasn't all that hot.
We thought we could control it, and could not.

What More It May Take

They had brilliance, wisdom, Latin, knowledge, pluck.

They copied the Roman in the Capitol.
For the Cathedral, they copied the Goth. It all
bode well. They took the best, when the best was known.
For the rest, they'd see. They'd pray. They'd throw the bones.

Against anticipated folly of the demos
they set *Education,* and crossed their fingers. Doubt
obtruded, but *Liberty* proved polysemous,
leaving room to leave a little out.

Against the tip toward tyranny—the alpha
problem, ever our threat, again we note—
they set a Cerberus against himself,
in hopes no gnash would ever catch a throat.

And there you had it: the Great Experiment,
designed by men who knew what peril meant.
Foreseeing ways their dream could go amiss—
did Jefferson never once imagine *this*?

Could it have been they weren't acquainted with fools
as vulgar and venial, as equally unfit?
Could it have been that they failed to frame the rules
no future umwelt might discomfit?
                                                    Spit.

For luck.

Boy Toys

Look at the tiny senators!
they almost could be real.
Their action-figure joints so smooth—
see how they kneel!

Their smiles are a little rigid, maybe,
but their stomachs sure are strong.
Let's try to remember, when the Big Boy's gone,
who's gone along.

It's Not What They're For

1. Aesthetics

The Constitution guarantees our gun.
Are we not men? We like *bang bang*. It's fun.

Plus, who am I and who are you to fool
With the Founders' fancies? Guns are *beautiful*.

It's fine the Founders thought to make Amends.
The Second earns our hottest hot Amens.

Though we might also wish they'd guaranteed
The freedom of unimpeded movement. Speed

is fun. Are we not men? We like *vroom-vroom*.
The elephant was not yet in the room

to unrestrict my motor vehicle,
so I could shout it isn't cars that kill,

it's men. Are we not men? We like our fun.
Don't pry it from our fingers till we're done.

2. *Footnote*

If anyone knew what *to be a man* meant
it was the Lord (God love him), whose Commandment—

the Second on his Tablet, thumbed to *Txt*—
was: no force fiercer than aesthetics, sexed

as it sometimes is, as it is in the case of guns,
whence sins of the fathers ventilate the sons.

3. *Moral*

It's not what they're *for,*
it's what they *are*. In the palm.
Sweet whisper. Like war.

Devil to Ares

Drink? Thanks for asking. What were we— *War?*
War's not working so well, anymore.
We used to be able to count on it to pull
the best and bravest out of the breeding pool.
You could always depend on the finest, fiercest one
to scamper up the muzzle of an automated gun,
whilst on the blitzed Home Front—well, self-
sacrifice was a concept you could *sell.*

I'm sure you're right. All's changed. Hostilities
just aren't what they used to be. A sterility's
set in, I'd say. Not only the random explosives,
but the gas . . . the drones . . . Jesus, Mary, and Joseph,
nuclear suitcases! Autonomous weapons systems!
Where's the *aristeia?* I question the wisdom—

Still, we have to adapt. We need a "flexible
response" (excuse the scare-quotes). Exit polls
suggest that never in the history of human conflict,
providing we shall have neither failed nor flagged,
and assuming of course that current trends continue,
may so many owe so much to so few.

Europhile

I've become increasingly aware

that, despite our "regional cuisines," Europeans still eat better.
More than that. More than health care. Even their toilets
work better, have you noticed that? Hot water's
quicker and more abundant there. Let's
not pretend their windows (tall, casement-style,
with brass fittings) aren't more functional and elegant.
Their cities are *cities*. They do not sprawl. I'll
bet you a dollar the war of all against
all doesn't fairly describe their concept of economy.
Also, having for so many consecutive generations drowned
in their children's blood, they're weary of that. The enemy
is that. They understand that. We ought to write that down.

Where, you say. *Where*.

#Satyr

(EMPTY PLINTH WHOSE PLACARD READS: *THE VATICAN MUSEUMS HAVE REMANDED THIS STATUE TO PERMANENT STORAGE IN THE BASEMENT.*)

Removed from the plinth
he leaves a leer on the air,
where he's been seen since.

Say *no*. Just say *no*?
Don't they know who he is, old
Papposileno?

Silence! *De jure*
rules. What's real? Counsel's advice:
shoot the messenger.

This marble prism,
scattering human nature.
The god is what is.

204 B.C.E.: *A New Cult*

That the Carthaginian monster be expunged from Italy—

On authority of the Senate and the People of Rome,
certified by the priesthood of the Books of Fate,
and with the blessing of Delphi, a black meteorite
called Magna Mater was sought in Phrygia, conveyed
to the city, installed on the Palatine Hill. Her rites—
(odd garb, mad dance, ecstatic street parade,
the frenzied trance of self-castrating acolytes,
and the like) contrasted strongly with the staid
traditional religion Romans knew. Decried
at first, the new cult would assimilate.
Rome changed around the stone. Tell now: in light
of Hannibal's defeat, did this price paid,
albeit in advance, seem slight? A sleight
of history: and then not-Rome was Rome.

But *What Was the Cybele Meteor?*

Trojan origin? Lost lodestone?
Stolen holy of holies, religious
pillage? Purling bullet
spalled off some exploded planet,
pollinating Rome's worst nightmare?
Mere metal-rich extraterrestrial substrate?
Stay fruit-pit Big God gob-spat
phhht through Jupiter's gravity-sling,
skirling an eon-long careen
around the solar system,
destined to oxidize over Phrygia—
jaw-dropping, jewel-bright trajectory—
jarring to an ox-cart-crawl
crossing elephant-haunted Italy?
Little ort of Unreason?—Asian excess!—or
orison to the Great Mother,
rather: Gaia Protectress
blessing meteor-struck
Republican Rome
from her time of need unto
a time of tyranny?
Uterine wisdom wicking luck? Or
uranium seed
needled into a tumor,
ticking?

Helical

What is the Covenant? I fain would learn.
That's the handshake deal we struck with God,
wherein we agreed to grovel in return
for being named His Favorite Tetrapod.

What are the Homeric Hymns? I ask.
These are a record of the consequence
when Middle School emotions wear the mask
of Heaven. Heaven knows how that tale ends.

The double-helix of the West!—two strands,
rooted in old pots, long intertwining,
rise like smoke from fire in the Holy Lands,
rise like spinal nerves whose braid, defining

what soul dipped in earth can know—*life*—
whose wick we may cut, once we have enough knife.

Necessity

Re: *rain*, and the long theological stalemate
concerning its origins, a tale Talmudic
in nuance, Homeric in scope: this was classic Lachrymism
vs. vulgar Micturism, paired like the chromosomes
of our tradition. At stake: the nature of Heaven.
At issue: the source of life, in rain. In the event,
the conclusive stroke was dealt by the geochemists,
who by the closing years of the last century had amassed
data demonstrating the identity of rain and tears
to the 97th part, in a theorem which survived rigorous peer
review. By contrast, undistilled urine assayed
as correlative only to the 60th part, notwithstanding acid
precipitates, adjusted mathematically, allowing for a salt-
correction constant. The question was settled.
Of course, rear-guard Micturian die-hards and tenured
professors with careers at stake and minds too inured
to the old way of thinking continued to cavil. Attempts
to impeach experimental procedure failed. Die or adapt:
the science proved solid. And we were happy, were we not?
Sure, though Heaven knows one cannot count on Nature
to conform to human preference, none could deny
a private relief at the proof: the tragic mind of Adonai
might henceforth be petitioned. The vulgar Eiron
was cast down. Earth bloomed. Heaven wept pure thereon.

*

The droughts began in the second decade following.
Crops failed in successive seasons. Fields lay fallow.
We attempted public supplications, under open skies,
the sadness of our plight sharpened by rhetors, our cries
drawn taut by singing masters, our kennings
pitched by poets to the asymptote of pity, razor-keen.
Still God withheld His tears. We sacrificed.
We burned incense, livestock, houses, towns. We revisited
more ancient screeds. With stricken reluctance
unimaginable to any human not so fated, we looked
into the red eye of Necessity, and agreed to begin
sacrificing the children again.

*

We will not be judged. Our lamentations exonerate us. Arraign
ineluctable fact in the court of the real. Physics
was never of our choosing. We must have rain
or die. One must live in the world as it is.

Questions for Delphi

1

Sing, Muse—

              If we, while thinking a thing untrue,

try it on the face of the world,

willing the lie may ameliorate that future

fissuring sheer before us, that black beckon,

begging only that our poppycock not seem too arrant,

our rants and ritual mutterings and queer ceremonial suits too risible—

Sibyl, speak: tell me, when we do that—

                            do we do right?

2

To repeat:

When drives dress themselves in a few abstractions,
bridle themselves with a few thready strictures

and get themselves promoted to the prefrontal cortex
salaried as *ideas*, diacritics

over serotonin, so to speak, sophist
shaking his shaman's rattle in the high glass office—suffice

it to say, we have *civilization*.
When such *ideas,* exhaled against the sky's silvering

precipitate in clouds. . . .
That is, when ideas graduate as gods,

garbed in the advanced fashions of the upwardly mobile,
braille-bright, labile

as one would expect of a personified whirl-
wind, as it were—

well, that circle would seem complete.

3

In a more up-to-date case:

When we make of a magma and mantle planet
a guise called *Gaia,*
when we propose of her gas-lit slime-thin skim of biology

a god to adore,
adorning our postures and censures with sanctimony
in Her name

do we vouchsafe a future for our children?
Chill
the answers

on the question's face.

Madonna in Blue

An aneurysm in the sun, a gravity-wave.
A beating of rainbows against the windowpane.
The angel, a lunge, an ejaculation of lilies, kneels,
knowing. Nods past her upstretched palm: he *knows*.

Against her will her womb suborned by a god,
incubating a future so far-fetched and odd
how could its knowledge from its power culled
but show? Her pose: a cobalt spring recoiled.

And what should a watching voyeur feel then? Rage?
The Ovidian horror? Again the seized girl, again Kore
covered by ungoverned god, as known is by strange,
as Past by Future—*this* one, where there are no angels,
no seraphim but us, its mobbing choir?
What *happened*? Didn't the painter's brush catch fire?

The Birth of Tragedy

Syntax rides mahout on an ancient python,
wrestling that sine-wave till it's kenned
a superscript, encoded in the writhing
muscle of emotional intent.

And so *Pan sapiens* invents *tomorrow*,
and *yesterday*, and *Rome*, and *maybe not*,
and all the grammars swaddling his sorrows
in that abyss between what is and ought.

But in the petri dish where glass pipettes
drop glucose *here*, and *here* a drop of lye,
the little one-celled creature senses death,
and edges toward a future otherwise.

The Greeks knew this, who copied faithfully
the diptych of the ancient primate mask:
one *Yes*, one *No*. Hath holy Pythia
another answer, ever? We can ask.

Meanwhile, in the Pantheon, a moment later
made its difference. As so it did to Rome.
As so, to moon: see now, *the terminator
cuts across her like a microtome.*

XI.

VANISHING

Another moon—sssh—

hear crescent, *then* crescent?*—that's*

the sound of the shears.

Follow-up Questions for the Pythia

Does money make greed possible—
the germ, itself, of the sin?
Or simply make greed visible,
as confetti would, wind?

Did syntax set the human mind,
with music, painting, dance?
Do verbs spin the cogs of time
or only track a trance?

What's fire? A magic hat?
Does *burn* mean *oxidize*?
What flickers in the ziggurat
of carbon, in the eyes?

Is love love without embrace?
Can love live in reserve?
May certain values be their face?
What's courage, lacking nerve?

I wish I knew. I'd bet good money
on dreams without a snoozing,
dreams like some folks, who, unfunny,
sometimes are amusing:

sometimes the world's hidden fees
are queasy in our sleep;
sometimes they say it won't be easy
when they mean it won't be cheap.

Meanwhile, I'll watch a bunch of birds
kerfuffle down a breeze
astir like metal in the purse
to vanish in some trees.

Good as a Mile

The sky replies to questions posed
by human senses, only those.
The sky is coy that way. It gulls.
It flimmers to the human pulse.

As nights are that which is not days,
the mirror dimples to our gaze.
Cast and casting; call, response,
candle daylit in the sky's sconce—

Askance I saw it, then. How else?
(the steering-wheel was carousels)—
our complement is all outdoors;
a fair likeness, too, of course.

Here's a story, by the bye
of how a mote caught in my eye—

*

Today, driving, I glimpsed the moon.
A half-moon, to be more precise,
small smear on an afternoon—

And all of a sudden as it struck my eyes
it wasn't *the moon,*
man-tracked, myth-worn, penny-sized,

nor retinal nick, nor rhyme on *rune,*
but a rock on the windshield, white as the Christ,
an immense, nonce, fully round

planetary thing,
locked in a gravitational partner-swing
with everything.

*

Not "the moon," I'm telling you! Not a pale communion-wafer,
but an astral entity, curving, stippled, dented, an entire rock
sky yawing steeply away on the shadowed side, adrift. It was
bigger than gibbous. It looked sensational as one of those
artist's impressions of "Callisto rising, as seen from the surface
of Ganymede." It felt like science fiction. I almost swerved
the car.

*

Can I hope to make you see this as I did?
Haven't you, too, yawned late, to witness—what,
some astral smirch or other—forecast aurora—
aphelion eclipse—the guaranteed closest approach
of Mars, or Jupiter, or any dirty comet
pinking its horizon, per advertisement,
commending mind to empyrean,
murmuring wan words like *there?*—then
there? forefingering night—well, haven't you?—
and, just as in this failed linguistic instance,
missed it?

What Am I?

On a blue glass beach
a prehistoric shark tooth
you can't reach?

The Candle in Daylight

Only look askance. Can't
see it otherwise. Crescent
on the wrought sky-sconce—

flakelike paring—moth-
wing—windscreen with wet petal—
glacial tablecloth's

crisp fabric cobwebbed
in what icewater-pitchers
aclink with ice cubes

do: *that* hyaline,
membranous skirting, unsquare
whirl, linen alive

with it, the flicker-
of likening, the not-there
of it, the for-lack-

of-words delighting,
blue future's egg-tooth, truth, the
candle in daylight.

Slow Blue

As time's canopy
where the cut tree shivering
slightly can appear

stopped: that blink eon
before stupendous motion,
so this saurian

slow blue, the heron,
when the breast muscle ignites
its deep furnace here,

and the tidepool soughs
and stirs, and the long eyelid
of the wing lifting.

Plants, Animals

Consider this:
if the fibrillating willow,
water as it mostly is,

is a sort of slow
fountain,
that leaves all of us, aloft, alow

—if, granted,
swifter over the ground,
moreover—

more of a river.

Other Water Clocks

Rings

Drips from a shipped oar
behind the gliding dory:
little orrery.

Prairie

Gone sea. Corn stubble.
The tidal rip's strong here still,
if resistible.

Hulk in Estuary; Horizon

What's disorganized
from wood boat to nails in mud?
Old wild surmise.

Moon and Stars

From Tree Full Moon

Luteal (if not
at all unlutely) lifting
from its little net.

*

Dryad Impossible

A starlit forest's
photosynthesis?—slight surge,
sugar to the root?

Tidal

Patient, the sea-seiche,
sorting according to size
cobbles down the beach.

Here's Ocean's wheeze—seas
clicking into sentient speech
in Demosthenes—

Think, then, tide on stone,
self-organizing no end.
Large; small; smaller; none.

And More Vivalding

1. Symphonic

March upcrumples expostulate sky
like a mongoose on a doily,
welcoming sun as thumb to eye,
while treating robins roily.

Green ferns bend a breeze
under summer's awning;
windows wide in libraries
and books and hammocks yawning.

Autumn whooms in fire first,
sumac, oak, and maple:
napalm bloom soon doused in mist,
and rain straight as cable.

Solstice doldrum, wool-chill,
the world in cold pajamas,
her icicles all prism-still
as air is, after hammers.

2. *Redirect*

What's the point of penning verse
like this? Why not erasures?
Something edgy, fresh, fierce,
on sex, or race, or glaciers?

If we'll just slice the spinal nerve
the sun'll settle still.
It won't bank, swoop, or swerve.
We'll study it at will.

That's good advice. Cerebral. Apt.
All rhyme I'll soon rescind-O . . .
I'd do it now, except I keep
glancing out the window.

The Graving Yard

FOR JOHN DELANEY

1. The Oceanographer

An ocean's pumped back in. Immense placental
engines labor. Lubbers, we have shore-leave until
midnight, when we'll board, too. Mantid cranes
wipe sky. One sways up the submersible,
belling. More cable-whine and whistle. Vessel groans
against its wharf.
                          Below, empty sample-
bottles chatter a little on a steel bench.
At 2°C in a berth below in the black benthos
of the napping oceanographer's dream, crimson
tubeworms, bacterial mansions, impossible basalt
spires outgassing. Archaeozoan something-or-others. Drumskin
lithospheres slipping on their puddings far from the Esquimault
Graving Yard, in a watery, igneous elsewhere, in a sherbet
of ammonia, maybe, on the second moon of Jupiter.

2. *Anaerobe*

You, yolk
too, sound
in the steel bubble
submersible.
Touch swollen tonsils:
gill slits.
Inside eyelid: slimelight.
Cheek: shark.
Here foreknown
we've dived
down dawnless
microbial snows,
phosphor blue to blue-
black, to black.
Fend fish. Find
the saffron curb
of the sulfur vent,
veering voiceless
again into the segmented,
swaying, white,
toothed tube-
worm, Time.

If One of Us

—*should die,* she laughs, *I shall go to heaven,*
which sounds not only confident, but gallant,
too, until you think about it, given
the difference in our ages. A land
of unlikeness. What would that be, for her? A blessed
realm, I suggest, turgid with ski instructors, solar
energy entrepreneurs, and software moguls
with mighty abs and intelligent eyes, their opalescent
intentions confessed in wines aswirl, from cellars
certified in France, n'est-ce pas? *My goal's
otherwise,* she says, growing serious,
which is the last thing either of us wants. Thin
smiles ensue. The land of unlikeness, eerie
as ever. But *really*? she says. Really? What, then?

Vanish, then? Live alone among strangers?—
tap an umbrella on the porches of old hotels,
the kind with tea-rooms and oaken bannisters
and baths down the hall, anywhere not Paris? Oslo,
maybe, Pittsburgh . . . Pittsburgh?—no, Tangiers . . .
Which would it be? *Hygge* by the purpling Jøtul,
watching fjord-fog crawl, or swirling anisette
in a sweating glass on a lime-white, blinding terrace, slow
ceiling fan batting at the noon stun?

                             Tinctures
of the fountain pen, that water-clock: you'd tell
it longhand, in a blank book titled *Finisterre,*
that phantasy of anywhere not home, solo,
quotidian, fossicking that lifelong midden,
dabbing at doing what I said I'd do, and didn't?

Love

Bees thick enough to cast
a shredding shadow on the grass.

Migrating birds on Doppler radar.
The Little Bear above the Greater.

The full moon muzzy through the fog.
Droplets off a shaking dog.

The seconds off the clock's éclat . . .
Like anything particulate

these things have shapes, but they don't have edges.
So, what does? Give me a *such as:*

The razor, slicing, feels no skin.
The noun seems neither out nor in.
Where does anything begin?

Parting Glass

MAEVE

Here's to the leopard who'd launder his spots,
the proactive traveler packing some prunes;
here's to gazpacho in coppery pots,
here's to the helium bobbing balloons.

Here's to the moons of Jupiter, here's
to the whistling steeplejack waving his cap.
Skoal to starshine, sharp as shears,
and the heat on the hearthstone upholstered in cat.

Here's to the pollster who's wondering whether;
here's to the whiskery frost on the pane.
Here's to your shadow, and here's to its tether;
here's to the thuddery roof under rain.

Woof to your mother and thump to my sons,
and kisses for maidens, their aprons askew;
salutes to some strangers I may have met once,
and a glass for my ghosts and pookas—boo:

Toast to my tailor whose needle's bespoke,
for Adam and Eve and the coop that they flew;
clink to the mirror whose dubious joke
is leaving me less of a him than a who,

who hopes you'll perceive, Maeve, it's hardly adieu
(and this is the magic, all mirror and smoke)
when the glass is the goblet he's raising to you.

Vanishing Point

CAROL

The kissed fingerpad
touched wet with wine
orbiting a crystal rim: ring,
ring,
a shuddering wrung into rhyme,
a moment's longbow
drawn to vanishing.

Annus Mirabilis

In this place still called *The*
Pantheon,
where once upon

a time it was no pinhole *camera*
obscura clamorous
with French, American

and Japanese, we wed
with no priest but old words
and a witness. What

place was that? Not this,
exactly. Thus
is the analog light-stream digitized. *The*

(we said) *Pantheon,*
and kissed therein. Then
Time, the god-yawn.

Signs

The Perseids are cinders, now,
the summer stars dissolved in wine,
the conflagration of the bough
extinguished in an Autumn rain.

Orion's back in the black. Behind,
where moonshine suffocates in cloud,
sling other nouns, like Charles's Wain
(or Bear, as some prefer, or Plough).

Below—blind. What words occlude!
Stars tangle in the trees' runes,
rising, setting. . . . Our ups and downs
were never in their lights aligned.

Mind how the breeze outside bassoons
and susurrates this cozy house.
It swoons like a tuning fork whose tines
twist in wind, or a wand whose dowse

divines love, instead of water,
divines love, instead of future,
divines nothing in these signs.

Acknowledgments

I'm indebted to the S. Wilson and Grace M. Pollock
Endowment at the University of Washington for support
during the decade of this book's assembly. I'm especially
grateful to colleagues and friends at the Friday Harbor
Laboratories, whose hospitality has meant much to me, and to
the Helen Riaboff Whiteley Center there, where many of these
poems were written or chastened. For those rigors, salutes to
Carol Light, Jason Whitmarsh, and Cody Walker, to whom the
book owes much of its shape. For the rest, a grateful wave to
Deb Garrison, Todd Portnowitz, Bonnie Thompson, and Rita
Madrigal at Knopf.

Warm thanks to Mott Greene (my Geometer, in "The Drake
Equation") and Adam Summers, for long and patient science
advisory. Also to Sholeh Wolpe, who walked me through the
literal translation of the Rumi poem, and to Christopher
Merrill at the International Writing Program, whose auspices
in partnership with the U.S. State Department made that
occasion possible.

The scraps stitched into the cento on pages 132 and 133
originate in Larkin, Auden, and Frost.

Finally, I'll thank the editors of the following magazines,
where many of the poems were accepted for first publication,
some in earlier versions or under different titles:

Agni: "Muted," "Leadership," "Another Sunset"

The Antioch Review: "Cave, Reversed" originally published as "Chiaroscuro," "*Pan sapiens* 2," "Questions for Delphi," "Follow-Up Questions for Pythia"

The Hampden-Sydney Poetry Review: "Cubicle," "Blackboard," "Farm," "D-Train," "Gym," and "Surgery" originally published together as "Places." A selection of chapter-section epigraphic verses, "Our Shimmer of Days," "From Sound Sleep, Isaac," "Sales Spike with the Toll," "Another Soon: Sssh," "Hobbes Obtrudes. Rousseau," and "There's Nothing Any," originally published together as "Six Discouraging Epigrams."

The Hopkins Review: "The Bad News, Straight," "Science Tuesday"

Light: "Boy Toys," "Tattered Coat"

Mare Nostrum: "The," "From Tree Full Moon," "Rings"

The Monarch Review: "Poetaster in Paris," "The Arcturan Vivesectionist Explains," "Global Citizen," "It's Always Yourself That You Find in the Sea," "Foreboding"

Narrative: "Easter Wings," "How?" "Vanishing Point," "The Apparition of These Faces," "Spring Wedding," "When I Lose," "Jeopardy," "Family Men," "Money, Worse," "Time Change," and "Vanishing Point." "December's Plans" and "May's Plans" originally published together as "Plans."

The New Criterion: "Numbers"

Plume: "If One of Us," "Madonna in Blue," "A Winter's Tale" and epigraph for Section VII first appeared as "And That?" as part of "Six Blessings"

Poetry: "The Drake Equation," "Anaerobe," "March"

Poetry Northwest: "Plants, Animals," "Day Moon," "Other Water Clocks" originally published as "Waters," "Slow Blue," "And More Vivalding," "Very Well, Thank You," "Memento Mori," "Love," "Afterlife," "Sword Upstairs"

The Sewanee Review: "Necessity"

Slate: "I'm Going to Have to Fire the Dream Master"

Southwest Review: "Annunciation"

Terrain: "Definitions," "Good as a Mile," "Terminator," "Tidal"

The Yale Review: "Pax," "Afterlife," "Over Coffee"

Author's Note

Outtake, Concerning This Book's Aggressive Title:

Hat-swoops to Hollywood!—that's de rigueur,
I guess. Regards to Mr. Schwarzenegger,

by all means, no *mens sana* meatier.
My title, though (see Wikipedia)

refers to the other firmament, where a moon's
chiaroscuros curve like nesting spoons—

I'll illustrate. Pretend it's night. Look up,
like the man-moth, eyeball pressed against the egg-cup

moon. Now gently drape your optic nerve
across that vocative, like so: not curved

across the middle, like the letter θ
(that's, as any kid knows, the *equator*),

but rather pole-to-pole, like uppercase Φ:
That line's ***the terminator***. It defines

a moving shadow, shearing light from dark,
the day/night line. You'll note its crawling arc

(which sickles everything) bisects this book,
too—the valley down the middle, if you look.

*

That valley splits the mirror halves of the poem titled
"Memento Mori." Here I tried to do in words what I saw in
Florence once, in paint. I've never found that panel again; I'll
imagine it tucked away in the Uffizi's Renaissance attic. Like
a number of other trompe l'oeil works of the period (not to
mention winking refrigerator art of the 1950s), the painting
was figured on a corrugated surface, which made the two-for-
one trick possible: standing to one side, you'd see a lovely young
woman; moving across, you'd see her turn to bones. Passersby
often did a double take, sidling back to find that point in the
arc where both apparitions vanish.

At any rate, this book attempts something like the same trick.
It's divided into chapters, five on either side of the medial abyss.
This is partly to keep sugars from vinegars, and partly to check
exhaustion—following Poe, it seemed to me that a long book
might hospitably be measured in a string of "single sittings,"
one coffee spoon each, and that's my recommendation here.

Last caveat: When Freud amusedly writes to his wife, "If one
of us should die, I shall go to Paris," it's one thing. When in
Frost's "Home Burial," the speaker to his wife predicts, "I shall
laugh the worst laugh I ever laughed," it's another. Death and
its modal auxiliary have lighter and darker shades, and so have
these poems. If *chiaroscuro* is the painter's word for it, those
syllables are in the correct order here: intermittent sunshine to
the left of the terminator; steady discouragement to the right,
remitting somewhat before moonset.

Richard Kenney is the author of four previous books of poetry: *The Evolution of the Flightless Bird, Orrery, The Invention of the Zero,* and *The One-Strand River.* His work has attracted recognitions, among them the Yale Series of Younger Poets Prize, a Lannan Literary Award, the Rome Prize in Literature, and fellowships from the Guggenheim and MacArthur Foundations. He teaches at the University of Washington and lives with his family on the Olympic Peninsula.

A NOTE ON THE TYPE

The text in this book was set in Miller, a transitional-style typeface designed by Matthew Carter (b. 1937) with assistance from Tobias Frere-Jones and Cyrus Highsmith of the Font Bureau. Modeled on the roman family of fonts popularized by Scottish type foundries in the nineteenth century, Miller is named for William Miller, founder of the Miller & Richard foundry of Edinburgh.

Composed by North Market Street Graphics,
Lancaster, Pennsylvania

Printed and bound by Berryville Graphics,
Berryville, Virginia

Book design by Pei Loi Koay